Metaphysics and the Representational Fallacy

In this refreshingly original and accessible investigation into the nature of metaphysics, Heather Dyke argues that for too long philosophy has suffered from a language fixation. Where this language fixation leads philosophers to reason badly, she calls it the "representational fallacy". She illustrates the various ways it can lead philosophers astray and argues that metaphysics can be better done without it. She discusses the philosophy of time as an illustration of how a metaphysical debate about the nature of time was needlessly transformed into a sterile debate about language and of how, once the focus on language is dropped, a new metaphysical strategy emerges. Dyke shows how the same applies to other debates in metaphysics and how this promises fruitful new research programmes, where the focus is on ontology rather than on language. The clear and accessible way in which current practice in metaphysics is brought under the spotlight will challenge philosophers to examine their own methodology.

Heather Dyke is Senior Lecturer in Philosophy at the University of Otago in New Zealand. She is the editor of *Time and Ethics: Essays at the Intersection* and author of several journal articles on metaphysics and the philosophy of time.

Routledge Studies in Contemporary Philosophy

1. Email and Ethics
Style and Ethical Relations in Computer-Mediated Communication
Emma Rooksby

2. Causation and Laws of Nature
Max Kistler

3. Internalism and Epistemology
The Architecture of Reason
Timothy McGrew and Lydia McGrew

4. Einstein, Relativity and Absolute Simultaneity
Edited by William Lane Craig and Quentin Smith

5. Epistemology Modalized
Kelly Becker

6. Truth and Speech Acts
Greimann & Siegwart

7. Fiction, Narrative, and Knowledge
A Sense of the World
Edited by John Gibson, Wolfgang Huemer, and Luca Pocci

8. A Pragmatist Philosophy of Democracy
Communities of Inquiry
Robert B. Talisse

9. Aesthetics and Material Beauty
Aesthetics Naturalized
Jennifer A. McMahon

10. Aesthetic Experience
Edited by Richard Shusterman and Adele Tomlin

11. Real Essentialism
David S. Oderberg

12. To be announced

13. Metaphysics and the Representational Fallacy
Heather Dyke

14. Practical Identity and Narrative Agency
Edited by Catriona Mackenzie and Kim Atkins

Metaphysics and the Representational Fallacy

Heather Dyke

NEW YORK AND LONDON

First published 2008
by Routledge
270 Madison Avenue, New York, NY 10016

Simultaneously published in the UK
by Routledge
2 Park Square, Milton Park, Abingdon, Oxon OX14 4RN

Routledge is an imprint of the Taylor & Francis Group, an informa business

© 2008 Taylor & Francis Group

Typeset in Times New Roman by
Taylor & Francis Books
Printed and bound in Great Britain by
Biddles Ltd, King's Lynn

All rights reserved. No part of this book may be reprinted or reproduced or utilized in any form or by any electronic, mechanical, or other means, now known or hereafter invented, including photocopying and recording, or in any information storage or retrieval system, without permission in writing from the publishers.

Library of Congress Cataloging in Publication Data
Metaphysics and the representational fallacy / [edited by] Heather Dyke.
   p. cm. – (Routledge studies in contemporary philosophy ; 13)
Includes bibliographical references and index.
  1. Metaphysics. I. Dyke, Heather.
  BD111.M5525 2007
  110–dc22
      2007015922

British Library Cataloguing in Publication Data
A catalogue record for this book is available from the British Library

ISBN: 978-0-415-95669-7 (hbk)
ISBN: 978-0-203-93371-8 (ebk)

For Ian and Ruby

Contents

	Preface	x
	Introduction	1
1	Metaphysics and the origins of the representational fallacy	14
2	A new metaphysical strategy: lessons learned from the philosophy of time	37
3	The representational fallacy: or how not to do ontology	63
4	The relationship between language and reality	89
5	The methodological map	105
6	The overlooked strategy in practice: moral discourse	132
7	Some further applications of the overlooked strategy	143
	Notes	171
	References	174
	Index	180

Preface

When I first began research into the philosophy of time as a Ph.D. student at the University of Leeds, I was puzzled by the fact that, while much of the literature claimed to be investigating the nature of time, what it appeared to be investigating was the nature of temporal language. The research question was, "Is time tensed or tenseless?" But philosophers set about answering that question by asking a different one, first, "Can tensed sentences be translated by, or reduced to, tenseless sentences?" And then later on, "Can tensed sentences be given tenseless truth conditions?" I eventually set aside my initial puzzlement, thinking that this focus on language was merely apparent. When philosophers asked for the truth conditions of tensed sentences, what they were asking was, "What must temporal reality be like to make these tensed sentences true?" Thus, what appeared to be a question about language was really a question about ontology, but couching that question in terms of truth conditions allowed for a regimented and systematic approach to answering it. Nevertheless, some of that initial puzzlement lingered on in the back of my mind.

The position in the philosophy of time that I came to defend is called the new B-theory of time. According to that theory, tense in language is irreducible even though time itself is tenseless. Thus, according to this view, the linguistic issues about tense do not settle the metaphysical issues about the nature of time. I came to think that if this is the case in the philosophy of time, then maybe it is also the case in other metaphysical issues. Maybe we have been mistaken in thinking that the way to do metaphysics is via language. I eventually came to the conclusion that proceeding to answer metaphysical questions via their linguistic counterparts could lead one to reason very badly. Sometimes it was as if the ultimate point of asking the linguistic question (to get an answer to the metaphysical question) was forgotten; all that really mattered in metaphysics were the linguistic questions. Other times, it seemed to be assumed that an answer to the linguistic question automatically delivered up an answer to the metaphysical question without any need for bridging principles to get from the linguistic to the metaphysical realm. Either way, language had, almost unquestioningly, been put on a pedestal as far as ontology was concerned. That nagging puzzlement that I had earlier set aside came flooding back, but this time as thoroughgoing suspicion. So it was that the idea for this book came about.

Much contemporary metaphysics has, for too long, been too fixated on language. Where this language fixation leads to bad reasoning I call it "the representational fallacy." Much of this language fixation is inadvertent, so part of my aim in this book is to draw philosophers' attention to it. But my primary aims are to illustrate the sort of bad philosophy that grows out of it and that metaphysics can well do without it.

In the early stages of my thinking about these issues, after I had formed the intention to write a book about them, John Heil presented a paper to the Otago Philosophy Department's seminar entitled "Language, Thought and Reality," later to become part of his book *From an Ontological Point of View* (2003). The ideas expressed in that paper so closely aligned with my own that I almost gave up on this project there and then, thinking that my ideas were not, after all, original; that they had already been expressed, and no doubt much more eloquently than I could ever express them. Nevertheless I was encouraged to continue with the project by many people, including John Heil, to whom I am deeply indebted. I owe a particular debt of thanks to Alan Musgrave, who provided gentle encouragement, penetrating criticism, and an unfailing belief in the importance of this project. I am grateful too to many other people who have made invaluable contributions to my thinking on these issues. They include Colin Cheyne, John Divers, Emily Gill, Cynthia Macdonald, James Maclaurin, Stephen Mumford, Daniel Nolan, Nathan Oaklander, Josh Parsons, Charles Pigden, J. J. C. Smart, Amie Thomasson and Brad Weslake.

Parts of this book have been presented as papers at the University of Leeds, the University of St. Andrews, the Joint Session of the Aristotelian Society and the Mind Association at the University of Kent, 2004, the Australasian Association of Philosophy Conference at the University of Sydney, 2005, a workshop on Presentism and Passage at the Centre for Time, University of Sydney, 2005, the Australasian Association of Philosophy (New Zealand Division) Conference at the University of Otago, 2005, and the Departmental Seminar at the University of Otago. I am grateful to the audiences on all these occasions for their criticisms and contributions. I also thank the Philosophy Programme at the School of Advanced Studies, University of London, for awarding me a Visiting Fellowship from February to September 2004, where much of the research for this book was carried out. I am particularly grateful to Tim Crane, Barry Smith and Shahrar Ali.

An earlier version of Chapter 6 appeared as "What Moral Realism Can Learn From the Philosophy of Time" in *Time and Ethics: Essays at the Intersection* ed. Heather Dyke (Dordrecht: Kluwer Academic Publishers, 2003: 11–25). Part of Chapter 2 appeared in my "Tokens, Dates and Tenseless Truth Conditions," *Synthèse* 131(4): 329–51. This material appears here with kind permission of Springer Science and Business Media. Parts of

Chapters 1, 2 and 7 will appear as "Tenseless/Non-Modal Truthmakers for Tensed/Modal Truths" in *Logique et Analyse* (2007, forthcoming). I am grateful to the editors and publisher for permission to use this material here.

Heather Dyke
Dunedin
February 2007

Introduction

Much recent and contemporary work in metaphysics takes itself to be investigating the fundamental nature and structure of reality. One of the most widely used methodologies in pursuing that aim involves taking language about the world, either ordinary language, or some modified version of it, as our starting point and asking what we can learn about the world by examining that language. In this book, I call this methodology into question, arguing that it is a fallacy to argue from facts about language to conclusions about the fundamental nature of reality, one that is widely committed. I call it "the representational fallacy." Here is an example of the representational fallacy at work in a make-believe metaphysical dispute.

> PHILOSOPHER A: I am a lurch-realist. I think that reality includes entities called lurches. To see that this is so, one merely has to recognize that there are many true sentences that include the term "lurch". For example, the sentence "The teacher's resignation left the students in the lurch" is true (let us suppose), and in order for it to be true, every referring term in that sentence must succeed in referring to some entity in extralinguistic reality. If it fails so to refer, that would render the sentence false, but, by hypothesis, the sentence is true, so the term "lurch" must refer to an entity in extralinguistic reality: a lurch.

> PHILOSOPHER B: I deny that reality includes lurches. I concede that the sentence "The teacher's resignation left the students in the lurch" is true. However, I deny that recognizing the truth of this sentence commits me to the existence of lurches. Admittedly, it may appear to do so, but that is merely an appearance. No, the sentence "The teacher's resignation left the students in the lurch" can be paraphrased by another sentence that more clearly reveals its true ontological commitments. For example, the sentence "The teacher's resignation left the students in a difficult situation" makes no mention of lurches and so does not commit us to their existence.

What Philosopher B claims to have achieved with this paraphrasing strategy is to have provided a replacement for the original sentence that has the same meaning, so conveys all the same information, and describes the same facts or states of affairs as the original, but which lacks its unwanted ontological commitments. Philosopher B then appeals to the principle of parsimony, or Ockham's razor, to support his claim that the translation, rather than the original, gives a more accurate representation of reality, ontologically speaking. If we do not need to recognize the existence of lurches, then we should not.

Philosopher A will rejoin that Philosopher B's proposed translation of the original sentence will not do, as it fails to convey all the information conveyed by the original. That being the case, there must be some aspect of reality that corresponds to the information conveyed by the original, but not the translation. The inadequacy of the proposed translation is, thus, further evidence, according to Philosopher A, of the existence of lurches. This position is supported by the respectable claim from semantic theory that idioms are not fully translatable, or translatable without loss of meaning, by non-idioms. The debate will continue, with Philosopher B offering further suggested translations of the original sentence that do not make reference to lurches, and Philosopher A arguing that these suggested translations are just as inadequate as the first one. Before you know it, what started off as an ontological question (are there lurches?) has been transformed into a question about the meanings of sentences that include the term "lurch".

This make-believe metaphysical dispute is patently absurd, and in more than one way. Philosopher A is mistaken if she thinks she can argue from the fact that the term "lurch" appears in true sentences to the conclusion that lurches exist. Philosopher B is equally mistaken if he thinks the right way to reject Philosopher A's conclusion is to attempt to find paraphrases of these sentences that have the same meaning but do not appear to imply the existence of lurches. By opting for this strategy, Philosopher B is tacitly accepting Philosopher A's assumption that we can arrive at ontological conclusions about the nature of reality by examining the nature of the language we use to describe it. Since he feels the need to find paraphrases of Philosopher A's sentences, he must think that, were he unable to do so, he would be committed to the existence of lurches. Both philosophers, in other words, are guilty of committing the representational fallacy.

To return, briefly, to the ontological status of lurches, the positions of Philosophers A and B are not the only options available. Two further protagonists may make their appearance and argue as follows:

> PHILOSOPHER C: I too deny that reality includes lurches, but I also deny that Philosopher B's paraphrasing strategy is successful. The sentence "The teacher's resignation left the students in a difficult situation" does not have the same meaning as the sentence "The teacher's resignation

left the students in the lurch," so it is not possible to paraphrase away all reference to lurches in ordinary language. The lurch sentence does indeed refer to lurches, so if it is true it commits us to the existence of lurches. Since there are no lurches, the sentence must be false. Thus, despite appearances, lurch sentences are false.

PHILOSOPHER D: I also deny that there are any lurches, and like Philosopher C I see little chance of success for Philosopher B's paraphrasing strategy. Unlike Philosopher C, however, I cannot bring myself to reject lurch sentences as false. But there is a different strategy available. Perhaps lurch sentences are, despite appearances, not capable of truth or falsity at all. They appear to be descriptive, fact-stating sentences, but really they are not; they have some other linguistic function.

Philosophers C and D also tacitly accept Philosopher A's assumption that we can arrive at ontological conclusions about the nature of reality by examining the nature of the language we use to describe it. However, they have come up with different strategies for consistently denying the existence of lurches in the face of the linguistic "evidence". Philosopher C offers us an error theory of lurch discourse, and Philosopher D gives us a non-cognitivist account of it.

In response to the strategies of Philosophers C and D, Philosopher A might re-enter the fray at this point and argue as follows: the paraphrase strategy of Philosopher B has been an outright failure, so linguistic analysis has shown us that lurch talk cannot be reduced to talk of any other kind of entity. That shows us that lurches cannot be identified with any other kind of entity. But it doesn't show us that there are no lurches. On the contrary, since some lurch sentences are true but are not reducible to any other kind of sentence, lurches must be "higher-level" entities that supervene on some "lower-level," presumably physical, entities.

No one should take a metaphysical dispute like this seriously. Its purpose has been to illustrate how absurd it is to think we can derive conclusions about the nature of reality from considerations about the nature of language. But one of the claims I will argue for in this book is that the sort of mistake that drives this absurd metaphysical dispute is also being made in much subtler ways in other, respectable metaphysical disputes.

The four positions I have described with respect to the ontological status of lurches are instances of positions on what I call the commonly accepted "methodological map," which I discuss in detail in Chapter 5. All of these positions accept that the way language is can inform us about the way reality is. I argue that there is a position that is often concealed by the methodological map. This position involves accepting (1) that lurch sentences (or whatever) are objectively true; (2) that they are descriptive or fact-stating; and (3) that they are irreducible to, or untranslatable by, any other sentences that do not use the term "lurch"; while denying (4) that the truth of such sentences implies the existence of lurches. If the sentence is true, then there is something about the world that makes it true, its "truthmaker". Our aim in metaphysics ought to be to investigate the nature of the truthmakers of our true sentences. Truthmakers may or may not involve the existence of the entities apparently referred to by terms in the sentence. If there are good reasons for denying the existence of lurches, as there surely are, then that is a reason for thinking that the truthmaker for the sentence "The teacher's resignation left the students in the lurch" does not involve the existence of a lurch. This overlooked strategy does not, by itself, tell us anything about the truthmakers of our true sentences. It merely gives us a framework for approaching many metaphysical issues that can be supplied with content in a variety of ways.

I want to deal immediately with a possible objection to my project. A critic may argue as follows, "You recommend abandoning the practice of beginning our metaphysical investigations with linguistic representations of reality and asking what they tell us about the nature of reality itself. But surely you are not denying that language can tell us *anything at all* about reality. After all, you want to affirm some metaphysical theses, and in order to do this you must express them in language. For example, you want to affirm a B-theoretic metaphysics of time, such that there is no ontological distinction between the past, present and future. And in order to do this, you must say things like 'There is no ontological distinction between past, present and future.' That is a linguistic claim (in so far as it is a linguistic entity; a sentence), and it is one that you think tells us something about reality. But," the critic continues, "you cannot claim that this sentence tells us something about reality if you insist that facts about language can tell us nothing about reality. In general, your recommendation is that we attend to reality itself, rather than to language, when doing metaphysics. But how exactly do we do this? We come up with theories that we express in sets of sentences that we take to be true. Now, with respect to these sets of sentences, either you are, at this level, endorsing a language-to-reality move, and committing the representational fallacy yourself, or, if you are to be consistent, you must deny that even these sentences can tell us anything about reality."

This objection misunderstands the nature of the representational fallacy. Of course, when articulating our theories, we must *use* language. But this is not to draw conclusions about reality from facts about language. It is, rather, to *say* what the world is like, *using* language. So long as the reasons that support our claims about what reality is like are not themselves to do with language, then the representational fallacy has not been committed. The reasons that I invoke in support of my claim about the ontological nature of time are metaphysical and scientific reasons, not linguistic ones. Consequently, I do not commit the representational fallacy when I say that there is no ontological distinction between past, present and future. By contrast, an A-theorist, who says that there are tensed facts and supports that conclusion by appealing to the fact that sentences like "World War II is past" are true, tensed and irreducible to tenseless sentences, does commit the representational fallacy. The reasons appealed to by this A-theorist to support her metaphysical conclusion are facts about linguistic representations of reality. This objection to my project ultimately rests on a use–mention confusion. It fails to see the difference between claims about descriptions of reality, which *mention* those descriptions, and claims about reality itself, which *use* them. The representational fallacy occurs when claims about descriptions of reality are taken to generate a metaphysics, not when claims about reality itself (which, of course, are couched in language) are taken to do so.

The critic may continue. She may concede that it is a fallacy to draw ontological conclusions from facts about descriptions of reality but insist that it cannot be a fallacy to draw ontological conclusions from the *truth* of a description of reality. That ontological conclusions do follow from true descriptions is a simple consequence of the truth schema. That schema tells us, for example, that "Trees exist" is true if and only if trees exist. The objection here cannot be that this instance of the truth schema, by itself, entails that trees exist. If so, then another instance of the truth schema, "Unicorns exist" is true if and only if unicorns exist, would similarly entail that unicorns exist. So the objection must be that an instance of the truth schema together with the claim that the sentence occurring on its left-hand side is true entails the ontological conclusion in question. But then, what ontological conclusions are we to derive from the following instances of the truth schema, together with the claim that the sentence on the left-hand side is true? "Eating people is wrong" is true if and only if eating people is wrong; "There are prime numbers greater than a million" is true if and only if there are prime numbers greater than a million, and even "The teacher's resignation left the students in the lurch" is true if and only if the teacher's resignation left the students in the lurch. Are we to take the truth of these sentences, together with these instances of the truth schema, to entail the existence of, respectively, moral properties, numbers and lurches? Surely not (Musgrave 1993: 266–7).

No one thinks (or should think) that semantics by itself can give us metaphysics. Semantics is just concerned with meanings, and false sentences have meanings just as much as true sentences do. In order to arrive at metaphysical conclusions, as the proponent of the above objection rightly points out, you need *true* sentences. But one of the claims I make in this book is that it is not enough to have true sentences about reality in order to generate a metaphysics. Just knowing that a sentence is true does not tell you what makes it true. Call this its truthmaker. If it is possible for two or more non-synonymous sentences to have the same truthmaker, as I will argue that it is, then it is not sufficient to focus our attention on those true sentences to find out what their common truthmaker is. In order to do that, we must appeal to metaphysical and scientific considerations. However, it is my contention that much contemporary metaphysics limits itself to a consideration of the nature of true sentences and takes it that this can inform us about the nature of reality.

I have just alluded to one claim that I will be arguing for in this book, which is that it is possible for two or more non-synonymous sentences to have the same truthmaker. One implication of this claim is that it is not the case that there is exactly one way to truly describe the world. There are many ways of truly describing the world. However, this does not commit me to any kind of antirealism. To illustrate my point, suppose physicalism is true. The truthmakers for all true statements are physical entities describable in the language of physics. But it does not follow from this that all true statements must be translatable into, or derivable from, statements couched in the language of physics. Many metaphysicians seem to accept the view that the sentences of some domain, F, are either translatable into the language of fundamental physics, or they refer to entities that exist in addition to the entities described by fundamental physics, or, lastly, that the entities they apparently refer to do not really exist. This is a false trilemma. The sentences in question can be true, untranslatable by the language of physics, and yet the only things that need exist in order to make them true are things that can be described by the language of fundamental physics.

The central example that I will be using to argue for this view is the new B-theory of time, according to which a tensed and a tenseless sentence can be non-synonymous and yet have the same truthmaker. However, there are simpler examples that can help illustrate and clarify my view. Suppose that something, o, is lilac in virtue of having a certain molecular structure, P. This is not to say that every purple thing has this structure, but this one does. We can describe P using the language of physics, and this description holds of o because o is P. However, there are lots of other ways we can truly describe o, and all these other descriptions will be true of *o in virtue of the fact that o is P*. For example, o is lilac, o is purple, o is colored, o has a color that falls between blue and violet on the spectrum, and so on. What we get from physics is our best account of the nature of P, which is the truthmaker for all these different descriptions. What we get from physics, on this account, is the "deep story" about P, which is of interest to us because the fact that o is P is the feature of the world in virtue of which lots of non-synonymous descriptions of o are true.

The alternatives to this view are to adopt one of the following strategies: either argue that, since "o is lilac" is true and "o is P" is true, but the former sentence cannot be translated into the latter sentence, the predicate "is lilac" must denote a property over and above the property denoted by "is P." Alternatively, attempt to offer a way of translating talk of being lilac into talk of having the molecular structure P. These attempts are usually unsuccessful, because there are lots of other things that are lilac in virtue of having a different molecular structure. The third alternative is to argue that since "o is lilac" cannot be translated by "o is P," and since there are no other properties in the world besides those described by fundamental physics, it must be, despite appearances, false that "o is lilac." Each of these strategies is mistaken because it assigns too much ontological significance to the language we use when truly describing the world.

Similar things can be said about the relationship between tensed and tenseless descriptions of some event, e. Suppose e occurs at time t_0. At time t_1 we can truly say that e is past, e occurred one unit of time ago, e was present, and so on, and all these tensed descriptions are true because they are uttered at time t_1, which is later than the time at which e occurs. What we get from the new B-theory, on this account, is our best description of what it is about the world that makes both tensed and tenseless descriptions of e true. The new B-theory gives us the "deep story" about what it is in the world that makes true both tensed and tenseless descriptions of events.

The term "the representational fallacy," then, does not refer to one particular invalid argument or form of argument. It refers to a general strategy of reading metaphysics off language. This can be done in different ways. The debate about the ontological status of lurches is one of the less subtle manifestations of the strategy, and I doubt that anyone would think this was a good way of settling metaphysical questions. But, in the course of this book, I will show that there are much more subtle ways of reading metaphysics off language. My aim is to expose some of these fallacious ways of reasoning about metaphysics.

One of the more subtle ways in which the representational fallacy is committed in metaphysics is by assuming, implicitly, that there is a privileged true description of reality, the sentences of which (a) stand in a one-to-one correspondence with facts in the world, and (b) are structurally isomorphic to the facts with which they correspond. I call this the Strong Linguistic Thesis (SLT). It may be that, if asked directly, no philosopher would assent to this assumption, but I argue that many metaphysical disputes only make sense if the disputants are understood to have assumed it. I argue against SLT by showing that two or more non-synonymous true sentences can have the same truthmaker, so it should be clear that we cannot move from linguistic facts about any of those sentences to conclusions about the nature of their common truthmaker.

Another, related way in which the fallacy is committed is by thinking that the range of available positions with respect to some metaphysical dispute is limited to those I describe as constituting the methodological map. With respect to some domain of discourse, for example, moral, tensed, or aesthetic discourse, these positions are realism, reductionism, eliminativism or an error theory, noncognitivism, and conceptual relativism. I argue that it is the tacit acceptance of SLT that is responsible for philosophers seeing this range of options as exhaustive. Once SLT has been rejected, so the inference from the nature of language to the nature of reality has been exposed as fallacious, a new metaphysical position emerges. According to positions of this ilk, sentences from some such domain of discourse can be true, descriptive or fact-stating, irreducible to any other kind of sentence, and yet have truthmakers that do not involve entities apparently referred to by the terms peculiar to the domain of discourse in question.

A third way in which the fallacy is committed is by conflating claims about descriptions of reality with claims about reality itself. For example, metaphysical realists believe that there is just one way that the world is. Opponents of metaphysical realism often (mis)represent this by saying that metaphysical realists believe that there is just one correct way of describing the world. But the realist claim is a claim about reality, while her opponent's claim is a claim about descriptions of reality. The opponent thus conflates reality with descriptions of it.

In the course of my discussion, I will give examples of the representational fallacy in practice, and I will contrast these with discussions of philosophers who do not reason in this fallacious way. For my claim is not the extremely implausible one that all philosophers, or all metaphysicians, can reliably be thought to commit the representational fallacy. My claim is the more modest one that reasoning in this fallacious way is more widespread than we might have thought, and that it ought not to play a part in our metaphysical investigations.

Outline of the book

This book is an investigation into metaphysics: its aims, scope, methodology, and practice. I argue that metaphysics should (and on the whole does) take itself to be concerned with investigating the nature of reality, and I suggest that the ontological significance of language has been grossly exaggerated in the pursuit of that aim. I begin, in Chapter 1, with a brief examination of the origins of the representational fallacy, which lie in the "linguistic turn," a philosophical revolution which took place in the early part of the twentieth century, and which saw language come to occupy centre stage in philosophical enquiry. The logical positivists, who were largely responsible for the linguistic turn, were reacting against the metaphysical excesses of the neo-Kantian tradition. They rejected any metaphysical speculation about extralinguistic reality as meaningless and argued instead that the only meaningful philosophical assertions are those about language itself. They denied that we could reach any philosophical conclusions about the world as it is independently of any linguistic framework.

In the aftermath of the linguistic turn, an alternative view of the philosophical significance of language came to the fore. Proponents of this view accepted the positivists' emphasis on the philosophical significance of language but rejected their claim that we can draw no philosophical conclusions about the nature of extralinguistic reality. Instead, these philosophers thought that a philosophical investigation into language could itself yield philosophical results about the nature of extralinguistic reality. Their view was that language gives us a picture of the world. The ordinary-language picture of the world is a distorted one, presenting the world as if through textured glass. It is the job of the philosopher to clarify that picture, by employing logical analysis to arrive at the correct logical form of ordinary language. The language thus arrived at is the "ideal language," the one that gives us the most accurate picture of the ontological form of reality.

In the remainder of Chapter 1, I show how this attitude towards the relationship between language and reality still prevails in contemporary metaphysics and contributes to some philosophers falling prey to the representational fallacy. I consider the relationship between metaphysics and science, and I examine a typical methodology that is widely used in metaphysics. It involves taking our prephilosophical ways of representing reality and asking what sorts of entities their truth implies the existence of. Philosophers who want their ontological inventory to include entities of a certain kind will appeal to these prephilosophical representations to support their case. Opponents of the existence of such entities will seek to paraphrase away any reference to them in our ordinary language. My contention will be that this methodology is deeply flawed and that it can only be thought to yield results if the problematic view of the relationship between language and reality is accepted. Finally, I take another, brief, historical detour to consider three reasons why language has come to be so important in philosophy. I argue that, if we keep in mind our goal in metaphysics, which is to discover the fundamental nature and structure of reality, then this focus on language may have been leading us astray.

In Chapter 2, I take as a case study the recent debate over the metaphysical status of tense in the philosophy of time. I show that, in its early incarnation, it was an example of the flawed methodological strategy introduced in Chapter 1. That debate takes as its starting point our ordinary temporal language and asks what this tells us about the nature of time itself. I argue that both A-theorists, who think that tensed language demonstrates the existence of tensed facts, and old B-theorists, who think that tensed language can be replaced by tenseless language, which demonstrates the existence only of tenseless facts, commit the representational fallacy. They both think that we are justified in deriving ontological conclusions from facts about our representations of reality.

I argue that proponents from both sides in this debate implicitly assume that there is one true description of temporal reality. I further argue that this notion is ambiguous. According to one interpretation of it, which I call the Weak Linguistic Thesis (WLT), it states that there is a true description of reality that includes all of the truths that there are. This is not the thesis that drives the debate between the A-theory and the old B-theory of time. Proponents from both sides in that debate would both accept this thesis, and it would not generate any further disagreement between them. Where they disagree is over the ontological significance of true tensed sentences.

There must, therefore, be an alternative interpretation of the notion that there is one true description of temporal reality. This interpretation, SLT, has it that there is one privileged, true description of reality, the sentences of which (a) stand in a one-to-one correspondence with facts in the world, and (b) are structurally isomorphic to the facts with which they correspond. This thesis brings out the disagreement between A-theorists and old B-theorists. For A-theorists, the one true description of temporal reality contains tensed sentences, and since there is a fact corresponding to every truth in the one true description, it follows that there are tensed facts. For old B-theorists, it only contains tenseless sentences, so there are only tenseless facts corresponding to those sentences.

I then present the truth-conditional variant of the new B-theory, which appears, at first sight, to be more concerned with ontology than with language and, thus, to break out of the representational fallacy. However, I argue that it ultimately commits that fallacy, by drawing conclusions about the nature of time from features of a particular language: the tenseless metalanguage in which it states the truth conditions of tensed sentences. Finally, I turn to the truthmaker variant of the new B-theory, and I argue that this theory does not commit the representational fallacy. Unlike its predecessors and its opponents, it starts with ontological premises and derives ontological conclusions from them. It rejects SLT, implicitly assumed by its predecessors and opponents. It is this position which, I want to suggest, has analogues in other metaphysical debates that have gone largely unnoticed because of the emphasis on language as our starting point in metaphysical enquiry.

In Chapter 3, I focus in on SLT, arguing that, while few, if any, philosophers explicitly adhere to it, implicit adherence to it is widespread, and this can be seen from the way many philosophers argue. I illustrate and criticize adherence to SLT and argue that it is false, focusing mainly on its component claims that truths stand in a one-to-one correspondence with facts and that they are structurally isomorphic to them. I discuss the difference between truth conditions and truthmakers, suggesting that a conflation of these two notions is another of the culprits responsible for the representational fallacy. I then discuss the notions of truthmaking and truthmakers and their role in doing ontology. Finally, I argue for the ontological insignificance of the method of paraphrase.

I turn, in Chapter 4, to focus on the component of SLT that states that there is a privileged true description of reality. I argue that it is false and that the main motivation for thinking it true is a commitment to the ontological thesis of realism: that there is just one way the world is that is independent of our means of describing it. I argue that the ontological thesis of realism is consistent with there being many ways of accurately describing reality. To think otherwise is to confuse descriptions of reality with reality itself.

I examine Putnam's arguments against the view that there is just one true description of reality and show that, contrary to what he thinks, they do not undermine the ontological thesis of realism. I then examine a particular problem for anyone who thinks that there is a privileged true description of reality, in the restricted sense of SLT, and who further combines this thesis with an austere physicalism such as Quine's. This is the problem of how to account for apparently descriptive language that is not part of the privileged physical description. I explore three suggestions for dealing with such language and argue that none of them is satisfactory. They are (1) Quine's noncognitive account, (2) reductionism, and (3) the view that there are facts over and above purely physical facts. I argue that there is an alternative to these options, which is that the truths of other domains of discourse are made true by physical facts, while not being synonymous with, or reducible to, any physical truths. I further suggest that the fact that this alternative has been largely overlooked is due to a tacit confusion of descriptions of reality with reality itself.

I then turn to a possible objection to my view, which is that I unjustifiably draw general conclusions about the relationship of language to reality on the basis of a particular and idiosyncratic type of language: tensed language. Tensed language is idiosyncratic because it is context dependent while, it is thought, language in general is not. I argue that, on the contrary, much of what we say is context dependent because what we choose to say involves our perspective on, and interest in, extralinguistic reality. I also suggest that consideration of this point gives us a further reason for rejecting the language-to-reality move that constitutes the representational fallacy. If two sentence-tokens differ in meaning, we cannot conclude that they also differ in the extralinguistic facts they each refer to, as the difference in information conveyed may be information about our perspective on and interest in the extralinguistic fact that is their truthmaker.

In Chapter 5, I expand the boundaries of my investigation from considering just realist strategies in metaphysics to include antirealist options as well. I suggest that it is widely agreed that there is a range of positions available with respect to any given domain of discourse and that this range has been thought to be exhaustive. I go on to argue that, just as in the case of the traditional methodological structure of a metaphysical debate, there is a position that has been overlooked, and it is that suggested by the strategy of the new B-theory of time. For some domain of discourse that involves predicates of kind K, the five main positions are:

1. There are facts of kind K corresponding to the truths of kind K (K-realism).
2. Truths of kind K are reducible to truths of kind L, and these are made true by facts of kind L (K-reductionism).
3. "Truths" of kind K are actually all false *because* there are no facts of kind K (error theory of K-discourse and eliminativism).
4. "Truths" of kind K are, despite appearances, not really fact-stating, so they are not candidates for truth or falsity (noncognitivism about K-discourse).

5. Truths of kind K refer to facts of kind K, so K-facts exist, but only relative to the domain of K-discourse (conceptual relativism).

Of course, this is a very "broad-brush" statement of the methodological map, but I show how different philosophers have accepted that these options are exhaustive and how different theories such as emergentism, supervenience theories, and different kinds of reductionism, all fall into one or other of these categories. The strategy that has been overlooked is:

6. Truths of kind K are not reducible to truths of kind L, but nevertheless, truths of kind K are made true by facts of kind L.

I argue that there are good reasons for pursuing the overlooked strategy in many metaphysical disputes, as it potentially has a number of advantages over the traditional options. We can accept, with the K-realist, that the sentences of a given domain of discourse are descriptive, or fact-stating, and literally true, as common sense would have it, but without being committed to K-realism's proliferation of nonnatural facts and properties. We can find naturalistically palatable truthmakers for these true sentences, without having to follow the lead of the K-reductionist and find naturalistically palatable sentences to which we can "reduce" them. Consequently, none of the antirealist options need even be considered. Our view can be a realist one without the attendant ontological drawbacks of K-realism.

In Chapter 6, I discuss the metaphysical issue over the status of moral discourse, illustrating how the various positions available within that debate instantiate four of the five main positions on the methodological map. I discuss in detail the position of moral realism, explaining its motivation and some problems it faces. I then examine an argument for moral realism, illustrating the striking resemblance it bears to the argument for tensed facts from tensed language that A-theorists endorse in the philosophy of time. I also illustrate that the different positions one can take with respect to the status of moral discourse are analogous to the different positions one can take with respect to the status of tensed discourse. I then point out that, within the moral debate, there is a position analogous to that adopted by the new B-theory of time. This is to accept that moral sentences are determinately true or false, not reducible to nonmoral sentences, and yet made true by nonmoral facts. I call this position truthmaker naturalism.

Finally, in Chapter 7, I take the overlooked methodological strategy, as exemplified by the new B-theory of time and truthmaker naturalism, and consider whether there are any other metaphysical debates to which it might apply. I suggest that there are, and that they include debates about material constitution, modality, causation, mathematics and vagueness. I briefly examine each of these debates, showing how many of the positions with respect to them that have been adopted are instances of the positions on the methodological map. I suggest how the overlooked strategy might be introduced and the sort of position it would generate. I thus suggest new research programs that can be taken up by those working in these fields, as the application of this strategy to each of these debates can be filled out with content in different ways, depending on the sorts of fact one takes to be the truthmakers for the truths of each domain of discourse.

1 Metaphysics and the origins of the representational fallacy

The term "the representational fallacy" refers to a general philosophical tendency to place too much emphasis on the significance of language when doing ontology. We shall see, in the course of this book, that this tendency can manifest itself in various ways, and with different results. To begin this investigation, it will be instructive to examine some of the movements and revolutions in the recent history of philosophy that led to the representational fallacy getting a grip on current philosophical thinking.

The Kantian turn

The starting point for an investigation into the origins of the representational fallacy is the work of Immanuel Kant. One of the driving forces behind Kant's philosophical program was the desire to rescue human knowledge from the perils of skepticism. Prior to Kant, the threat of skepticism was thought to be particularly acute, largely as a result of the view that humans do not directly perceive reality; what we have direct epistemic access to are our perceptions, or sense impressions. The human mind, philosophers reasoned, is presented with perceptual impressions picked up by the sense organs and not with reality itself. That being the case, what grounds have we for the claim that there really is a reality out there at all, let alone one that is causally responsible for our sense impressions, or that is adequately represented by them? Kant sought to undermine this skeptical threat by focusing attention not on reality but on our perceptual impressions themselves which, due to our direct access to them, are not similarly threatened by skepticism.

Another driving force behind Kant's philosophy was a desire to avoid the excessive metaphysics of the rationalist philosophers. By anchoring human knowledge to the perceptual and conceptual features of human experience, which are universal, in the sense of being common to all humankind, and to which we have direct epistemic access, he intended to exclude from serious consideration the elaborate, speculative metaphysical systems like those of the rationalists. These were merely ad hoc philosophies; what Kant wanted was a philosophy grounded in certainty and supported by empirical evidence.

Unfortunately, Kant's intention to avoid excessive metaphysical systems backfired, and spectacularly so. His strategy of anchoring human knowledge to the perceptual and conceptual features of human experience involved arguing that the objects of human knowledge are mere appearances, in part constituted by the knowing mind, and not to be confused with objects that are independent of human knowledge. He thus distinguished between the world of appearances, the "phenomenal" world, and the world of things-as-they-are-in-themselves, the "noumenal" world. The only world we can have knowledge of is the phenomenal world. Furthermore, the phenomenal world, being the object of our knowledge, is partly constituted by the imposition on our sensory input of our a priori, categorizing concepts.

There are two features of this strategy that were seized upon by those wishing to perpetuate the excessive metaphysical system-building that Kant was seeking to avoid. First, by drawing the distinction between the phenomenal and the noumenal worlds, Kant's view permitted speculation about the transcendent realm of reality that lies beyond mere appearance. Thus, instead of undermining speculative metaphysics, Kant's philosophy legitimized it as a discipline distinct from science, with its own subject matter and methods of enquiry.

The second feature of Kant's strategy that caused it to backfire was his claim that phenomena, the objects of knowledge, are partly constituted by the knowing mind. Kant argued that we cannot have knowledge of anything without using our conceptual apparatus, and he concluded that the objects of our knowledge are the product of the operation of our conceptual apparatus upon the information received via our senses. Thus, far from being independent of humans, and part of the external world, the things we have knowledge of are, at least in part, the product of human conceptual activity. Now, for Kant, the conceptual apparatus employed in generating the objects of human knowledge is universal, so the products of this activity are the same for everyone. However, many neo-Kantians dropped this feature of Kant's philosophy, while retaining the idea that the objects of knowledge are generated by the imposition of our concepts and categories on sensory input. The upshot of this deviation from Kantianism was that humans, or cultures, with different conceptual schemes would generate different objects of knowledge; different worlds. Thus, Kantianism gave way not just to elaborate metaphysical theorizing as to the nature of the noumenal world but also to a brand of relativist constructivism, according to which, in so far as human beings think about the world in different ways, they actually live in different phenomenal worlds.

Despite its popularity, one of the central arguments for Kantian and neo-Kantian metaphysics is deeply flawed. This is the argument from the premise that we cannot know things without using our conceptual apparatus, or employing our cognitive faculties, to the conclusion that we cannot know things-as-they-are-in-themselves; we can only know things-as-conceived-of-by-us. This argument was identified by David Stove (1991: 140) and labeled the Gem.[1] The premise of the Gem is a tautology. It states that we cannot conceive of things without employing our conceptual apparatus, or, alternatively, we cannot think of things without bringing them under the categories of our thought, or, what comes to the same thing, we cannot think of things without using our minds. Its conclusion, however, is not tautological. It is that we cannot conceive of things that exist independently of us, or things-as-they-are-in-themselves. The tautological premise concerns the human cognitive activity of knowing things, or conceiving of things. The conclusion concerns the objects of our knowledge, or conceptual activity. Since no tautological premise can, by itself, validly yield a non-tautological conclusion, the Gem is an invalid argument.[2]

The impact of the Kantian and neo-Kantian episode in the history of metaphysics on the development of the representational fallacy is most noticeable, as we shall see in the following section, in the way in which the logical positivists, and their successors, reacted against it. However, before moving on to that stage in the history of metaphysics, it is worth reflecting briefly on the role of representations in the Kantian conception of metaphysics. According to Kantians, the aim of metaphysics is not to investigate the nature of mind-independent reality; mind-independent reality is essentially (and almost by definition) inaccessible to human minds. Consequently, if that were the goal of metaphysics, it would be a futile enterprise. Instead, the object of metaphysical investigation is the human conceptual apparatus itself. Furthermore, since, for the Kantian, the world of appearances is partly constituted by the operation of the human conceptual apparatus, by studying the latter we will, in effect, be studying a world of some sort: the phenomenal world.

The only legitimate object of metaphysical enquiry, then, according to the Kantians, is the human conceptual scheme, and the representations it consists of. Such an enquiry cannot provide us with knowledge of the reality that these representations are representations of, even for those who accept that there is such a thing. The representations thus constitute a barrier between us and the world, making it essentially inaccessible to us. Thus, the Kantian is, in a sense, immune from committing the representational fallacy. The fallacy is only committed when one claims to derive *ontological* conclusions from premises about representations of reality. The Kantian, however, denies that any ontological conclusions can be drawn from *any* premises. Her study of our representations is purely intended to achieve a picture of the conceptual scheme which we employ to represent, and partially construct, the phenomenal world. Given the Kantian's denial that we can have any knowledge of mind-independent reality, it is natural for her to focus her attention on the nature and structure of our representations, since that is all we can have knowledge of, according to her. It is possible that this focus on representations and conceptual schemes within the Kantian tradition has encouraged a general acceptance of the view that representations are a legitimate object of metaphysical enquiry. However, I do not think that this is the principal source of the representational fallacy. We shall move a step closer to identifying that by examining how the logical positivists reacted against neo-Kantian metaphysics.

The linguistic turn

Just as Kant had tried (and failed) to rescue philosophy from the speculative metaphysical system-building of the rationalists, the logical positivists attempted to rescue philosophy from the speculative metaphysical system-building of the neo-Kantians. As we have seen, Kant's distinction between the phenomenal and noumenal worlds had opened up new possibilities for extravagant metaphysical theories about the ultimate nature of reality. Furthermore, these theories were not subject to any empirical standards for assessing their truth, since empirical standards applied only to investigations into the phenomenal world. All this horrified the scientifically minded positivists, who sought to find a way to throw out the entire neo-Kantian metaphysical enterprise. They focused their attention on the nature of the philosophical project itself.

The positivists concentrated on language, and on its logical analysis. There are a number of reasons for this. One significant one was that the method of analysis had already delivered promising results when deployed against certain unattractive metaphysical theories. Russell, for example, had shown that Meinong's ontology of nonexistent objects could be avoided by adopting his account of the logical form of sentences involving definite descriptions that have no referent (Russell 1905). His theory of types (1903: 523–8) was seen to offer an even more devastating weapon against unsavory metaphysical systems. Russell employed that theory to argue that certain set-theoretic statements, which appeared to be grammatically correct, could be shown, by logical analysis, to be meaningless strings of symbols.

The positivists leapt upon this strategy of using logical analysis to demonstrate not merely the falsity but also the meaninglessness of whole classes of assertions they deemed to be unsavory, and it became central to their overall aim of undermining metaphysics. Russell's deployment of his theory of types showed that it was possible for statements that appeared to be perfectly coherent and meaningful to be shown to be, as a matter of fact, incoherent and so meaningless. The positivists were thus able to target entire realms of discourse with which they took issue and to argue that they were no more than meaningless nonsense.

Another reason for, or perhaps an outcome of, the shift in philosophical focus to questions of language was that it gave the positivists a way of securing a legitimate domain of enquiry for philosophy, distinct from that of science, while being able to avoid the speculative metaphysics they so deplored. As we have seen, the neo-Kantians saw philosophy as prior to science because it investigated the ultimate nature of reality, while science merely investigated the nature of phenomenal reality; a distinctly second-class activity.

The positivists denied that philosophy was prior to science in this sense, upholding science as the privileged intellectual discipline, but they still wanted to recognize a role for the philosopher. They found a means for distinguishing the two domains by appealing to the idea that before one is in a position to determine whether a statement is true or false, one must at least have understood what it means. They took this distinction between meaning and truth to reflect the different domains of investigation of the philosopher and scientist. The philosopher, by her investigation into which statements are meaningful and which are not, defines the limits of scientific investigation. Only those statements deemed meaningful by the philosopher are worthy of investigation into their truth or falsity by the scientist.

Whatever the reasons for this "linguistic turn" – the shift in philosophical focus to questions of language – it is important to note that it did not merely generate a single view of the philosophical significance of language. Many of the positivists, as we have seen, used linguistic and logical analysis to argue that metaphysical claims were meaningless. Other philosophers, for example Russell, used it not to attack metaphysics, but to do metaphysics; to argue against one ontological view and in favor of another. The later Wittgenstein had different motives again for focusing his attention on language. He thought that the role of philosophy was to uncover the true logical form of ordinary language statements and that this would have the effect of dissolving all philosophical problems, which were thus revealed to be merely "pseudo-problems" (Wittgenstein 1953). Other philosophers, for example, Ayer, rather than rejecting all philosophical claims as meaningless assertions about the extralinguistic world, attempted to reconstrue what he took to be the legitimate ones as significant assertions about language itself (Ayer 1946). He says, for example, "What has contributed as much as anything to the prevalent misunderstanding of the nature of philosophical analysis is the fact that propositions and questions which are really linguistic are often expressed in such a way that they appear to be factual" (Ayer 1946: 57–8).

Not only were there, in the aftermath of the linguistic turn, multiple views of the philosophical significance of language, and of what we could establish by focusing our attention on it, there were also two different views of the relationship between language and extralinguistic reality. The official line of the positivists was that philosophical assertions about the nature of extralinguistic reality were meaningless. The only meaningful philosophical assertions were those about language itself. Thus, philosophical investigation into the world as it really is was systematically replaced by philosophical investigation into the language we use to talk about the world.

The positivist view on the relationship between language and reality is captured by the idea that all knowledge of the world is relative to language. Any claim apparently about the world is either meaningless or, if meaningful, is in fact a claim about how we use language. This idea was most fully developed by Carnap, and his views on this matter received their most developed presentation in his paper "Empiricism, Semantics and Ontology"

(1950). In that paper, Carnap argued that apparently ontological questions, such as "Are there numbers?" are not to be understood as questions about the nature of extralinguistic reality. Understood in that way, they would be meaningless. Instead, they can be given two possible interpretations. They can either be interpreted as internal questions, or as external questions. If they are treated as internal questions, then they are questions that are asked from within some linguistic framework. Treated in this way, the answer to them will be determined by appeal to the framework itself. So, from within the linguistic framework of mathematics, the question "Are there numbers?" receives an affirmative answer simply because the linguistic framework itself employs number terms. If they are treated as external questions, they are pragmatic questions about whether or not we ought to adopt the linguistic framework of mathematics. So, metaphysical assertions, such as "There are numbers," which appear to be about reality, are treated either as assertions about the rules of particular linguistic frameworks or as pragmatic proposals for adopting those linguistic frameworks.

For the positivists, then, language constitutes a barrier between us and extralinguistic reality. Any claims we might wish to make about the world are, in fact, claims about language, and any knowledge available to us about the world is relative to a linguistic framework. There is no sense in which we can find out about the world as it is independently of any linguistic framework. Given this picture, the positivists, just like Kant, are effectively immune from committing the representational fallacy. If we simply cannot find out about the world as it is independently of any linguistic framework, then we cannot find out about the world by examining language.

The alternative view of the relationship between language and extralinguistic reality that emerged from the aftermath of the linguistic turn was that, although the proper object of philosophical investigation was language, this investigation *could* yield results about the nature of extralinguistic reality. For example, Russell and the early Wittgenstein thought that there was a correspondence between the ideal language (the language obtained by applying the methods of logical analysis to ordinary language) and the reality that it represented, such that it was legitimate to infer the nature or structure of the world from that of the ideal language. For them, the logical structure of the propositions of the ideal language correspond to, or "picture," the ontological structure of the facts or states of affairs they represent. For Wittgenstein, for example, the propositions of the ideal language picture possible states of affairs, and those that are true picture actual states of affairs. By examining the true propositions of the ideal language, then, we are effectively examining pictures of reality.

Russell, too, thought that we could infer the nature or structure of the world from that of language. In *An Inquiry into Meaning and Truth*, for example, he writes, "Some modern philosophers hold that we know much about language, but nothing about anything else....For my part, I believe that, partly by means of the study of syntax, we can arrive at considerable knowledge concerning the structure of the world" (Russell 1940: 347). Not only does Russell here explicitly deny the positivist idea that the extralinguistic world is inaccessible to us, he actually endorses the contrary idea that there is a definite relation between the logical form of sentences and the ontological form of the facts they represent. He further thinks that by examining the logical structure of sentences we can learn about the ontological structure of the facts represented.

Another philosopher who endorsed the idea that there is an ideal language was Bergmann. He thought that the ideal language is the one that provides a true representation of the extralinguistic world. Bergmann's view was, thus, in stark contrast to that of Carnap. According to Bergmann, one does not choose the linguistic framework of the ideal language on purely pragmatic grounds. Instead, one discovers that it is the one language that provides a true representation of reality. His view as to the relationship between the ideal language and the extralinguistic world was that, "philosophical discourse is not just about the ideal language but rather, by means of it, about the world" (Bergmann 1959: 93).

According to this brand of philosopher, whom we might label "picture theorists," language provides a picture of the world. The picture provided by ordinary language is imperfect, and it is the job of the philosopher to clarify it until a perfectly accurate one is arrived at. This is done by reformulating ordinary language, by means of logical analysis, into the ideal language, which is the one that presents the one true picture of reality. The true picture of reality is one that, by its logical form, represents the ontological form of reality. These philosophers thought that the ideal language mapped so perfectly onto reality itself that the ontological features of reality could be ascertained by examining the logical features of the ideal language.

The positivists were unhappy with the claims to metaphysical knowledge of the picture theorists, and also with the idea that there is only one true, or ideal, language. The picture theorists were, in turn, unhappy with the positivist conclusions that there can be no knowledge of reality independent of any linguistic framework, and the inevitable relativism that this generated. They were also unhappy with the positivist idea that there was no privileged linguistic framework. Just like the positivists, they were keen to banish the speculative metaphysical system-building of the neo-Kantian tradition and return philosophy to a more respectable, scientific basis, but the positivist strategy for doing so led straight back to a similar metaphysical picture as that endorsed by the Kantians. The picture theorists adopted the focus on language that the positivists had recommended, as a way of securing the scientific respectability of philosophy, but rejected the positivists' view that there can be no knowledge of extralinguistic reality. Instead, they claimed that the study of language could itself yield knowledge of the nature of extralinguistic reality.

In the early part of the twentieth century, there appeared to be two views on offer about the relationship between language and reality. One was that philosophical assertions about extralinguistic reality were meaningless, or they were to be understood as assertions about language (the positivist view). The other was that language generates a picture of reality and that there is, or at least could be, an ideal language which is a perfectly accurate picture of extralinguistic reality, such that by studying the former you can learn about the latter (the picture theory). Since the positivist view led to a kind of Kantianism, the picture theory was adopted as the only viable, and available, alternative. As noted above, the positivist view, like the Kantian view, is effectively immune from committing the representational fallacy. The picture theory, however, is far more prone to it. The very core of the picture theory is that the ideal language is a perfectly accurate picture of reality and that the logical features of the ideal language are representative of the ontological features of reality. With these ideas in place, it is a short step to the position that we can derive conclusions about the nature of reality from premises about the nature of language. It is, however, a fallacious step.

The question that we need to ask at this juncture is: are these two alternatives exhaustive? If we reject the strategy of the picture theorists, is our only alternative the unappealing metaphysics of the positivists? It is my view that these two alternatives are not exhaustive. It is not the case that, having identified and rejected any strategy that employs the representational fallacy, we are condemned to a relativist, antirealist metaphysics. It is quite possible to be a realist, in the robust, metaphysical sense of the term, while denying that we can learn about the nature or structure of reality from the nature or structure of the language we use to describe it. The positivists rejected the picture theorists' claim that there is just one true, or ideal, language, but they thought that this committed them to the view that the way the world is, is relative to the different languages used to describe it. The picture theorists denied this conclusion and thought that the only way to do so was by asserting that there is just one true description of reality: the "ideal" language. I will argue in Chapter 4 that both parties to this dispute have made the mistake of conflating descriptions of reality with reality itself. As we shall see, it is possible for reality to be just one way, while there are many different ways of accurately describing it.

This brief, potted history of some of the pivotal moments in recent philosophical thinking has, I hope, revealed that the representational fallacy came about largely as a result of the linguistic turn. This revolution had the result of elevating language to the prominent position of being the only legitimate focus of philosophical investigation. It was further encouraged by the ultimate collapse of the positivist strategy since that was seen to lead to a kind of neo-Kantian metaphysics, together with the belief that the only alternative to this strategy was that of the picture theorists. If language is the proper focus of philosophical investigation, and extralinguistic reality *is* accessible to us then, it was thought, the study of language must be the proper route to knowledge of it.

The contemporary metaphysical project

The practitioners of contemporary metaphysics in the analytic tradition have rejected the positivist project along with the Kantian conception of metaphysics. It is reasonable to think that proponents of the picture theory led the way in this reaction against positivism which, in turn, has led to the dominant strategy in contemporary metaphysical thought. The proponents of the picture theory, as we have seen, thought that while language was the appropriate object of philosophical study, nevertheless extralinguistic reality is not beyond our epistemic reach. This idea that metaphysics is the study of reality itself, rather than of our thought about it, or representations of it, is one that is strongly endorsed by contemporary metaphysicians. It represents a return to the traditional Aristotelian conception of metaphysics and a rejection of the Kantian conception. Most contemporary metaphysicians in the analytic tradition take the primary concern of metaphysics to be the systematic study of the most fundamental structure of reality as a whole (Lowe 1998: 2).

Like scientific disciplines (biology, physics, chemistry, for example), metaphysics is concerned with the nature of reality, of what exists in the world. But scientific disciplines are each concerned with a particular portion of reality: living things, for example, or molecular structures. The subject matter of metaphysics, by contrast, is reality *as a whole*. That is not to say that metaphysics is equivalent to the sum total of every other scientific discipline. It differs from them both in scope and in methodology, and I will elaborate on these differences below. Metaphysics studies the nature of existence, what kind (or kinds) of things exist. Its subject matter is reality itself, and its aim is to discover the nature and structure of that reality.

It is on this point that the Aristotelian conception of metaphysics differs from the Kantian conception. As we have seen, Kantians hold that reality itself is not something the human mind can access. Thus, metaphysical knowledge as understood by the Aristotelian is something that cannot be achieved, according to the Kantian. However, the Kantian endorses another kind of activity under the name of metaphysics. Where the Aristotelian seeks to study and articulate the nature and structure of reality, the Kantian seeks to study and articulate the nature and structure of human thought about reality. The difference between the Kantian and the Aristotelian conceptions of metaphysics can be captured by focusing on how they each see the relationship between minds, representations, and reality. When we think about the world, of necessity we can only do so by employing our concepts and our cognitive equipment. Thus, our knowledge is never wholly independent of the thinking involved in acquiring it. The Kantian concludes from this (via the Gem) that the world as it is independently of our thinking about it is inaccessible to us. That is, our representations of the world constitute a barrier between us and the world, making it ultimately inaccessible to us. By contrast, the Aristotelian sees our representations of the world not as barring us access to the world but as constituting our means of accessing it. As Michael Loux puts it,

> Traditional [Aristotelian] metaphysicians...insist that we manage to think and talk about things – things as they really are and not just things as they figure in the stories we tell. They will insist that the very idea of thinking about or referring to things presupposes that there are relations that tie our thoughts and words to the mind-independent, language-independent things we think and talk about; and they will insist that so far from barring us from access to things, the concepts we employ in our thinking are the vehicles for grasping the things to which they apply. They are not screens or barriers between us and things; they are, on the contrary, our routes to objects, our ways of gaining access to them.
>
> (Loux 2002: 10–11)

In a similar vein, E. J. Lowe writes, "Our thoughts do not constitute a veil or curtain interposed between us and the things we are endeavouring to think of, somehow making them inaccessible or inscrutable to us. On the contrary, things are accessible to us precisely because we are able to think of them" (2002: 14). Thus, the Aristotelian conception of metaphysics sees minds as capable of achieving access to reality, and it is via our representations of reality that we achieve that access.

I take it that the majority of metaphysicians working within the analytic tradition consider themselves to be employing the Aristotelian conception of what metaphysics is. That is, they take themselves to be involved in the systematic study of the fundamental nature of reality itself and not of the nature of our thought about reality, or of our conceptual scheme. I, for one, see this as what I am doing when I am engaged in metaphysics. However, given this return to the Aristotelian conception of metaphysics that focuses on the study of reality itself, two questions reemerge. First, what is the relationship between metaphysics and science? Are they distinct disciplines, and if so, how do they differ from each other? Second, how do metaphysicians carry out this investigation into the nature of reality? I will address these questions in the following two sections.

Metaphysics and science

If metaphysics is concerned with investigating the nature and structure of reality, how does it differ from science, which also has that aim? I noted above that one difference between metaphysics and the scientific disciplines is in their scope. Metaphysics is concerned with reality as a whole, while the various scientific disciplines are concerned with particular portions of reality. Furthermore, even if we consider the subject matters of all of the sciences put together, the scope of metaphysics is wider still. The combined subject matters of the physical sciences, for example, constitute physical reality, but whether reality is exhausted by physical reality is a metaphysical question. Many philosophers think that there are abstract objects, such as, for example, propositions, numbers, universals, possible worlds, and God. If such entities exist, then an investigation into their nature falls within the purview of metaphysics, but not of any of the empirical sciences. And it is equally an exercise in metaphysics, but not in science, to establish their nonexistence if they do not exist. There are other entities too, the nature of which is studied by metaphysics, but not by science. What it is to be a person, for example, is a metaphysical question. According to some philosophers, being a person involves possessing an immaterial soul, but other philosophers think persons are physical entities. Even if the latter philosophers are right, however, the nature of persons is still not a scientific question, although it may be a question to which science is relevant.

Metaphysics also asks questions the answers to which are presupposed by science. Physics, for example, investigates the properties of, and relations between, objects in the natural world. Metaphysics asks whether there really are any properties, relations, and objects, and if so, what are the natures of these entities? Physics also appeals to putative causal laws in explaining the behavior of objects in the natural world. Metaphysics asks whether there really is any such thing as causation, and, if so, what is its nature? So the empirical sciences begin their investigations into reality with certain assumptions in place, and one of the tasks of metaphysics is to examine those very assumptions. In this way, the metaphysical enterprise is at once wider in scope than, and prior to, the various scientific enterprises.

Lowe remarks on a further difference between metaphysics and the empirical sciences, while trying to justify the pursuit of metaphysics as an intellectual enquiry independent from science. He states that "Empirical science at most tells us what *is* the case, not what *must* or *may be* (but happens not to be) the case. Metaphysics deals in *possibilities*" (1998: 5). This claim seems to be, if not in direct conflict, then at least in tension with the view, endorsed by Lowe, that metaphysics is the study of the fundamental nature of reality. An investigation into what reality might be like is not the same thing as an investigation into what reality is in fact like. For one thing, there are many ways the world might be, but there is just one way the world actually is. If metaphysics is concerned with finding out what the world might be like, then it stops short of telling us what it actually is like. And if empirical science is concerned with finding out what the world is actually like, then in this respect it is more informative than metaphysics.

Lowe seems to be aware of this tension, even if only implicitly. As I noted above, he raises this point while attempting to distinguish metaphysics from empirical science. But in spite of the differences between metaphysical enquiry and scientific enquiry that I have already noted, there is a sense in which they share a common aim: to discover the nature of reality itself. But if the world is the way it is merely contingently, then, as Lowe concedes, "only [empirical] evidence could reveal to us that the world we inhabit has one contingent structure rather than another which it is equally possible for the world to have had" (2002: 10). Thus, if metaphysics is a nonempirical enquiry that is concerned with possibilities, then it is unable to achieve its aim of discovering the nature of reality itself. At this point Lowe comments that

> This kind of consideration, then, may seem to drive us in the direction of regarding metaphysical knowledge, to the extent that it is possible at all, as being a species of *empirical* knowledge. But then it is not clear, after all, that metaphysics can legitimately claim to be distinct from, and in any sense prior to, natural science.
> (Lowe 2002: 10)

It is clear, however, that Lowe emphatically wishes both to reject the claim that metaphysical knowledge is a species of empirical knowledge and to endorse the claim that metaphysics is distinct from, and prior to, natural science.

In the face of this situation, Lowe responds as follows:

> [W]here a metaphysician asserts the existence of some fundamental structural feature of reality which he deems to be *contingent* in character, then, indeed, he should acknowledge that this claim is answerable to empirical evidence, at least in part. But it is important to see that such a claim is not answerable *solely* to empirical evidence. For where a metaphysician makes such a claim, it is incumbent upon him to establish ... that the existence of that feature is at least *possible*.
> (Lowe 2002: 10)

Thus, Lowe concedes that metaphysics is answerable to empirical evidence, but, he thinks, this is not sufficient to establish that metaphysical knowledge is a species of empirical knowledge. Furthermore, he believes he has done enough here to secure the claim that metaphysics is distinct from, and prior to, natural science. Metaphysics is concerned with establishing which features of reality are possible, and this is not something that can be done either by appeal to empirical evidence or by empirical means of enquiry. However, by characterizing metaphysics in this way Lowe threatens to render it redundant. If a metaphysician asserts the existence of a contingent feature of reality, and the existence of that feature is confirmed by empirical evidence, then there is no need to establish that the existence of that feature is possible, since what is actual is *a fortiori* possible.

At this point, Lowe seems to be withdrawing from his earlier position that metaphysics is concerned to discover the fundamental structure of reality. Now it seems that metaphysics is concerned to discover the range of possible fundamental structures of reality. But insofar as we want to discover what the world is actually like, metaphysics, it seems, is unable to help us. The best it can do is tell us what the world is not like, since discovering the range of possible fundamental structures of reality involves ruling out of contention any *im*possible fundamental structures of reality. As Lowe remarks, "Having charted the possibilities, the question will remain as to which of many mutually incompatible possibilities for the fundamental structure of reality *actually* obtains – and this question can only be answered, if at all, with the aid of empirical evidence, and then only tentatively and provisionally" (2002: 11).

But this position seems at odds with what most metaphysicians, Lowe included, take themselves to be doing. They clearly see themselves as arguing that reality *is* such and such a way, not that it *might* be, and I think they are right to do so. What seems to be driving Lowe away from this position is his concern to distinguish metaphysical enquiry from scientific enquiry, together with his recognition that no conclusion regarding the existence of some contingent feature of reality can possibly be arrived at without appealing to empirical evidence. But these two concerns need not be in tension.

Lowe is evidently reacting against Quine's naturalism, and, in particular, his view that philosophy is merely a part of natural science and that its methods and resources are no different from those of the sciences (Quine 1966, 1969, 1975). However, in rejecting that view, and in an effort to preserve the status of metaphysics as an enterprise independent from science, he takes the view that the subject matter of metaphysics is the realm of possible ways reality might be, as this is clearly beyond the realms of any scientific enterprise. But, as I have suggested above, if this view is right, it is not clear how Lowe can retain the claim that the aim of a metaphysical investigation is to study and articulate the *actual* fundamental structure of reality. By retreating from the Quinean view in this way, he renders metaphysics far less informative than science. At the same time, Lowe does not want to deny the role of empirical evidence in arriving at one's metaphysical conclusions. Any metaphysical theory must be consistent with all of the available empirical evidence. But the role he assigns to empirical evidence in a metaphysical enquiry is a subsidiary one. I want to suggest, however, that it is possible to reject Quine's naturalized view of philosophy without rejecting the view that, in some respect, metaphysics is continuous with science.

For one thing, as we have seen, metaphysics differs from science in a number of respects, so the distinction between them can safely be maintained. Second, in order to accommodate the recognition that empirical evidence plays an essential role in deriving conclusions regarding the existence of contingent features of reality, all the metaphysician need do is admit that, *in this respect*, metaphysics is continuous with science, and not a discipline apart. We should recognize that there are two stages involved in a metaphysical enquiry. First, as Lowe suggests, we must explore the possible ways the world might be, ruling out of contention any ways that it is not possible for the world to be. Then we must argue that one of these ways the world might be is the way the world actually is. This latter step needs to appeal to empirical evidence, and so in this respect metaphysics is continuous with science.

The methodology of metaphysics

Another respect in which metaphysics differs from science is in its methodology. Empirical science appeals to the results of experiments and observational data to test its hypotheses and support its conclusions; metaphysics typically does not. According to the conception of metaphysics currently under consideration, its practitioners see themselves as investigating and articulating the fundamental structure of reality. How do they go about undertaking this project? Like any other investigation, a metaphysical investigation must have some preliminary data, consideration of which constitutes its starting point. It is widely agreed that the data for a metaphysical investigation are our ordinary thought and talk about (or our representations of) the world (Laurence and Macdonald 1998: 6; Loux 2002: 16).

Loux suggests that metaphysical disputes typically display a certain general structure (2002: 16). They are often organized as responses to a question about the existence of things of a very general type or category, for example, are there properties? Are there propositions? Are there events? He continues,

> In each case, there is a body of prephilosophical facts that function as data for the dispute. One party to the dispute insists that to explain the relevant prephilosophical facts, we must answer the existential question affirmatively. The other party claims that there is something philosophically problematic in the admission of entities of the relevant sort into our ontology, and argues that we can account for the prephilosophical facts without doing so.
>
> (Loux 2002: 16–17)

Loux does not suggest that all metaphysical disputes are structured in this way, but rather that this is a common formula. Metaphysical investigations often begin with existential questions about very general kinds of entity. The prephilosophical facts that constitute the data for these disputes are our ordinary conceptual representations of the world. Such a dispute then revolves around whether these representations require the existence of the entities in question.

Van Inwagen concurs with this account of the structure of a metaphysical debate (1998: 16–19). He presents, as a case study of a metaphysical dispute, the problem of universals. He asks how we are to resolve the dispute between Platonists and nominalists. Platonists think that properties, construed as abstract entities, exist; nominalists deny this. Following Quine, van Inwagen suggests that we should examine the beliefs we already have and see whether any of them commits us to the existence of properties. If any of them does, then we have a reason for believing that properties exist, namely, the reason we had for holding the original belief in the first place, together with the general epistemic principle that if I become aware that my belief that p commits me to the belief that q, then I should either believe that q or relinquish my belief that p. Van Inwagen goes on to suggest that we might, on examining our beliefs, discover the belief that "Spiders share some of the anatomical features of insects" among them. He then remarks that it is plausible to think that this belief commits us to the existence of anatomical features, and that, furthermore, it is reasonable to think that anatomical features are properties. So, we have a case of prima facie commitment to the existence of properties, where our starting point is our set of prephilosophical beliefs about the world.

How does the nominalist, who denies that there exist any properties, respond to this? Van Inwagen suggests that there are four possible responses available to the nominalist: (1) become a Platonist; (2) abandon her belief that spiders share some of the anatomical features of insects; (3) attempt to show that it does not follow from this belief that there are anatomical features; or (4) admit that her beliefs are apparently inconsistent, affirm her commitment to nominalism, and resolve to find a fault in the argument from ordinary beliefs to Platonism. Of these four options, the only viable ones, I want to suggest, are (1) and (3). If the nominalist is concerned to retain as many of her prephilosophical beliefs as possible, then (2) is not a viable option. (4), on the other hand, is merely a promissory note.

So a nominalist must either reject nominalism and become a Platonist, as option (1) suggests, or attempt to show that the existence of properties does not follow from her prephilosophical belief about spiders and their anatomical features. Of these, van Inwagen notes, the nominalist is most likely to take up option (3). The way in which she will do this is to try and find a paraphrase of that sentence. The paraphrase will be one that allows her to convey all the information conveyed by the original sentence but which does not have the unwanted ontological implication. If successful, she will be in a position to affirm that the prima facie commitment to the existence of properties entailed by her endorsement of the original belief was merely apparent.

Van Inwagen's presentation of this case study of a metaphysical dispute brings into focus a methodological tool that is widely used in such disputes, that of paraphrase. Some sentences of ordinary language appear to have ontological implications; they seem to imply that entities of various kinds exist. It is commonly agreed that there are two ways in which a metaphysician can proceed. She can either accept the apparent ontological implications of some sentence of ordinary language, or she can attempt to find a paraphrase of it which conveys all the same information, but which does not have the unwanted ontological implications. Metaphysical disputes then centre on whether a candidate paraphrase really does convey all the information of the original ordinary language sentence. Proponents of the existence of the entities in question will argue that any suggested paraphrase fails to convey the same information as the original, and so is an inadequate paraphrase. They conclude that there are some things that can only be said using the original ordinary language sentences. If we can only accurately describe reality using such sentences, then there must *exist* some aspect of reality that can only be described using those sentences. Their opponents argue for the adequacy of any suggested paraphrase. It is in this way that metaphysical disputes are transformed into disputes about language, and about what various sentences "really" mean.

But is it the case that, in metaphysical disputes which are structured in this way, these are really our only options? I think there is an alternative option, and that its existence has been hidden by an implicit commitment to the view that the way our representations of reality are must reveal the way reality itself is. But that view, as we shall see in the course of this investigation, is false.

An historical interlude: why has the significance of language been upgraded in philosophy?

Both of the positions in the common methodological structure just described depend on seeing language as highly significant in the development of a metaphysical position. We have already seen some of the reasons for the linguistic turn above. In this section I will examine some of the key lines of thought that led to the upgrading of the importance of language in metaphysics, and in philosophy more generally, and also consider whether its significance has in fact been overstated.

In "Language and Philosophy," Hilary Putnam (1975) offers two reasons why the importance of language has been upgraded in philosophy, both of which have their roots in the work of the logical positivists in the early part of the twentieth century. In order to set these developments into their historical context, Putnam gives a characterization of the philosophical scene immediately prior to their occurrence. It is generally agreed, he says, that some of the tasks of philosophy are to study our ideas or concepts of, for example, matter, cause, duty, good, and so on. Up until the early twentieth century, it was universally thought that ideas and concepts were mental entities: images, or mental presentations of some kind. Thus, philosophers took it to be their job to engage in introspective psychology. If we want to find out about our concept of cause, for example, and concepts are mental entities, then it is natural to think that we should turn our attention inwards and study the mental entity that is our concept of cause. But, Putnam notes, the more philosophers concentrated on purely mental matters, the harder it became to refute the idealist view that "mental matters" are all there is. In this way, philosophy dug itself deeper into what he calls an "idealist swamp."

How, then, did philosophers break out of this idealist swamp? Putnam outlines two different, albeit related, ways in which this happened. The first is due to Wittgenstein (1953) who challenged the conception of concepts or ideas as mental entities. According to that view, an organism possesses the concept of, say, a chair if it has a mental image of a chair. Wittgenstein's alternative view was that an organism possesses the concept of a chair if it can successfully employ the usual sentences containing the word "chair" in some natural language. Someone might have that very complicated ability without possessing any chair images, and in that case we would say that she possessed the concept of a chair. Conversely, someone might possess chair images without having the ability to use the word "chair" correctly in ordinary language, and in that case we would say that she lacked the concept of a chair. So, possessing mental images of a chair is neither necessary nor sufficient for possessing the concept chair. It is, at best, correlated with it. But having the very complicated ability to use the word "chair" successfully in ordinary language is, according to Wittgenstein, both necessary and sufficient for possessing the concept *chair*.

Contemporary philosophers of mind would no doubt baulk at Wittgenstein's account of having a concept in terms of having the ability to use certain words correctly as being overly behaviorist. Nevertheless, if Wittgenstein is merely right about rejecting the identification of concepts with mental entities, then the method of investigating philosophical issues via introspective psychology can be seen to be fundamentally misguided. But Wittgenstein's account of what it is to possess a concept also suggests an alternative, and potentially more fruitful, way of investigating such concepts. If possessing the concept of cause is possessing the ability to use and understand the word "cause" in ordinary language, then we should turn our attention away from introspecting the contents of our minds and onto the way in which we use the word "cause".

This is potentially more fruitful than the method of introspective psychology for two reasons. First, there is no public way of assessing the reliability of someone's report of her mental images, but the way in which we use the word "cause" is well within the public domain. Second, we would be lucky to find two philosophers with the same mental images corresponding to the word "cause," but we can expect a high level of agreement among philosophers as to how the word "cause" is properly used. This latter kind of enquiry is a public, rather than a private one, and so, in this way, philosophy becomes more akin to scientific enquiry, subject to public methods of scrutiny and assessment. Thus, by performing a Wittgensteinian analysis of the notion of what it is to possess a concept, and rejecting the idea that the way to make progress in philosophy is by introspection, we are led to the conclusion that the proper focus of a philosophical enquiry is language.

An enquiry along the lines suggested by Putnam and Wittgenstein will, indeed, be a lot more fruitful and reliable than one in which philosophers merely inspect the contents of their minds in an attempt to gain insight into the nature of philosophical concepts. But let us be clear about the aims of such an enquiry, whether it be of the Wittgensteinian or the traditional variety. What these two very different kinds of enquiry share is their view of what is the proper object of a philosophical enquiry. They both agree that philosophy is concerned with (among other things) our *concepts of* matter, cause, duty, good, and so on. If our aim in philosophy is to produce an account of these concepts, then we can pursue that aim in either the traditional or the Wittgensteinian way, and of these alternatives, the latter will be more fruitful, so we will make more progress in philosophy by concentrating on language than on mental entities. But is it really the case that our aim in philosophy is to produce an account of concepts such as these?

Certainly, many philosophers have thought, and still think that it is. According to Michael Jubien, for example, "The study of concepts plays a central role in all of philosophy. In fact it is often held that philosophy is nothing more than the study of certain very general, characteristically "philosophical" concepts – for example, existence, truth, knowledge, justification, mind, and goodness" (Jubien 1997: 1), and progress can be made in philosophy because

> the meanings of the words and phrases of our language are the result of the linguistic activity of its (past and present) speakers. To understand these words and phrases is to have a grasp – possibly imperfect – of these meanings. In other words, it is to have some idea of the concepts associated with the terms.
>
> (Jubien 1997: 8)

Jubien has clearly taken up the philosophical program generated by Wittgenstein's analysis of what it is to possess a concept. He sees the objects of philosophical study to be various philosophical concepts, such as the concepts of cause, truth, and goodness. He also endorses the view that the proper way to go about investigating those concepts is to examine the ways in which we use the words "cause", "truth", and "goodness".

But this account of the aim of philosophy is at odds with that endorsed by metaphysicians such as Loux, Lowe, and others, whose program is the focus of this enquiry. According to them, as we have seen, the aim of metaphysics is to present and defend a theory of the fundamental nature and structure of reality itself and not of our concepts. Contemporary metaphysics in the Aristotelian tradition is less interested in our concept of cause and more interested in whatever it is in the world (if anything) to which our concept applies. If we understand a metaphysical enquiry in that way, then it is at best an open question how useful it will be to focus our attention on language.

The second way of breaking out of the idealist swamp described by Putnam is found in the work of Rudolf Carnap, although it is also suggested by the work of Russell. In *The Logical Syntax of Language*, Carnap

(1937) suggested that traditional philosophical problems might best be considered by looking at the theoretical relations between whole systems of sentences. Putnam describes Carnap's treatment of the philosophical theory of phenomenalism. This is, roughly, the view that material objects are nothing but "bundles of sensations." Traditionally this thesis would have been examined by looking, introspectively, at our idea of a material object and considering whether or not it was the same idea as that of a bundle of sensations. Carnap suggested instead that if there is anything to this view then it must be that for each sentence about material objects there is a corresponding sentence about sense data which expresses all that is expressed by the first sentence. The idea behind Carnap's suggestion must be that if phenomenalism is right, then it must be possible to say all that can be said using the language of material objects, by using the language of sense data instead.

As Putnam notes, one effect of taking Carnap's suggestion seriously is that at least part of the traditional philosophical dispute about phenomenalism can be raised to a scientific level. The phenomenalist has a tangible goal: to define a mapping from material-object sentences to sense-datum sentences that, at the very least, preserves truth value. Any proposed mapping can be subjected to scrutiny to see if it really does preserve truth-value. If she is unable to supply such a mapping, then phenomenalism does not have to be taken seriously. So, the Carnapian reason for upgrading the importance of language in philosophy, just like the Wittgensteinian reason, has a significant virtue, which is to render the practice of philosophy more scientific and more open to public scrutiny. Perhaps as a result of this virtue, it is easier to see how progress can be achieved in philosophy by the combined efforts of all those involved in it.

Another implication of Carnap's treatment of phenomenalism, noted by Putnam, is that it reveals that there are in fact two different versions of phenomenalism, where it was thought that there was only one. These are:

(I) Ontological Phenomenalism: Material things *are* bundles of sensations.
(II) Linguistic Phenomenalism: Thing-sentences can be 'translated' into sense-datum sentences, by a 'translation' that preserves truth-value, according to the phenomenalist.

(Putnam 1975: 19)

Carnap's point was that it is only if the phenomenalist asserts (II) as well as (I) does she assert anything testable, and if she asserts (II), then we can carry out research to determine whether any proposed translation is successful. Indeed, Carnap went on to conclude, after much investigation, that (II) is, in fact, false. It seems very likely that material-object language cannot be translated into sense-datum language, so at least some "material object" notions must be taken as primitive in any language adequate for science. So, by following Carnap, not only do we make philosophy more scientific but we can actually achieve significant results.

This is, of course, all very well. But it seems to me that at least one question has been overlooked, and that is: what is the relationship between (I) and (II)? Carnap himself, of course, thought that (I) had no factual content, so the closest we could get to a meaningful approximation to (I) was (II). But suppose we shelve that positivist assumption for the moment and assume, along with contemporary metaphysicians, that we are capable of asserting philosophical claims about reality that have genuine factual content. Furthermore, let us suppose that Carnap has established the falsity of (II). As far as I can see, that doesn't tell us whether (I) is true or false. On the one hand, (I) does not entail (II), so refuting (II) does not refute (I). On the other hand, (II) does not entail (I), so proving (II) would not prove (I). Carnap's claim is that the closest we can get to a testable version of (I) is (II). But just how close is (II) to (I)? What does rejecting (II) tell us about the status of (I)? Rather than being a "testable version" of (I), (II) simply changes the subject from a claim about material objects to a claim about material-object sentences; it changes the subject from reality to language.

I suggested above that the idea behind Carnap's program must be that if phenomenalism is right, then it must be possible to say all that can be said using the language of material objects, by using the language of sense data instead. If this is not possible, and if we assume that we are capable of asserting philosophical claims about reality that have factual content, then the language of material objects is capable of expressing some facts about the world which the language of sense data is incapable of expressing. It then seems to follow that there must *be* some fact in the world that can only be described using the language of material objects. All this seems to be taken for granted, but it is, as I shall argue in Chapter 3, far from obviously true.

Yet another reason for the upgrading of the importance of language, in particular of sentences, in philosophy is suggested in an aspect of Quine's work, which echoes that of Russell. It is Quine's so-called second milestone of empiricism: "the shift of semantic focus from terms to sentences" (1981: 67), or the primacy of sentence meaning. If we take individual terms to be the primary vehicles of meaning, then we seem to be led inevitably to the conclusion that the world contains far more entities than science would have us believe. For example, there must be fictional and mythological entities corresponding to names and definite descriptions such as "Harry Potter" and "the whomping willow"; universals, such as the property of redness, corresponding to predicates; some kind of entity corresponding to logical connectives (logical glue?); and so on for every kind of expression. Naturally, this conclusion is in violent conflict with Quine's austere worldview. It also conflicts with his empiricism, as it suggests that our grasp of our familiar language gives us direct acquaintance with objects that are not evident to our senses. But it can be avoided if we change the focus of our attention from individual terms to whole sentences.

If the primary vehicle of meaning is the sentence rather than the word, then the meanings of individual words can be explained in terms of the roles they play in meaningful sentences in which they occur. We understand a word, or grasp its meaning when we know how to use and understand the sentences in which it occurs. This insight of Quine's, it will be noticed, bears a striking resemblance to Wittgenstein's analysis of what it is to possess a concept, discussed above. However, Quine applied it in some interesting ways. First, as already noted, we can stop looking for some object that functions as the referent of a predicate and focus instead on the roles of predicates in sentences. This allows space for a nominalist position, such as Quine's. Second, we can account for the roles played by the term "meaning" itself, without having to introduce meanings as abstract objects. In "On What There Is," Quine argued that the two main purposes served by talk of meanings are those concerned with the significance of a term and with synonymy between terms, and we can say everything we want to say about these notions without assuming that there is some meaning that every meaningful expression has (Quine 1948).

Perhaps most importantly for our purposes here, Quine associates the thesis of the primacy of sentence meaning with Russell's use of paraphrase, particularly as it occurs in his theory of descriptions (Russell 1905). We appear to refer to properties with singular terms, such as "redness". But we can paraphrase talk of redness by talk of red things. This does not give us an analysis of the word "redness", but it (arguably) gives us an account of all the sentences in which it occurs. According to Quine, only the primacy of sentence meaning can explain why such analyses seem satisfactory. If word meaning was primary, any analysis of the meaning of a sentence would have to contain a clarification of the problematic words. The primacy of sentence meaning frees us from this requirement. An adequate paraphrase of an allegedly misleading sentence need contain no term corresponding to the problematic term in the original.

The paraphrase technique is supposed to take a problematic sentence and provide another, less problematic sentence, which reveals the content of the original. The primacy of sentence meaning, according to Quine, explains why this technique appears to offer a satisfactory analysis, and thus why a focus on language (i.e., finding paraphrases for problematic sentences) is philosophically respectable. Two questions naturally arise at this point. First, what is problematic about the original sentences? And second, what is the relationship between a problematic sentence and its unproblematic paraphrase? I shall address these questions in turn.

Presumably, a sentence such as (1) "Redness is a color" is thought, by Quine, to be problematic because it contains a singular term "redness", which appears to refer to a universal. Quine wants to reject the existence of universals because they are not objects of scientific study and because we are not acquainted with them via our senses. Since he wishes to reject their existence, he seeks to find paraphrases of sentences like (1) which do not contain terms that appear to refer to universals. But Quine's notion of the primacy of sentence meaning undermines his reason for finding sentences like (1) problematic in the first place. If the word is not the primary bearer of meaning, then, as Quine himself realizes, we do not have to accept that there is some entity that is the referent of every word. We can explain the meaning of the word "redness" by explaining how it contributes to the meanings of sentences in which it occurs. And this does not require us to find some entity to which the word refers. Why then do we need to find paraphrases for sentences containing the word "redness"? If we follow Quine in adopting the primacy of sentence meaning, then it seems that we no longer need to see sentences like (1) as problematic, so we should be relieved of the burden of finding unproblematic paraphrases of them.

To turn to the second question, what is the relationship between "problematic" sentences and their unproblematic paraphrases? According to Russell (1905), the paraphrases provide analyses of the originals. They reveal the underlying, true logical or grammatical structure that was present in the original but concealed by the misleading trappings of ordinary language. If this is right, then we might still wonder what motivates this search for the true logical form of ordinary language sentences. Is it merely an attempt to "tidy up" or regiment ordinary language? Or is there some further belief about the relationship between the true logical form of sentences and the reality described by those sentences?

I think it is clear that in Russell's case there is an explicit belief that the true logical form of sentences somehow reveals to us the true ontological form of reality. So his desire to provide unproblematic paraphrases of problematic sentences is motivated by his belief that ordinary language gives us a misleading picture of what the world is like, but if we can reveal the underlying, true logical form of sentences of ordinary language, that will give us a much more accurate picture of what the world is like. But what reason have we for thinking that there is one true logical form of ordinary language, or of all ordinary languages? And, more importantly, even supposing that there is a single, true logical form of ordinary language sentences, what reason have we for thinking that reality somehow matches up to that form, such that we can "read off" the nature and structure of reality from the nature and structure of logical form?

Quine takes a weaker view than Russell on the relationship between "problematic" sentences and their unproblematic paraphrases. Two such sentences, he suggests, can serve the same purpose, but the paraphrases are preferable because they are clearer (Quine 1960: 214). So, according to Quine, if we stopped using the original sentences and used only the paraphrases, we would still be able to say everything we could previously say, and we would avoid the possibility of being misled by the surface features of ordinary language. This aspect of Quine's view can be subjected to testing.

We can examine any pair of sentences constituted by a "problematic" sentence of ordinary language and an unproblematic paraphrase of it to see whether it really is possible to say everything with the latter that could be said with the former. We shall see in Chapter 2 that there is at least one domain of "problematic" discourse whose sentences have no unproblematic paraphrases that are capable of saying all that is said by the originals.

But let us, for the moment, grant Quine his view about the relationship between ordinary language sentences and their paraphrases. The question still arises, as it did with Russell, what motivates the search for unproblematic paraphrases of ordinary language sentences? Once again, as with Russell, I do not think it is any yearning on Quine's part to tidy up ordinary language. Rather, I believe it is driven by a belief that the paraphrases are ontologically more perspicuous than the originals. So, even a weaker view than Russell's on the relationship between problematic sentences and their paraphrases is driven by the view that language has some ontological significance and that if we want to find out about reality we should avoid ordinary language, which will give us a false account of its nature and structure, and turn instead to unproblematic paraphrases of ordinary language sentences, which will give us an accurate account. But once again, why should we think that even a tidied-up version of language can reveal to us the way reality is? There is an assumption in the work of both Quine and Russell, that at some level it is legitimate to move from the nature and structure of certain privileged sentences about reality to the nature and structure of reality itself.

We have considered three reasons why the importance of language to philosophy has been upgraded in the past 100 years or so. These were: (1) the move from thinking that concepts, a natural focus of philosophical enquiry, were mental entities to thinking that the possession of a concept consists in the ability to use language; (2) the transformation of puzzling philosophical theses into linguistic theses, where, unlike with the former, real progress could be made in answering the latter; and (3) the shift from the primacy of word meaning to the primacy of sentence meaning, which freed us from having to look for some entity which is the referent of any meaningful term. While acknowledging the benefits these shifts in focus have had in philosophy, I have suggested that, if our goal in metaphysics is to discover the fundamental nature and structure of the world itself, then this concentration on language may in fact be misplaced.

2 A new metaphysical strategy
Lessons learned from the philosophy of time

In the section "The Methodology of Metaphysics," of Chapter 1, I raised some questions about a common form of metaphysical dispute, which is structured around existential questions and according to which it is commonly thought that there are two available positions. One of these positions appeals to our ordinary linguistic representations of reality to support it, and the other employs the method of paraphrase in its support. Both positions thus take language to be highly significant for the purposes of answering existential questions. In this chapter, I want to examine a particular metaphysical dispute, the debate about the ontological status of tense, that originally had this sort of structure, and whose protagonists relied on facts about language in the way described. However, in the early 1980s, this debate radically changed, and a new position emerged that showed that the original two positions were not exhaustive as had originally been thought. I will show that, whether its proponents realized it or not, the possibility of advancing this new position depended on rejecting a particular, flawed view about the relationship between language and reality.

The A-theory and the B-theory of time

There are two basic metaphysical theories of time. There is the A-theory of time, according to which the commonsense distinction between the past, present, and future reflects a real ontological distinction. A corollary of accepting the reality of this distinction is that time is dynamic: what was future, is now present, and will be past. Then there is the B-theory of time, according to which there is no ontological distinction between past, present, and future. The fact that we draw this distinction in ordinary life is a reflection of our perspective on temporal reality, rather than a reflection of the nature of time itself. A corollary of denying that there is a distinction between past, present, and future is that time is not dynamic in the way just described.

Both theories recognize that, at the level of ordinary thought and talk, there are two different ways in which we conceptualize the ordering and location of events and moments in time. They disagree over the metaphysical significance of each of these ways of thinking about time. Consider, for a moment, the series of events that constitutes the entire temporal history of the universe. One way of thinking about this series involves the recognition that each event is located in either the past, present, or future, and that they can be ordered according to whether they are in the distant past, near past, present, near future, or distant future. The series of events conceived in this way is called the A-series, a label derived from McTaggart (1927: Chapter 33, §306). The other way involves the recognition that each event in this series is temporally related to every other event. That is, for any pair of events, e_1 and e_2, in this series, e_1 is either earlier than, simultaneous with, or later than e_2. Both the temporal locations of events relative to each other, and their temporal ordering, can be given in terms of these temporal relations, without any need to employ the concepts of pastness, presentness, and futurity. The series of events conceived in this way is called the B-series (McTaggart 1927: §306).

The A-theory of time is so-called because, according to it, A-series concepts are essential for an adequate metaphysical characterization of time. While it recognizes that events stand in temporal relations to each other, and so constitute a B-series,[1] it holds that this is insufficient to characterize the true metaphysical nature of time. A tensed attribute, such as "three hours ago," "50 million years hence," or "today," when ascribed to an event, assigns it a position in the A-series. The metaphysical nature of time is such that there are tensed facts: facts involving the pastness, presentness, or futurity of events, or the tensed properties of pastness, presentness, and futurity.

According to the B-theory of time, the B-series ordering of events is sufficient for an adequate metaphysical characterization of time. Although B-theorists recognize that the distinction between past, present, and future is one that we constantly allude to in everyday life, this says more about us and our epistemic access to temporal reality than it does about the metaphysical nature of time. Our use of tensed concepts merely reflects the fact that, when we use them, we do so from a particular temporal point of view. If I describe an event as present, I do so at a particular time, and what I say is true if, and only if, the event happens simultaneously with my description of it. Similarly, if I describe an event as past (future), my description is apt if, and only if, the event is temporally located earlier (later) than the time at which I so describe it. No tensed facts are needed to ground the truth of any true description that employs a tensed concept. That job can be done by the tenseless temporal relations that events stand in to each other.

I have spoken, in my characterization of the A- and the B-theory, of facts, specifically tensed facts. The term "fact" is used with many meanings in much recent and contemporary philosophy. It can be used to mean, among other things, "true sentence," "true proposition," or "structured entity." In order to avert any confusion over this issue, I will explain what I intend to convey by my use of the term "fact" and the associated notion of a truthmaker.

I take a fact to be simply a portion of reality, a bit of the world, a way some part of reality is. I am, thus, not using the term to denote a linguistic entity: a true sentence or proposition. I am, instead, using it to denote an extralinguistic entity: a part of the world. Picking out a part of reality by calling it a fact does not require that it have any particular structure. It does not require, for example, that it consists of a particular possessing a property or two particulars standing in a relation. Calling something a fact implies nothing whatsoever about its constitution. It is simply a way of picking out something that is part of the world, or a way some part of the world is, rather than picking out some way of describing some part of the world. It is a means of talking about parts of the world rather than linguistic entities.

Facts, considered in this way, can be responsible for making sentences about them true. So I use the terms "fact" and "truthmaker" interchangeably. If a sentence describing some part of the world is true, it is true in virtue of the way that part of the world is. Consequently, in such a case, I would say that the fact in question makes the sentence true. I would also say that the sentence has a truthmaker, which just is the fact that makes it true. As a further clarificatory point, a tensed fact is a fact that requires for its existence an ontological distinction between past, present, and future. This may involve that fact including, as a constituent, a tensed property, one of the properties of pastness, presentness, or futurity, or some more fine-grained variant of these, such as "being three days past."

But not all A-theorists recognize the existence of tensed properties. Many presentists, for example, deny that anything is past or future, so they deny that anything could possess properties of pastness or futurity. Furthermore, they deny that there is a property of presentness, taking the term "present" to denote instead the sum total of reality (Craig 1997). For an A-theorist like this, the question of what the truthmakers for past- and future-tensed sentences are is a live issue.[2] According to some presentists, the truthmakers for past- and future-tensed sentences are past- and future-tensed propositions, which are abstract objects. For others they are past- and future-tensed properties of the world. But one thing is certain. Whatever the truthmakers for past- and future-tensed sentences are, according to a presentist, they will be of a different ontological kind from the truthmakers of present-tensed sentences. So, as stated above, tensed facts, for the presentist, will be facts that require for their existence an ontological distinction between past, present, and future. There are many varieties of A-theory, but they do all have something in common. They all recognize an ontological distinction between past, present, and future. They merely have different ways of cashing out this distinction. Therefore, my account of a tensed fact as one that requires for its existence an ontological distinction between past, present, and future, should encompass the sorts of facts that all A-theorists take to exist.

The A-theory's argument from language to reality

The focus of much early work by proponents of the A-theory of time was the irreducibility, or ineliminability of tensed language (Gale 1968; Schlesinger 1980). These philosophers argued that tensed expressions could not be eliminated from natural language without some attendant loss of meaning. They concluded from this claim about temporal language that temporal reality itself was irreducibly or ineliminably tensed. At least one of their arguments for their metaphysical conclusion, thus, moves from premises about temporal language to conclusions about temporal reality.

The main argument that A-theorists employed to arrive at the conclusion that temporal language is ineliminable is that no tenseless sentence conveys as much information as a tensed sentence. One way to see this was highlighted by Richard Gale (1968: 91). There, he argued that tensed sentences entail tenseless sentences, but the converse entailment relation does not hold. For example, the tensed sentence, S1, "X is present and Y is future" entails the tenseless sentence, S2, "X is earlier than Y," but S2 entails nothing about the A-series locations of X and Y. Thus, by uttering the tensed sentence, we convey more information than we would convey by uttering the tenseless sentence. Since S2 is the best candidate for being a tenseless translation of S1, and it fails to convey all the information conveyed by S1, Gale concluded that no tenseless sentence can convey all the information conveyed by a tensed sentence, so no tenseless sentence has the same meaning as any tensed sentence.

A more vivid illustration of the difference in information conveyed by tensed and tenseless sentences was given by Gale in an earlier paper (1962) using the following example. Joe's job is to inform his military company when the enemy are within 100 yards of their position. If Joe shouts the tensed sentence, "The enemy are now within 100 yards," his company is duly warned of their position and may take appropriate action. If, however, he tries to capture the information contained in this tensed sentence in terms of the tenseless relations between the event he is reporting and his utterance of the sentence, or the time at which he utters it, he will be unable to warn the company of the danger. If, for example, Joe shouts "The enemy are within 100 yards at 2.15 P.M.," his company will not be warned unless they also know that it is *now* 2.15 P.M., and this is a piece of tensed information.

The A-theorists concluded that, since tensed expressions convey more information than tenseless sentences, there must exist something in reality that corresponds to this additional information conveyed. For example, Gale states that, "A-expressions are ineliminable because they do convey some kind of factual information" (1968: 56). William Lane Craig states that, "if some tensed sentences are true, then reality must be tensed, since such sentences purport to ascribe ontological tenses" (2000: 22). As a final example, Quentin Smith believes that "an argument for the untranslatability thesis [the thesis that tensed sentences are untranslatable by tenseless sentences], along with a defense of the logical coherency and scientific viability of the tensed theory of time, provides adequate evidence for the tensed theory" (1993: 3). Thus, according to the A-theorists, since tensed expressions *are* needed to give a complete description of reality, there *is* a feature of reality to which they refer. That is, there really is an objective distinction between past, present and future, and time really does flow. As we shall see shortly, however, the validity of this inference has been challenged by proponents of the new B-theory of time. They argue that it is quite possible to hold that tensed language is ineliminable and that temporal reality is tenseless.

A more recent example of an A-theorist who claims that we can draw metaphysical conclusions about the nature of time from linguistic facts about temporal language is Peter Ludlow (1999). Ludlow's book constitutes an extended argument for both an A-theory metaphysics of time (specifically, presentism) and an A-theory semantics of tense. But his arguments for these two positions are not independent of each other. He suggests throughout that there are good reasons to suppose that if the A-theory conception of tense in language is correct, then the A-theory conception of the metaphysics of time follows. The following quotations illustrate how firmly he endorses this line of reasoning:

> I think he [Whorf] was correct in thinking that one can argue from the structure of human language to the nature of reality.
>
> (Ludlow 1999: xiii)

> The structure of language does have metaphysical consequences, but the structure of language does not differ in relevant ways between English and Hopi, between French and Farsi, or between Chinese and Urdu. It follows that humans all share the same metaphysics – the same reality.
>
> (Ludlow 1999: xiv)

> [W]e have good reasons to suppose that there is a close (if not isomorphic) relation between the semantics of tense and the metaphysics of time.
>
> (Ludlow 1999: 137)

> I argued for a strong connection between semantics and metaphysics, but I also hinted that there might be the possibility of an even stronger relation – one that takes the structure of language and the structure of the world to be isomorphic to each other.
>
> (Ludlow 1999: 171)

With his assumption about the connection between language and metaphysics in place, the structure of Ludlow's argument for the A-theory's metaphysics of time becomes clear. He begins by arguing that the B-theory's semantics is deficient in a number of respects. He then defends the A-theory's semantics against a number of objections, concluding that we ought to prefer the A-theory's semantics. He also offers further psycholinguistic evidence in support of the A-theory's semantics. He concludes that the A-theory conception of time, the metaphysical A-theory, is preferable. His metaphysical conclusions thus depend entirely on semantic claims.

If Ludlow's argument is to work, it must be shown that there really is this strong connection between semantics and metaphysics that he alludes to throughout. However, his claim in the fourth quote above notwithstanding, it is hard to discern anywhere in the book an *argument* for the sort of connection between semantics and metaphysics that would licence Ludlow's inferences, as opposed to repeated assertions of it. One would expect to find such an argument in his pivotal chapter entitled "Drawing Metaphysical Consequences from a T-Theory," but even there, one finds only the assertion that "we will be committed to whatever objects serve as semantic values in a correct T-theory for natural language" (Ludlow 1999: 66). Without an argument justifying the inference from facts about temporal language to conclusions about temporal reality, there is no reason to suppose the inference is valid.

Another recent A-theorist who has argued explicitly from claims about temporal language to conclusions about temporal reality is William Lane Craig (2000). He presents what he calls the A-theorist's fundamental argument, the argument from the ineliminability of tense, which is essentially an argument from tensed language to the conclusion that time is tensed. It goes as follows:

1. Tensed sentences ostensibly ascribe ontological tenses.
2. Unless tensed sentences are shown to be reducible without loss of meaning to tenseless sentences or ontological tense is shown to be superfluous to human thought and action, the ostensible ascription of ontological tenses by tensed sentences ought to be accepted as veridical.
3. Tensed sentences have not been shown to be reducible without loss of meaning to tenseless sentences.
4. Ontological tense has not been shown to be superfluous to human thought and action.
5. Therefore, the ostensible ascription of ontological tenses by tensed sentences ought to be accepted as veridical.

(Craig 2000: 22; numbering of premises changed)[3]

The argument moves from the premise that tensed sentences ostensibly ascribe ontological tenses to the conclusion that this ought to be accepted as veridical. Craig insists that, in order to avoid its conclusion, the B-theorist must either show that tensed sentences can be translated into tenseless sentences (thus refuting premise 3) or that tensed facts are not required for human thought and action (thus refuting premise 4). However, it is open to a B-theorist to reject premise 2, but Craig does not seriously consider this possibility. He thinks that in premise 2 he has offered the B-theorist her only escape routes from the conclusion of his argument; she must either show tensed sentences to be reducible to tenseless sentences without loss of meaning, or she must show that tense is superfluous to human thought and action.[4] But this is a false dilemma. The B-theorist can maintain that tense cannot be eliminated from language without loss of meaning, and that there are some human activities that cannot be fully explained without the use of tensed sentences. Nevertheless, all these essential and true tensed sentences are made true by tenseless facts.

I have shown in the foregoing discussion that A-theorists past and present have relied on claims about tense in language to reach their conclusions about tense in reality. I have also suggested some ways in which the new B-theorist responds to their arguments. Before developing that line of thought in more detail, I want to consider the old B-theorist's position with respect to the relationship between temporal language and temporal reality.

The old B-theory's translation project

According to the B-theory of time, there are no tensed facts and no tensed properties. The old B-theory tried to prove this by showing that tensed expressions could be eliminated from natural language (Russell 1915; Goodman 1951: 287–301; Quine 1960: §36; Smart 1963: 132–42). It claimed that any tensed sentence (a sentence locating an event or state of affairs somewhere in the past, present, or future) could be translated, without loss of meaning, by a tenseless sentence (a sentence locating an event or state of affairs in the static B-series). The idea behind this translation project was that if an expression-type can be shown to be eliminable from natural language, then it need not be employed to give an adequate description of the nature of reality. An eliminable expression-type is thus ontologically irrelevant. Proponents of the old B-theory of time appealed to the principle of parsimony, or Ockham's razor, to support their contention that it is the tenseless sentences rather than the tensed sentences that display the true nature of temporal reality. Tensed sentences imply the existence of tensed facts, but tenseless sentences do not, so tenseless sentences imply the existence of fewer kinds of entity than tensed sentences and are thus to be preferred.

The old B-theory concluded from its claim that tensed sentences are eliminable that, since tensed expressions are not needed to completely describe reality, there is no feature of reality that they describe. So the success of the translation project was thought to show that in reality there is no distinction between past, present, and future, and no flow of time. As it turned out, the translation project of the old B-theory of time failed. It is not possible to translate tensed sentences into tenseless sentences without some loss of meaning. This conclusion was originally arrived at by philosophers working in the philosophy of language, on the linguistic phenomena of indexicals and demonstratives. These philosophers established that no sentence containing a context-dependent expression, like an indexical or a demonstrative, could be translated by any sentence that was wholly context-independent (Castañeda 1967; Perry 1979; Wettstein 1979). Tense in language is a context-dependent phenomenon. Whether or not a tensed sentence is true depends on the time at which it is uttered, a feature of its context of utterance. So, the conclusions arrived at by these philosophers of language with regard to context-dependent sentences carried over to tensed sentences.

It is clear that proponents of both the old B-theory and the A-theory of time took temporal language to be ontologically significant. Implicit in both their positions is the idea that there is one true description of temporal reality, and once we have arrived at that description, the next step is simply to read off the nature and structure of temporal reality from the nature and structure of the representations contained in that one true description. To see that they do both make this assumption, we merely have to consider their disagreement. A-theorists argue that since there are true, ineliminable tensed sentences, reality contains tensed facts. Old B-theorists argue that true tensed sentences are eliminable in favor of tenseless sentences, so reality does not contain tensed facts. Their disagreement, therefore, is over whether tensed truths are eliminable. If they are not eliminable, the implication is that they are part of the ontologically privileged description, which informs us of the ontological nature of reality. If they are eliminable, the implication is that they are not part of the ontologically privileged description, which tells us something different about the ontological nature of reality. Thus, protagonists in this debate agree that there is a privileged, true description of reality, which can inform us about the ontological nature of reality, but they disagree over which truths that true description contains. The dialectic between them can be illustrated by Figure 2.1.

When we consider the dialectic in this way, we can see that, whatever answer is given to the initial question, a further assumption is needed to get from that answer to the ontological conclusion it is taken to yield. It is possible to hold the linguistic view that tensed sentences are not eliminable, in conjunction with the ontological view that there are no tensed facts.[5] Since this combination of views is possible, there must be a hidden assumption licensing the move from an answer to the initial question, which is purely linguistic in nature, to the ontological conclusion. Precisely how to formulate this hidden assumption is not clear. Obviously, since it is a *hidden* assumption, no one has explicitly declared it, so no amount of scholarship can help my cause here. However, it is my view that this hidden assumption is a particular interpretation of the idea that there is one true description of reality.

One true description of reality

There are at least two different ways of understanding this notion of "one true description of reality." According to the first interpretation, the one true description of reality is the collection of all the truths that there are.[6] This collection contains the truths of physics, and of the other sciences. It contains ordinary, everyday truths, political and economic truths, moral truths (if there are any), and so on. Since it contains all the truths that there are, and there are some tensed truths and some tenseless truths, it will contain both of these kinds of truth. The tensed truths, being context-dependent, may have to have their contexts of utterance made explicit in order to rule out the possibility of the one true description containing apparently contradictory "truths." For example, unless we make the context explicit, the one true description may contain the truth "It is raining" and the truth "It is not raining," which appear to contradict each other. Once we make the context explicit, however, we can see that they do not really contradict each other. The former utterance is produced at time t_1, when it is raining, and the latter is produced at time t_2, when it is not raining. I will call this interpretation of the notion of "one true description of reality" the weak linguistic thesis:

> WLT There is one true description of reality that contains all the truths that there are.

This cannot be the sense of "one true description of reality" over which the A- and B-theorists disagree. They both accept that ordinary tensed sentences can be determinately true. So they would not deny that there is a collection of all the truths that there are, where that collection includes both tensed and tenseless truths. There must be an alternative interpretation of the notion which allows for their disagreement.

An interpretation that permits the disagreement between A- and B-theorists is that there is one true description of reality which contains a subset of all the truths that there are. This subset of truths is ontologically

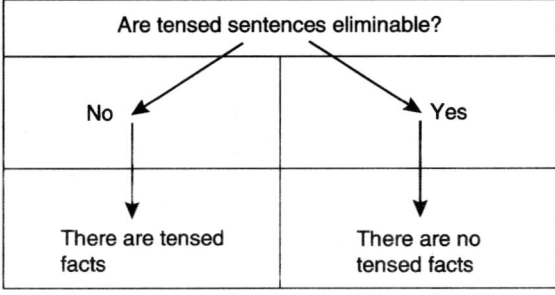

Figure 2.1

perspicuous, in that each truth in it reveals the nature of the fact that it describes, and that makes it true. In order for this to be the case, there can be no more than one truth per fact. If there were more than one truth per fact, then a choice would have to be made as to which was the most ontologically perspicuous. So this notion of the one true description of reality involves a commitment to the view that there is a one-to-one correspondence between truths in the one true description and facts in the world. I will call this interpretation of the notion of "one true description of reality" the strong linguistic thesis:

> SLT There is one privileged, true description of reality, the sentences of which (a) stand in a one-to-one correspondence with facts in the world, and (b) are structurally isomorphic to the facts with which they correspond.[7]

SLT captures the notion of "one true description of reality" implicitly assumed by both A- and B-theorists. Their disagreement is over which truths that description contains. For the A-theory of time it contains tensed sentences, and *because* it contains tensed sentences, reality contains tensed facts. In order to reach the conclusion that there are tensed facts from the premise that there are ineliminable tensed sentences in the one true description, one must think (1) that there is a fact corresponding to every truth in that description; and (2) that the truths are structurally isomorphic to the facts. Without (1), the A-theorist would not be able to infer that there are *any* ontological counterparts to her tensed truths. Without (2) she would not be able to infer that those ontological counterparts are *tensed*.

For the old B-theory of time, the one true description is given to us by a language purged of tensed expressions. Because, according to her, tensed sentences are eliminable in favor of tenseless sentences, the one true description contains only tenseless sentences. She concludes from this that reality contains only tenseless facts. Once again, in order to reach this conclusion she must think (1) that there is a fact corresponding to every truth in that description; and (2) that the truths are structurally isomorphic to the facts. Without (1) she would not be able to infer that there are *any* ontological counterparts to her tenseless truths. Without (2) she would not be able to infer that those ontological counterparts are *tenseless*. So, for the old B-theory, even though tensed sentences are true, they are not part of the one true description, as that is one that has a fact corresponding to, and discernible from, every sentence contained in it.

When presented with SLT, it may be that most, if not all, philosophers (and not just philosophers of time) would explicitly reject it. That is all well and good. I too think it is false, and I shall be arguing for that conclusion. But my point here is that whether or not one thinks it false when considering it on its own merits, the logic of the arguments of the A- and old B-theorists (and, I shall be arguing, of the arguments in some other metaphysical disputes) requires that it be assumed. Once we make it explicit, and then reject it, we can see that those disputes are, by and large, fruitless.

Both A-theorists and old B-theorists thought that an acceptable means of arriving at the one true description of reality, understood in the restricted sense of SLT, is the method of paraphrase. The idea behind the method of paraphrase is that it seems to offer a way out of being committed to the existence of entities apparently implied by the sentences of ordinary language. The aim of the method of paraphrase is to find a sentence that conveys all the same information as that conveyed by the original, problematic sentence, but which lacks the original's apparent ontological commitments. If a suggested paraphrase fails in either of these respects then the proponent of the existence of the entities in question can argue that the paraphrase is inadequate, and retain her commitment to their existence. Consequently, when the method of paraphrase is employed on a particular metaphysical issue, debate often centers on whether a suggested paraphrase really does convey all the information conveyed by the original sentence.

A-theorists argued that any tenseless paraphrase of a tensed sentence fails to completely capture the meaning of the original, and is thus an inadequate paraphrase. B-theorists argued that the tenseless paraphrases did indeed convey all the information conveyed by their tensed counterparts, so they were adequate paraphrases. However, the tenseless sentences lacked the unwanted ontological implications of the tensed sentences, and were, for that reason, ontologically more accurate descriptions of temporal reality. Consequently, in this, as in other metaphysical disputes, the debate about the nature of temporal reality was quickly transformed into a debate about the meanings of temporal sentences.

The truth-condition variant of the new B-theory of time

The new B-theory of time emerged in response to the failure of the old B-theory's translation project, and it made its appearance in two distinct stages. The first stage was the truth-condition variant of the new B-theory, and was propounded by, among others, J. J. C. Smart (1980), D. H. Mellor (1981) and L. Nathan Oaklander (1984).[8] The second stage was the truth-maker variant of the new B-theory, which was first put forward by D. H. Mellor (1998). I will first outline the truth-condition variant, and explain how it fails to escape completely from the false dilemma exemplified by the debate between the A-theory and the old B-theory of time, and how it too ultimately relies too heavily on facts about language in arriving at its ontological conclusions.

Proponents of the new B-theory accept that tense cannot be eliminated from natural language without some loss of meaning, but they deny that this implies that time itself is tensed. Proponents of the truth-condition variant argue that, while it is not possible to translate any tensed sentence into a tenseless sentence, it is possible to state the truth condition of any tensed sentence in entirely tenseless terms. For example, an utterance, u, of a tensed sentence such as:

S1: The enemy is now approaching.

may not be translatable by a tenseless sentence such as:

S2: The enemy's approach is (tenselessly) simultaneous with u.

but S2 states u's truth condition.[9] That is,

TC: Any utterance, u, of "The enemy is now approaching" is true if and only if the enemy's approach is (tenselessly) simultaneous with u.

The significance of this account of the tenseless truth conditions of tensed sentences is often thought, by its proponents, to be largely ontological. Mellor, for example, argues that, since the truth of any tensed sentence can be accounted for in entirely tenseless terms, that is, by stating its truth condition tenselessly, tensed facts are not needed to make tensed sentences true (Mellor 1981: 46). He further argues that the only reason there could be for admitting the existence of tensed facts is to make tensed sentences true, and since they are not needed to play that role, there is no reason for admitting their existence. One way of construing this strategy, then, is to see it as arguing from the fact that tensed sentences can be given tenseless truth conditions to the conclusion that temporal reality is tenseless.

But this is not the only way of understanding this approach. It is possible that a B-theorist may have independent arguments for the truth of the B-theory and offers an account of the tenseless truth conditions of tensed sentences, not as a direct argument for the B-theory but merely in order to show how the semantics of tensed sentences are compatible with the B-theory. I have no quarrel with this kind of approach. My quarrel is with the strategy of arguing from the fact that tensed sentences can be assigned tenseless truth conditions to the conclusion that temporal reality is tenseless. I will have more to say on the different ways of understanding this project below.

The problem with this variant of the new B-theory is that the notion of truth conditions is ambiguous between semantics and ontology. Talk of truth conditions is commonplace throughout philosophy, and it is generally thought that its significance is well understood. However, there are at least two kinds of significance that the notion of truth conditions is thought to have. On the one hand, it is thought to have significance for the meanings of sentences. This is suggested by platitudes like "to know the meaning of a sentence is to know under what conditions it is true," and "to give the truth condition of a sentence is to give its meaning." The intuition here is that there is some significant connection between the meanings of sentences and their truth conditions.

On the other hand, it is thought to have ontological significance. This is suggested by platitudes like "a sentence is true if and only if its truth condition obtains or is satisfied," and "the truth condition of a sentence states what the world must be like if that sentence is to be true." Here the intuition is that there is some significant connection between the truth condition of a sentence and the ontology that grounds the truth of that sentence if it is true. Since the notion of truth conditions has both kinds of significance, the project of stating the truth conditions of tensed sentences in tenseless terms can be interpreted as, on the one hand, a semantic exercise, concerned to provide a semantic analysis of tensed language, or, on the other hand, an ontological exercise, concerned to state what the world must be like given the truth of our true tensed sentences.

The possibility of interpreting the new B-theory's truth-conditional project in these two ways has been exploited by Quentin Smith (1993). He goes so far as to identify two different versions of that theory: what he calls the "new tenseless theory of time," and the "nonsemantic tenseless theory of time." He characterizes the new tenseless theory of time as "the theory that tenseless truth condition sentences provide a 'logically adequate representation of ordinary temporal language'" (Smith 1993: 13). He then remarks that one of its proponents (Smart 1980) "is concerned with the logical structure of ordinary language and is interested in how the meaning of ordinary expressions should be understood or represented in theories of meaning for ordinary language" (Smith 1993: 13). Thus, according to Smith, the aim of the new tenseless theory of time is purely to do justice to the semantic significance of the notion of truth conditions and is not at all concerned with the ontological nature of time. Indeed, he criticizes Oaklander (1991) for saying that the new tenseless theory of time serves the "'ontological' function of representing the metaphysical nature of time" (Smith 1993: 13). Thus, Smith sees the new tenseless theory of time as offering an account of the meaning of tensed language, but not an account of the ontological nature of time. On such a view, there would be no tenseless theory of *time*, just an account of what tensed language means.

Smith describes the nonsemantic tenseless theory of time as a theory that "considers the meaning or semantic content of ordinary tensed discourse as irrelevant – or at least as not crucial to the truth or falsity of [that theory]" (1993: 14). It merely represents the ontological nature of time, and has no significance for the meaning of the tensed language whose truth conditions it states.

Thus, Smith isolates the semantic and ontological aspects of truth conditions from each other to the extent of constructing two distinct B-theories, one "semantic," the other "ontological." Proponents of the new B-theory do not recognize different versions of that theory along these lines, but it is clear that there is both a semantic and an ontological significance to the notion of truth conditions, and Smith exploits this to undermine the project of the new B-theory.

50 A new metaphysical strategy

William Lane Craig seeks to drive a similar wedge between the semantic and the ontological function of providing truth conditions for tensed sentences. He writes:

> The giving of truth conditions is a semantic exercise; specifying grounds for a statement's truth concerns ontology. One can lay out the semantic conditions which will permit one to determine for any sentence whether that sentence is true or false without saying anything at all about the ontological facts which make that sentence true.
> (Craig 1996: 22)

This suggests that we are able to determine whether a sentence is true or false just by examining its truth condition, but this is not true. Examining its truth condition will tell us *what must be the case* for the sentence to be true. Once we know that, we turn to the world to determine whether or not the truth condition is satisfied; we must determine *what is the case*, and then see whether what is the case fulfils the sentence's truth condition. The attempts of both Smith and Craig to isolate the semantic and the ontological functions of giving a tenseless account of the truth conditions of tensed language is misguided because both functions are integral to that project. Nevertheless, the fact that an account of truth conditions has both these functions is the fundamental weakness of the truth-condition variant of the new B-theory.

To state the truth condition of a tensed sentence-token is to specify what the world must be like in order for that token to be true. This is the ontological function of the truth-condition project. If the truth condition only requires the existence of tenseless facts, then the project will have shown that tensed facts are not needed to account for the truth of tensed sentence-tokens. In addition, the truth condition explicates how the truth or falsity of a sentence-token depends on what its semantic constituents mean when produced in a given context. This is its semantic function. If the project as a whole is successful, it will, on the one hand, show that the world need not be tensed to account for the fact that we sometimes utter true tensed sentence-tokens, and on the other hand, it will also explain why the true tensed sentence-tokens we utter are true. The provision of truth conditions makes perspicuous both the relationship between truth and reality (the ontological function) and that between truth and meaning (the semantic function).

However, if we suppose, as I think we should, that the primary goal of the new B-theory is to arrive at an ontological conclusion regarding the nature of temporal reality, how is the project of providing tenseless truth conditions for tensed sentences supposed to assist in achieving that goal? One view is that it serves merely a supporting role. According to this view, the new B-theorist is convinced on independent grounds that a B-theoretic metaphysics of time is correct and offers an account of the tenseless truth conditions of tensed sentences merely as an adjunct to that metaphysical theory; it serves as a demonstration of how semantics might be done in a way compatible with the B-theory's ontology. A new B-theorist who holds this view does not illicitly draw ontological conclusions from facts about language, as the truth-condition project plays no positive role in arriving at the B-theory's ontological conclusions.

Another view is that the truth-condition project plays a part in the B-theorist's rebuttal of the A-theorist's argument from tensed language to tensed facts. According to this view, the A-theorist argues from the fact that tensed sentences are true and irreducible to tenseless sentences to the conclusion that temporal reality is tensed. The new B-theorist rebuts this argument by appealing to the fact that the truth of true, irreducible, tensed sentences can be fully accounted for in tenseless terms, and she shows how this can be done by giving tenseless truth conditions for tensed sentences. Since the new B-theorist is here using the truth-condition project to block an argument from language to reality, she is not, in this instance, guilty of committing the representational fallacy. The truth-condition project, according to this view, plays no positive role in establishing the B-theory's ontological conclusions.

Both of these views are innocent of any illicit moves from language to reality. Thus, it is legitimate for a new B-theorist to adhere to one, or indeed to both of these views. However, if a proponent of the truth-condition variant of the new B-theory thinks that by offering an account of the tenseless truth conditions of tensed sentences, she is thereby arguing for the ontological conclusions of the new B-theory, then she commits the representational fallacy. She is arguing for a metaphysical conclusion about the way temporal reality is on the basis of a fact about our temporal language, namely, the fact that tensed sentences can be assigned tenseless truth conditions. Despite the fact that she concedes the A-theorist's claim about the untranslatability of tensed and tenseless sentences, her strategy remains one of offering a language, the tenseless metalanguage in which the truth conditions of tensed sentences are stated, that is supposed to reveal the ontological nature of time. Thus, the truth-condition strategy of the new B-theory, conceived as an argument for a B-theoretic metaphysics, is essentially no different from the strategy of the old B-theory, and indeed of the A-theory, which was also to provide a language that is supposed to reveal the ontological nature of time.

I have argued that if the truth-condition project of the new B-theory is thought of as an argument for the B-theory's metaphysical conclusions, then it commits the representational fallacy. But do any philosophers think of it in this way? There is evidence that some proponents and opponents of the new B-theory have thought of it in this way. For example, in *Real Time*, Mellor offers his version of McTaggart's paradox to prove that there are no tensed facts. However, he also claims that "there is a simpler argument which should serve to sway more open minds" (Mellor 1981: 102). The simpler argument is this: the "tenseless truth conditions [of tensed sentence-tokens] leave tensed facts no scope for determining their truth-values. But these facts by definition determine their truth-values. So in reality there are no such facts" (Mellor 1981: 102). In his earlier work, then, Mellor sees the project of providing truth conditions for tensed sentences as doing more than merely supplementing his McTaggart-inspired rejection of tensed facts. That is, he does not see it simply as offering a semantics for tensed sentences that is consistent with the B-theory. Instead he sees it as a positive argument for the conclusion that there are no tensed facts.

Similarly, Anthony Brueckner, who is not a B-theorist, characterizes Mellor's project as follows: "since A-series sentences are not property-attributing at all, it cannot be that they attribute...A-series properties to events, properties with some special metaphysical status" (Brueckner 2003: 201). He goes on to compare Mellor's project with that of David Lewis with respect to modality, which he characterizes as follows: "David Lewis argues from the correctness of these truth conditions to the conclusion that *being actual* is not a special, distinguished property possessed by just one possible world" (Brueckner 2003: 201). Lewis has many reasons for believing that actuality is not a privileged property, and it is not clear to me that he does endorse an inference from the truth conditions of modal statements to this ontological conclusion. Nevertheless, Brueckner's Lewis endorses the inference, and by analogy, Brueckner's Mellor endorses it in the temporal realm. According to Brueckner, the reason why a B-theorist argues that tensed sentences have tenseless truth conditions is to prove that there are no tensed properties or facts.

As a final example, Michelle Beer sees her version of the new B-theory as one that permits ontological conclusions to be derived from linguistic claims. Her theory, which she calls the co-reporting thesis, is somewhat different from the standard truth-conditional variant of the new B-theory. Instead of offering tenseless truth conditions for tensed sentences, she claims that for every tensed sentence there is a tenseless sentence which reports one and the same event, even though no linguistic reduction is available from tensed to tenseless sentences (Beer 1988: 161). But this view is comparable to the standard view. Truth-conditional B-theorists claim that there is no linguistic reduction available from a tensed sentence to the tenseless sentence that states its truth condition, and they also assent to the claim that two such sentences report the existence of the same event or state of affairs. Insofar as there is a difference between them, it is that the truth-conditional B-theorist makes the further claim that there is a particular relationship between two such sentences, namely, that the tenseless sentence states the truth condition of the tensed sentence.

Beer makes the following claim on behalf of the co-reporting thesis:

> The Co-reporting Thesis thus establishes the identity of the A-series and the B-series, for it shows that an event or moment having an A-determination is identical with that event or moment being earlier than,

simultaneous with or later than some moment of time. But we can draw an even stronger conclusion, namely, that the A-series is reducible to, and thus is nothing more than, the B-series.

(Beer 1988: 163)

According to Beer, then, the fact that a tensed and a tenseless sentence are co-reporting is sufficient grounds for concluding that the A-series is reducible to the B-series. The linguistic evidence is taken to support the ontological conclusion that there are no A-properties or facts.

The truth-condition variant of the new B-theory, conceived as an argument for a B-theoretic metaphysics, accepts SLT. For its proponents, the one true description is the one given by the tenseless metalanguage in which the truth conditions of tensed and tenseless sentences are stated. A true tensed sentence is true because its tenseless truth condition obtains, and the statement of that tenseless truth condition corresponds to the fact that makes it true. Furthermore, the statement of the tenseless truth condition is structurally isomorphic to the fact with which it corresponds. As a result of this, the proponent of the truth-condition variant of the new B-theory is in a position to move from the premise that tensed sentences have tenseless truth conditions to the conclusion that reality contains only tenseless facts. For her, the route to discovering the ontological nature of time is via the statements of the tenseless truth conditions of tensed sentences.

The problem with the strategy of identifying a language that purports to reveal the ontological structure of reality is that it assumes that it is legitimate to "read off" features of reality from features of the language used to describe it. And that is to commit the representational fallacy. To see that it is a fallacy in this case, one just has to realize that it is possible for an A-theorist to accept the new B-theorist's account of the truth conditions of tensed sentences and still to maintain that there are tensed facts. Quentin Smith, for example, takes this line. However, it is interesting to note that he does so by insisting that tensed sentences have a *further* truth condition in addition to their tenseless one. He concedes that tensed sentences have a tenseless token-reflexive truth condition but insists that they have a tensed truth condition as well (Smith 1993: 98–105). Thus, he too takes the strategy of supplying truth conditions for tensed sentences to have ontological implications.

The truth-condition variant of the new B-theory of time found a way of breaking out of the apparently exhaustive alternatives offered by the A-theory and the old B-theory of time. Those alternatives were to accept the apparent ontological implications of tensed language or to find a way of translating tensed language into tenseless language without any loss of meaning. The truth-condition variant of the new B-theory accepted that tensed language cannot be translated into tenseless language without loss of meaning but denied that it was thereby forced to accept the A-theory's account of the ontological nature of temporal reality. Its proponents argued instead that the truth conditions of tensed sentences could be stated in entirely tenseless terms. But, in so far as they saw their account of the tenseless truth conditions of tensed sentences as a premise in an argument for a B-theoretic metaphysics, they committed the representational fallacy. Like their opponents and their predecessors, they thought that one can identify a language of some sort and then proceed directly from the nature and structure of that language to a conclusion about the nature and structure of the reality described by it. However, even if the truth-condition project of the new B-theory fails to establish its ontological conclusions, it should not be discarded. It shows that the A-theorist's argument for her ontological conclusion is invalid, and it remains a powerful and explanatory account of the semantics of tensed language.

The truthmaker variant of the new B-theory of time

Consideration of the ontological significance that truth conditions are thought to have, suggests an alternative strategy for the new B-theory, one which was developed by D. H. Mellor (1998). That significance was thought to be that by stating the truth condition of a sentence one states what the world must be like to make that sentence true. By focusing on this notion of "how the world makes a true sentence true" instead of on how to state the truth condition of a tensed sentence, one arrives at the truthmaker variant of the new B-theory. Proponents of this theory argue that the truthmaker of any true tensed sentence is a tenseless fact. The crucial respect in which the truthmaker variant differs from the truth-conditional variant is that it is a purely ontological thesis. Rather than employing an account of the semantics of temporal language to arrive at conclusions about the ontological nature of time, it employs an account of the ontological nature of time to explain the semantics of temporal language. The account of the ontological nature of time it employs is one that is arrived at independently of any semantic considerations.

How does the truthmaker variant of the new B-theory respond to the methodological structure of a metaphysical dispute exemplified by the debate between the A-theory and the old B-theory? Its proponents agree with the A-theory that tense cannot be eliminated from language, but they deny that this implies that time itself is tensed. The only way they can sustain this position is if they reject SLT, and its corollary, that paraphrase is ontologically significant. If SLT is true, then there is one privileged true description of temporal reality the sentences of which (a) stand in a one-to-one correspondence with facts in the world, and (b) are structurally isomorphic to the facts with which they correspond. That description will be either tensed or tenseless. If it is tensed, then reality itself is tensed, and if it is tenseless, then reality is tenseless. Given that this is the structure of the debate between A-theorists and old B-theorists, it should be clear that there is simply no room for the position of the new B-theorist, according to which language is irreducibly tensed, but time is tenseless, unless the underlying assumption, SLT, is relinquished. By asserting their position they must, therefore, whether they realized it or not, have rejected that underlying assumption.

The truthmaker variant of the new B-theory thus rejects SLT. It need not reject WLT, according to which there is a true description of reality, which is a collection of all the truths that there are. But it denies that the sentences of that description stand in a one-to-one correspondence with the facts in the world, or that those sentences need be structurally isomorphic to the facts that make them true. The ratio of true sentences to facts in the world can instead be many-to-one. For each fact there can be many ways of accurately describing it. Tensed sentences are true and irreducible to tenseless sentences, but it does not follow that there must be some extralinguistic fact corresponding to the additional information that they convey over and above that conveyed by tenseless sentences.

The debate between the A- and both versions of the B-theory of time can be illustrated by considering the following argument.

The argument from tensed language
1. Some tensed sentences are untranslatable into tenseless sentences without loss of meaning.
2. If there are tensed sentences which are untranslatable and true, then there are corresponding, irreducible tensed facts.
3. There are tensed sentences which are untranslatable and true.
4. Therefore, some irreducible tensed facts exist.[10]

According to the A-theory, this argument is sound. If some true sentence makes an ineliminable reference to the pastness (say) of an event, that must be because there exists a fact about the pastness of that event to which that sentence refers. So, according to A-theorists, the argument from tensed language establishes the existence of tensed facts.

The old B-theory thought that the argument from tensed language was unsound because premises 1 and 3 are false. It took the option of denying premise 3 by accepting that there are true tensed sentences, but denying that those sentences are untranslatable by tenseless sentences. Its proponents offered a variety of translation schemas which purported to show how any tensed sentence could be translated by some tenseless sentence without loss of meaning. Their reasoning was that if tensed sentences are translatable by tenseless sentences, then they do not refer to any tensed facts. Instead they are translatable by sentences that refer to tenseless facts. So the only facts referred to by both tensed and tenseless sentences are tenseless facts. But these attempts at translating tensed sentences into tenseless sentences failed.

The new B-theory also takes the argument from tensed language to be unsound, but it rejects premise 2. Tensed sentences are not translatable by tenseless sentences but it is not the case that the only alternative to this is that they refer to tensed facts. Indeed, premise 2 conceals the implicit, and illicit, inference from language to reality, which is precisely what new B-theorists reject. A tensed sentence can be irreducible, in that no tenseless sentence can capture the entire meaning conveyed by it, while still being made true by a purely tenseless fact. It thus rejects the notion that there is one true description of temporal reality, in the sense given by SLT, and that our goal is to arrive at that description and then simply to ascertain from its nature, the nature of temporal reality described by it.

What was accepted by the A-theory and the old B-theory, and rejected by the new B-theory, is that we can move by valid inference from premises about the nature of language to conclusions about the nature of reality. The A-theorist thought (and still thinks) that we can conclude that reality is tensed from the fact that ordinary language is irreducibly tensed. The old B-theorist thought that we would be committed to this conclusion if it was true that ordinary language was irreducibly tensed, but she thought that it wasn't. The new B-theorist, on the other hand, accepts that ordinary language is irreducibly tensed, but denies that reality is tensed. Therefore, she rejects any move from the nature of temporal language to the nature of temporal reality as fallacious.

The semantics of tense

What are the implications of this position for the semantics of tense, and for the metaphysics of time? According to the new B-theory of time, the semantic significance of tense is that tensed language is ineliminable. No tenseless sentence can convey all the information conveyed by any tensed sentence, so it is not possible to communicate using a purely tenseless language all that can be communicated using an ordinary tensed language. Another way of putting this point is that no tensed sentence has the same meaning as any tenseless sentence. However, an account of the tenseless truth conditions of tensed sentences goes at least some way towards explicating the meanings of tensed sentences.

Suppose an utterance, u, of the tensed sentence "The forest fire is now raging" is produced, and is true. According to one new B-theoretic account of the truth conditions of tensed sentences, the truth condition of u can be stated by the tenseless sentence, v, "The forest fire rages (tenselessly) simultaneously with u." I and others have argued for a token-reflexive account of the truth conditions of tensed sentences along these lines (Mellor 1981; Oaklander 1991; Dyke 2002b, 2003b). According to the truthmaker variant of the new B-theory that I advocate, the truthmaker for both u and v is the fact that the forest fire and u stand in the tenseless temporal relation of simultaneity to each other. That is, what makes u true is that u is produced simultaneously with the raging of the forest fire, and what makes v true is that u is produced simultaneously with the raging of the forest fire. There are a number of possible objections to this account that I want to address before moving on.

One might object that the fact that the forest fire rages simultaneously with *u* is not the right truthmaker for *u* because *u* is simply about the raging of the forest fire, and not about any utterance, and yet it has an utterance as a constituent of its truthmaker. This objection sails dangerously close to the idea that we ought to be able to read the truthmakers off our sentences. Consider the example, that I discussed in the introduction, of the sentence "*o* is lilac" whose truthmaker is the fact that *o* has molecular structure *P*. The sentence "*o* is lilac" is not about molecular structures, but that is no reason for thinking that the fact that *o* has molecular structure *P* cannot be the truthmaker for that sentence. Furthermore, if a sentence is context-dependent, as tensed sentences are, we should expect that some feature of the sentence's production makes its way into its truthmaker. In the case of *u*, it is *u*'s temporal relation to the event that it is about that is the relevant feature of its context of utterance, and that is precisely the feature that I claim is part of its truthmaker.

Another objection is that the forest fire would, presumably, be raging even if *u* were never uttered, so the sentence "The forest fire is now raging" could be true even if the particular utterance, *u*, were never produced. I take sentence-tokens to be the primary bearers of truth and falsity.[11] Thus, if no sentence-token is produced, the question of whether or not a sentence is true or false does not even arise. Of course, the forest fire would still be raging even if *u* were not uttered, but in those circumstances there would be no token requiring a truthmaker.

However, this objection can be developed into a potentially more damaging version. Surely, my opponent might argue, I do not want to deny that the sentence "There are no sentence-tokens now" can never be true, for it has been true (before language-users evolved) and it will be true again (once there are no language-users left in existence). But my position seems to entail that it cannot be true as, in order for it to be true, there would have to be a sentence-token uttered simultaneously with a time at which there are no sentence-tokens.[12]

My response to this objection follows similar lines to my response to the previous objection. I do not deny that there have been and will be times at which there are no sentence-tokens, but this is quite different from thinking that there can be a true token of the sentence "There are no sentence-tokens now." Any such sentence-token would be self-refuting, and that is just what we should expect. But from the fact that there can be no true tokens of that sentence it does not follow that there have been and will be no times at which there are no sentence-tokens. Of course, there have been and will be, and those times devoid of sentence-tokens will no doubt be constituents of the truthmakers of utterances such as "There have been times at which there are no sentence-tokens" and "There will be times at which there are no sentence-tokens." Once again, without a sentence-token, the question of whether truth or falsity can be correctly predicated of a sentence does not arise. But this is quite different from the world's being the way it is independently of some description of it. Indeed, this objection makes the mistake of confusing claims about reality with claims about descriptions of reality, about which I will have more to say in Chapter 4. From the fact that it is not possible truly to say "There are no sentence-tokens now," it concludes that it is not possible for there to be any times at which there are no sentence-tokens. But this is an invalid inference.

According to the new B-theory, then, true tensed sentences have tenseless truthmakers. Furthermore, true tenseless sentences also have tenseless truthmakers. It follows that it is possible for a true tensed and tenseless sentence to have the same truthmaker, even though they cannot translate each other and so do not have the same meaning. The fact in the world responsible for making true any true tensed sentence is a fact involving only events and the tenseless temporal relations between them. But the same fact could be responsible for making true a tenseless sentence about the temporal relations between those same events. What, then, is the relationship between two such sentences?

Consider again the utterance, u, of the tensed sentence "The forest fire is now raging," and the tenseless sentence-token, v, "The forest fire rages (tenselessly) simultaneously with u," and suppose they are both true. According to the new B-theory, v states u's truth condition. However, as we have seen, u and v are not equivalent in meaning. The utterance u is a token of a temporally context-dependent sentence-type, and v is a token of context-independent sentence-type and that is enough to ensure that they are not synonymous. However, according to the new B-theory, even though u and v do not have the same meaning, it is possible for them to have the same truthmaker. Their common truthmaker, according to the new B-theorist, is the fact that u and the raging of the forest fire stand in the tenseless temporal relation of simultaneity to each other.

The significance of this point is that it shows that it is possible for two sentences to be made true by the same fact, and yet not to have the same meaning. Given this possibility, it should be clear that any reason we might have had for supporting the idea that the way language is reveals to us the way reality is, has been completely undermined. If two sentences have different meanings, but are made true by the same fact, then we cannot, merely by inspecting the meanings of those sentences, ascertain the fact that makes them both true. It also undermines the other idea that drove the debate between the A-theory and the old B-theory: SLT. This idea, together with the notion that, once we have arrived at that description of reality we can, by inspecting its structure, ascertain the structure of the reality it represents, is completely defeated by the recognition that two non-synonymous sentences can be made true by the same fact. It shows that it is possible for the relationship between representations of reality and reality itself to be many-to-one, whereas SLT assumes that this relationship is one-to-one.

Given a tensed and a tenseless sentence that have the same truthmaker, there is a sense in which, according to the new B-theory, the tenseless sentence gives a more accurate description of their common truthmaker. But this is not to say that it is legitimate to "read off" the nature of a truthmaker from the nature of a tenseless description of it; that because the more accurate description is grammatically tenseless, reality must therefore be metaphysically tenseless. Instead, the tenseless sentence, more accurately than the tensed sentence, says or describes what the truthmaker is like. The reasons for thinking that reality is tenseless are, as we will see in the next section, not linguistic reasons, but rather, metaphysical and scientific reasons. So it is not because the tenseless sentence is a more accurate description of the truthmaker that we should think reality is tenseless, according to the new B-theory. Rather, we should think reality is tenseless for reasons that have nothing to do with language, and then we will be in a position to see that a tenseless sentence gives us a more accurate description of the fact that makes it, and possibly some other tensed sentence, true.

The lesson to be learned from all this is that we should stop looking to the meanings of our sentences in the hope that they will reveal to us the way things really are. We should instead look to the nature of reality itself, in particular, to the nature of those constituents of reality that are the truthmakers of our true sentences.

The metaphysics of time

Unlike the A-theorist and the old B-theorist of time, the new B-theorist does not seek an answer to the ontological question about the nature of temporal reality from facts about the semantics of tensed language. She does not begin with language and derive an ontology from it. Instead, she begins with reality itself, and asks how it makes our true sentences true. According to the new B-theorist, temporal reality need only be tenseless to account for the truth of every true tensed sentence. This, is not an argument that temporal reality must be tenseless, rather, it is an argument that temporal reality need not be tensed in order to account for the truth of every true tensed sentence. It is an argument designed to rebut the A-theorist's argument from the existence of true tensed sentences to the existence of tense in reality (Dyke 2003a).

According to the new B-theory of time, temporal reality is constituted by the temporal relations of earlier than, later than and simultaneous with. Furthermore, unlike the A-theory, the B-theory does not take temporal location to have any ontological significance. According to the A-theory, present events are more real than past or future events. By contrast, according to the B-theory, all events are equally real, no matter when they are located. However, its proponents do not claim to arrive at these metaphysical conclusions on the basis of any claims about the nature of tensed or tenseless language.

Proponents of the new B-theory recognize that, given the ineliminability of tensed language, it is possible for temporal reality to be either tensed or tenseless, at least in so far as each of these is a genuine metaphysical possibility. This is an important point. Identifying that, for example, some proponents of the A-theory have committed the representational fallacy does not entitle us to conclude that their view of the metaphysics of temporal reality is false. It merely entitles us to conclude that they are not entitled to their view of the metaphysics of temporal reality just on the basis of the linguistic considerations they invoke. A fallacy is just an invalid argument, and recognizing that an argument is invalid does not permit the inference that its conclusion is false.

How, then, do proponents of the new B-theory of time arrive at their metaphysical conclusions? Since semantic considerations cannot help, they need to appeal to other considerations. Typically, two kinds of consideration are invoked in support of the metaphysics of the new B-theory; one of them metaphysical, and the other scientific.

The metaphysical argument appealed to by many, but not all,[13] new B-theorists is an argument to the effect that any alternative to a B-theoretic account of the metaphysics of time is incoherent, and so is not a genuine metaphysical possibility. The main argument of this kind is one that has come to be known as McTaggart's Paradox, after its first proponent, J. M. E. McTaggart (1927; see also Horwich 1987: 18–20; Le Poidevin 1991; Mellor 1998: Chapter 7; Dyke 2002a). However, other arguments have been proposed which also claim to establish that certain A-theoretic accounts of the metaphysics of time are incoherent (Smart 1949; Williams 1951; Bourne 2002). I do not want to focus here on the details of any of these arguments, as that ground has been well covered. The point I want to make is simply that, in order to support their view of the metaphysical nature of temporal reality, new B-theorists should not, and need not, appeal to linguistic considerations. If a successful argument can be mounted to the effect that a given A-theoretic account of the nature of temporal reality is incoherent, then that will show that it is not possible for temporal reality to be as the A-theorists say it is, and therefore that it is not as they say it is.

Recall the two-stage process of a metaphysical enquiry into the nature of reality that I endorsed in the section, "Metaphysics and Science" of Chapter 1. I argued there that we must first explore the possible ways the world might be, ruling out of contention any ways that it is not possible for the world to be. This is the distinctively metaphysical stage of the enquiry, normally employing a priori reasoning. Then we must argue that one of these ways the world might be is the way the world actually is. And this latter step needs to appeal to empirical evidence, so in this respect metaphysics is continuous with science. The metaphysical arguments whose goal is to establish the incoherence of the A-theoretic account of the nature of temporal reality are arguments that exemplify the first stage in this process. They are attempts at ruling out of contention a candidate account of the nature of temporal reality, namely, the A-theory's account. If successful, they will not establish the truth of the B-theory's account of temporal reality, but they will rule out some alternatives to it.

The second stage in a metaphysical enquiry is to argue that one way the world might be is the way the world actually is, and this stage can appeal to empirical considerations. This is where the scientific considerations in support of the B-theory's account of the nature of temporal reality come in. We should look to our best current scientific theories, which are confirmed by empirical evidence, to support any proposed metaphysical account of the nature of time. Our best current scientific theory about the nature of time is the special theory of relativity, and that theory is both consistent with the B-theory's account of the nature of time and, prima facie, inconsistent with the A-theory's account of the nature of time.

According to the standard interpretation of the special theory, simultaneity does not obtain simpliciter, but only relative to a frame of reference. It may be the case that e_1 is simultaneous with e_2 relative to one frame of reference, but relative to another, e_1 is earlier than e_2, and relative to yet another, e_1 is later than e_2, Furthermore, no one frame of reference is privileged. It follows that there is no frame-independent way of marking out all those events that are simultaneous with the present moment, or with some event nominated as a present event, and thus are themselves present. An event which is present relative to one frame of reference may be past or future relative to another frame of reference, and neither of these frames of reference has a claim to being ontologically privileged. Consequently, there is no absolute (frame-independent) distinction between past, present, and future.

This is, prima facie, problematic for all versions of the A-theory, according to which there is an absolute distinction between past, present, and future, and furthermore, that distinction has ontological significance. According to presentism, for example, only what is present exists (Merricks 1994; Bigelow 1996; Craig 2000; Markosian 2004). Other versions of the A-theory hold that only the past and the present exist (Tooley 1997). Still others hold that the past and the future, while existent, are somehow less real than the present (Smith 2002). If it is a frame-relative matter which events are simultaneous with some event designated as present, and if presentness is supposed to confer ontological status on those events which possess it, then it follows that which events have that privileged ontological status is also a frame-relative matter. To put it simply, existence itself is not absolute, but relative. However, since the B-theory posits neither a distinction between past, present, and future, nor a privileged present moment, none of these constituents of the special theory is inconsistent with it. Considerations from the special theory of relativity, thus, tell against the A-theory's account of the nature of time, and support the B-theory's account of the nature of time.

A number of A-theorists have attempted to reconcile their theories with the special theory of relativity (Smith 1993; Tooley 1997; Craig 2001).

Whether or not they are successful has been challenged (Saunders 2002; Balashov and Michel 2003), and so is still up for debate. I have not argued that the special theory is irreconcilably inconsistent with the A-theory, merely that there is a prima facie inconsistency between the two theories, while there is a prima facie consistency between it and the B-theory.

The metaphysical view of the new B-theory has not changed since the days of the old B-theory. What has changed is its methodology. Some proponents of the old B-theory thought that the way to argue for its metaphysical conclusions was to show that tense could be eliminated from language. Then some proponents of the truth-conditional variant of the new B-theory replaced this methodology with that of providing tenseless truth conditions for tensed sentences. The truthmaker variant of the new B-theory eschews strategies like this. It relies only on metaphysical and scientific arguments to establish its metaphysical conclusions. Its response to the linguistically inclined debate between its predecessors is to say that even though tensed and tenseless sentences cannot have the same meaning, this need not have the ontological implications A-theorists take it to have. By arguing that a tensed and a tenseless sentence can both be made true by the same tenseless fact, they effectively reject the underlying assumptions of their predecessors that there is a restricted, true description of temporal reality, and that once we have arrived at it we can read off the nature of time from the nature of the description. Thus, they reject the idea that the way a certain privileged description of reality is reveals the way reality itself is.

3 The representational fallacy
Or how not to do ontology

The direction of fit between language and the world

According to the conception of metaphysics derived from the Aristotelian tradition and outlined and endorsed in Chapter 1, metaphysics is the study of the fundamental nature and structure of reality. The aim of metaphysics is to provide us with a map of the structure of all that exists. This analogy between language and maps as a guide to reality is illustrative. Granted, we can learn some things about reality from studying maps. If the map is a road map, then we can learn which towns we will pass through driving from Dunedin to Christchurch, for example. But we will not learn from such a map whether the terrain is hilly or flat, or what the weather will be like on the day of our journey. All maps are selective about the information they convey, and what information they convey depends on the interests of the mapmakers in making the map. So any map leaves open a range of possibilities about how the terrain actually is. It would be a mistake to think that there is only one way reality can be given the way the map is. Similarly, we can learn some things about reality from examining our true sentences about it, specifically, we learn which of our sentences have truthmakers, but we will not learn from studying those sentences whether those truthmakers are particulars or states of affairs, for example. Just like maps, true sentences are selective about the information they convey, and what information they convey depends partly on the interests of whoever asserts them. Furthermore, just like maps, they leave open a range of possibilities about how reality actually is. The mistake is to think that there is only one way reality can be given our true sentences about it, and that a close examination of those sentences will reveal the nature of reality.

Russell held that language, including logic, can inform us about the nature of the world. In *An Inquiry into Meaning and Truth*, for example, he writes:

> There is, I think, a discoverable relation between the structure of sentences and the structure of the occurrences to which the sentences refer. I do not think the structure of non-verbal facts is wholly unknowable,

and I believe that, with sufficient caution, the properties of language may help us to understand the structure of the world.

(Russell 1940: 341)

Russell, thus, endorses the line of thought alluded to in the previous paragraph, that given the nature of our true representations of reality, there is only one way reality can be, and we can discover its nature by studying "with sufficient caution" those true representations. It sees the "direction of fit" between language and the world as being *from* language *to* the world. That is, it sees language as our starting point in metaphysics and in explaining what the fundamental structure of the world is like. I think the real direction of fit is from the world to language. That is, I think the world must be our starting point, both in metaphysics and in explaining how our true sentences get to be true.

Consider a very simple language that consists of just proper names and predicates, and suppose that some sentences of that language are true. Even if we were, for some reason, to think that this language was the most significant language, a number of different ontologies would be consistent with its true sentences.[1] The nature of the language itself does not dictate that one particular ontology is the correct one. One natural interpretation of such a language is the ontology of immanent realism. According to that interpretation, proper names refer only to particulars, and predicates refer only to the universals of immanent realism. Universals are tied to particulars by the relation of inherence, whereby a universal inheres in a particular.

However, other interpretations would also be consistent with a simple language such as this, for example, Platonism. According to that interpretation, proper names refer only to objects in the world of appearances, and predicates refer only to the Forms. The relation that ties objects to the Forms is that of participation. We could go on: trope theory, resemblance nominalism, class nominalism, indeed any other variant of nominalism, would all be viable interpretations of such a language, and each comes with its own associated ontology. Furthermore, nothing about the language itself dictates which, if any, of these interpretations is the right one. The most we can say is that if we have some other metaphysical arguments that one of these ontologies is the right one, then we might be able to appeal to our simple language to help characterize that ontology. What this shows is that there is something fundamentally wrong with adopting a view like Russell's according to which we can examine the syntax and structure of our language and infer conclusions about the structure of reality.

To further illustrate the point that language does not favor any particular ontology over any other, consider the following example, adapted from one given by John Heil (2003: 41–2). We speak of objects possessing properties. We say, for example, that a billiard ball is red and spherical (and suppose this is true). So the term "billiard ball" bears the linguistic hallmarks of an expression denoting a substance of some kind, while the terms "is red" and "is spherical" bear the hallmarks of expressions denoting properties. Now, it is at least possible that there is just one substance: spacetime, for instance. In that case, ordinary objects, like billiard balls, would not be substances—there is just one substance—instead, they would be properties of spacetime; ways a certain region of spacetime is. Language cannot rule out this possibility. Our best scientific theories might tell us that billiard balls exist without telling us to which ontological category they belong. Similarly for terms that appear to denote properties. A sentence like "The billiard ball is red" may be true, but that it is true does not tell us that in virtue of which it is true. It may be true because the billiard ball possesses the property of redness, participates in the form of redness, belongs to a resemblance class of red things, has a red trope, or any number of other reasons. Knowing that it is true, even knowing what its truth condition is, does not tell us what it is about the world that makes it true.

The idea underlying Russell's claim is that the structure of language can inform us about the structure of reality. If we know what sorts of logical structures must be used to accurately describe reality, then, the thought goes, we can infer from that something about the structure of reality so described. Why did he think this? One clue as to the answer to that question appears in the chapter of *An Inquiry into Meaning and Truth* from which I have already quoted. He asks what the relation is between words and non-verbal facts and suggests that the available answers to that question divide philosophers into three broad types:

> A. Those who infer properties of the world from properties of language. These are a very distinguished party; they include Parmenides, Plato, Spinoza, Leibniz, Hegel, and Bradley.
> B. Those who maintain that knowledge is only of words. Among these are the nominalists and some of the logical positivists.
> C. Those who maintain that there is knowledge not expressible in words, and use words to tell us what this knowledge is. These include the mystics, Bergson, and Wittgenstein; also certain aspects of Hegel and Bradley.
> (Russell 1940: 341)

Having delineated the three categories of philosophers, Russell goes on to dismiss the third as self-contradictory, and the second on account of the fact that "we can know what words occur in a sentence, and that this is not a verbal fact, although it is indispensable to the verbalists" (Russell 1940: 342). He then remarks that "If, therefore, we are confined to the above three alternatives, we must make the best of the first" (Russell 1940: 342). But why should we think ourselves confined to these three alternatives? For one thing, as I have already argued, many different ontologies are compatible with a single language, so we have no reason to think we can infer properties of the world from properties of language. For another, it is, at the very least, plausible to think that there is a fourth alternative: that we can explain the properties of language, and how it relates to the world, once we have an adequate understanding of the world itself, and that this understanding need not proceed via an understanding of language.

The view about the relation between language and reality that Russell seeks to "make the best of" is, I think, a view that is committed to SLT. If one thinks that one can infer the properties of the world from the properties of language, then one must think that there is a privileged set of truths describing reality that is ontologically perspicuous. Otherwise, it would not be possible to draw the inference in question. In order to draw that inference, there must be a one-to-one correspondence between the truths in that language and facts in the world, and those truths must be structurally isomorphic to those facts. But once we recognize that many different ontologies are compatible with a single language, and that SLT is false, we must also recognize that it is not possible to infer the properties of the world from the properties of language. The direction of fit between language and reality is not from language to reality, but from reality to language.

Against SLT

I have already argued that some philosophers implicitly assume SLT, and that it is the driving force behind some debates in metaphysics. I have also argued that the very fact that certain other theories in metaphysics are tenable gives us reason to reject it. What I want to do in this section is, first, to provide evidence that adherence to it is more widespread than we might have thought and, second, to argue more directly against it.

SLT, recall, is the following thesis: "There is one privileged, true description of reality, the sentences of which (a) stand in a one-to-one correspondence with facts in the world, and (b) are structurally isomorphic to the facts with which they correspond." If one thinks that SLT is true, then one will think oneself justified both in attempting to identify the ontologically privileged language, and also in deriving one's ontological conclusions from an examination of it.

In a 2002 article, Mary Kate McGowan argues against metaphysical realism (m-realism), the view that "the world is individuated independently of us so that there is an entirely objective way that it is" (McGowan 2002: 7). She seeks to undermine m-realism by showing that there are occasions when what properties an object has depends on contextual factors, including our interests in those things. Here is one such case:

> Suppose, for example, that my friend Sue asks me to describe my friend Mike and I launch into a detailed description of the microphysical properties of his muscle tissue. Even if my description is true, it is nevertheless defective. Since Sue is interested in Mike's personality and

not the microphysical details of his muscle tissue...the information imparted is simply irrelevant.

(McGowan 2002: 8)

McGowan believes that this case illustrates that what properties an object has depends on relevance, which in turn depends on our interests. There are two possible interpretations of McGowan's critique, one more charitable than the other. The charitable interpretation is that she has simply made a mistake and is confusing properties with predicates. It may be true that what *predicates* are appropriate for a certain kind of description depends on the kind of description we are interested in, but it does not follow from this that what *properties* an object has depends on our interests.

The less charitable interpretation (but, alas, the one I think more likely to have been intended by McGowan) is that she believes that our choice of words when describing an object enables us to identify which properties that object has. In other words, she thinks that we can read off the properties of an object from the predicates that occur in the true sentences we use to describe it. She is implicitly assuming that any true sentence describing an object is structurally isomorphic to the features of the object so described, so that by examining the true sentence we can ascertain what those features are.

There is further evidence that the less charitable interpretation is the right one. Later on in the same paper, when discussing the notion of similarity, she claims that, "If all properties are on a par then any two things (no matter what they are like) are maximally similar to one another. This is so because there are infinitely many properties that the two things share" (McGowan 2002: 10). Once again, the charitable interpretation is that she is simply confusing "property" with "predicate" here. There may very well be infinitely many ways of describing an object, but why should we think that every object has infinitely many properties? The only reason for thinking so is if one also thinks that we can read off the properties of objects from the language we use to describe them; that *because* there are infinitely many ways of describing an object, there are infinitely many properties that the object has.

This part of McGowan's reasoning illustrates that she is committed to the "structural isomorphism" claim that constitutes part of SLT. That is, she thinks that any sentence truly describing some part of reality is structurally isomorphic to the part of reality it describes, which enables her to conclude that by examining the features of the true description we can ascertain the features of its ontological counterpart. If she is right, it follows that we are able to discover the properties of an object merely by examining the true sentences describing it.

Is there an alternative to McGowan's pattern of reasoning, one that does not rely on there being any structural isomorphism between language and reality? Let's consider her example of alternative true descriptions of her friend Mike. McGowan thinks that for any true description of Mike, the predicates of that true description stand in a one-to-one correspondence with properties that Mike possesses. So, if the sentence "Mike is athletic and outgoing" is true, then Mike possesses the properties *being athletic* and *being outgoing*. And if the sentences "Mike's muscle tissue has configuration C" and "Mike's brain cells have configuration D" are true, then Mike has the properties *having muscle tissue with configuration C* and *having brain cells with configuration D*. An alternative view about Mike and his properties that I would support would claim that, while all of these sentences describing him are true, there need not be a property corresponding to every predicate. It is true that Mike is athletic, not because he possesses the property *being athletic*, but because of facts about his physical constitution. It is true that he is outgoing, not because he possesses the property *being outgoing*, but because of facts about the state of his brain and his accumulated experience. The truthmakers for these statements about him need not be structurally isomorphic to the statements themselves. If they were not so isomorphic, it would not be possible to "read off" Mike's properties from the predicates used in statements that truly describe him.

A similar critique of the sort of reasoning employed by McGowan is put forward by John Heil. He identifies what he calls the picture theory, which is a family of loosely related doctrines concerning the relationship between language and the world. He notes that many philosophers would explicitly reject it, but nevertheless continue to endorse it implicitly in the manner in which they do philosophy. The core idea of the picture theory "is that the character of reality can be 'read off' our linguistic representations of reality – or our suitably regimented linguistic representations of reality. A corollary of the Picture Theory is the idea that to every meaningful predicate there corresponds a property" (Heil 2003: 6). It should be clear that the representational fallacy is prone to be committed by those who, implicitly or explicitly, endorse the picture theory. If one thinks that elements of the way we represent the world linguistically "line up" with elements of the world (Heil 2003: 6), then it would be natural to think that an investigation into the elements of our linguistic representations of the world will yield results about elements of the world.

This unspoken adherence to the picture theory has an important implication in the way philosophers reason when it comes to questions of ontology. Philosophers of a realist persuasion think that much of our ordinary talk about the world is descriptive, and literally true. When doing ontology they want to provide an account of what it is in the world that makes this ordinary talk true. If the picture theory is lurking in the background when they attempt to provide such an account, they will be inclined to think that the elements of our ordinary linguistic representations will be indicative of the elements of reality in virtue of which those representations are true. This, in turn, leads them to focus on features of the linguistic representation itself in an attempt to come up with an account of what it is in the world in virtue of which the representation is true. Part of the mistake that

McGowan makes here is due to the fact that she has succumbed to this pattern of reasoning.

Let's consider a different example. Suppose that the object before me is a desk. In that case, I would want to say that the sentence "The object before me is a desk" describes some part of the world, and is literally true. I would also want to say that there is something about the world in virtue of which that sentence is true. How do I ascertain what it is in the world in virtue of which that sentence is true? If I were attracted to the picture theory I might want to say that there is a particular substance standing in a certain, specifiable, spatial relation to me (the utterer) which has the property of being a desk. The reason I might want to say this is that the grammatical structure of the sentence is such that there is (1) a term referring to a substance, or particular; (2) a term denoting a spatial relation between that substance and me (the utterer of the sentence); and (3) a term denoting a property possessed by that substance. All this, a proponent of the picture theory would think, implies the existence of (1) a substance, or particular; (2) a certain spatial relation obtaining between that substance and the utterer of the sentence; and (3) the property of being a desk, possessed by that substance.

Let's focus now on the item apparently denoted by the predicate: the property of being a desk. We might ask what is it in virtue of which the object before me satisfies the predicate "is a desk"? If we were scientifically minded, we might want to say that it is in virtue of the object's being made up of certain fundamental constituents that are arranged in a certain way. However, lots of other objects could satisfy the predicate "is a desk" without sharing that fundamental constitution—the object before me is made of wood, but other desks are made of plastic, metal, or glass. Now the proponent of the picture theory will be in the following predicament: there is nothing at the fundamental level that all objects satisfying the predicate "is a desk" have in common, so either the property denoted by that predicate lacks extension, leading us to the conclusion that there are no desks, or the predicate must denote a "higher-level" property, which is "realized" by a possibly infinite range of "lower-level" physical properties.

A realist tendency, that is, a tendency to say that our ordinary linguistic representations of the world are literally true, and true in virtue of some way the world is independently of us and our representings, together with a commitment to the picture theory, leads inevitably to a hierarchical view of reality, according to which there are "levels" of being. Predicates like "is red" and "is a desk" are not reducible to lower-level physical predicates, because such a wide variety of entities can satisfy such predicates, so either nothing *really* satisfies those predicates (nothing is red, and there are no desks), or those predicates denote higher-level properties.

The sense in which there are "levels" of being, to which Heil is alluding and objecting here, should be distinguished from another sense in which we might say there are "levels" of being. We might say that my desk is made up of pieces of wood, and that these pieces of wood are made up of molecules, which in turn are made up of atoms. If we were to say that, then it would be natural to describe the atoms as existing at a lower "level" from the molecules, which in turn exist at a lower "level" from the pieces of wood, which exist at a lower "level" from the desk itself. All of these things exist, so there are levels of being. This sense in which there are levels of being is not problematic in the same way as the hierarchical view of reality that Heil is criticizing. It is compositional, or mereological, describing at greater levels of detail the fundamental constituents of objects. But it is not the case that with each new level of description, new entities come into existence. That is, these levels involve no addition of being. The problematic sense of levels of being is not compositional in this sense. It takes it that there are properties of objects that exist "over and above" their fundamental constituents, so on this picture there *are* additions to what exists at each new level of existence.

The doctrine of the picture theory that is explicitly responsible for this pattern of reasoning, according to Heil, is the doctrine he calls Principle Φ: "When a predicate applies truly to an object, it does so in virtue of designating a property possessed by that object and by every object to which the predicate truly applies (or would apply)" (Heil 2003: 26).

If one accepts Principle Φ, in conjunction with a commitment to the realist view that many of our ordinary language representations are literally true, and are true in virtue of the way the mind-independent world is, it is easy to see how one will be tempted into committing the representational fallacy. Being realists, we are interested in finding out what it is about the world that makes our true sentences true. Being committed to the picture theory in general will encourage us to think that we ought to begin our ontological investigation by considering our true sentences about the world. Being committed to Principle Φ, we will conclude that the predicates of any domain of discourse about which we want to be realists must denote real properties possessed by all the objects to which that predicate truly applies. For example, the predicate "is a desk" applies truly to many different objects, so it must denote a property, the property of being a desk, possessed by every object to which it truly applies.

Accepting this line of thought will reinforce the view that the way to identify what properties there are in the world is by examining the language we use to describe the world. You won't discover the property of being a desk by examining the fundamental constituents of objects we call desks, because there is a potentially infinite variety of them. Instead, you discover that being a desk is a property by attending to the language we use to describe the world, and noting that lots of objects can truly be described as desks. As Heil notes, this will be unappealing to anyone who thinks that properties (if they exist) are mind-independent (2003: 6). The lesson to be learned, therefore, is that we should not accept this line of thought.

Philosophers who argue in the way McGowan does, and adherents of the picture theory in general, clearly subscribe to the "structural isomorphism" component of SLT. Do any philosophers also subscribe to the rest of it?

McGowan thinks m-realism is committed to something very similar, if not identical, to it. She says, "There is a single objective way that the world is, according to m-realism and, in virtue of this uniqueness claim, m-realism is committed to the existence of a single correct and complete description of the world" (McGowan 2002: 13). According to McGowan, then, from the fact that m-realism thinks that there is just one way that the world is (an ontological thesis), it is committed to the linguistic thesis that there is a single correct and complete description of the world. I shall have more to say about this linguistic thesis and its relation to the ontological thesis of metaphysical realism in Chapter 4, but for now, let me just note that in order to draw this linguistic conclusion from the ontological thesis, one must think that, for any ontological component of the world, there is at most one true statement, in some privileged description of the world, that describes it. In other words, drawing this inference involves a commitment to the first part of SLT: that there is a privileged true description of reality, the sentences of which stand in a one-to-one correspondence with facts in the world.

I think that SLT is false. Since it is a complex thesis, there are different ways in which it can be rejected. One may, for example, deny that there is a privileged true description of reality, but still think that *any* true sentence stands in a one-to-one correspondence with a fact in the world, and that that sentence is structurally isomorphic to the fact with which it corresponds. Something like this line of thought seems to be at work in McGowan's reasoning, since she thinks that any sentence truly describing an object ascribes a unique property to it and that objects have infinitely many properties. I have already explained the way in which A- and old B-theorists of time are committed to there being a privileged true description of temporal reality; that description contains only a subset of all the truths that there are, and that subset of truths is ontologically perspicuous. I deny that there is a privileged true description of reality in this sense.

I do not deny that some descriptions of reality are better than others in that they *say* more objectively what reality is like. In general, the better descriptions will be ones whose truth depends less on features of their context of utterance, and in that sense are more objective, and less observer-dependent. For example, if the new B-theory of time is correct, the sentence "Event e occurs at time t" will be a better description of the temporal location of event e than the sentence "Event e is past," because it is a less observer-dependent description. Similarly, the sentence "Object o has molecular structure P" is a better description of o than the sentence "Object o is lilac" also because it is a less observer-dependent description. Admitting that there can be better and worse ways of describing reality in this sense is merely to admit that we are capable of *saying* more and less accurately (where accuracy here is something that comes in degrees) what observer-independent reality is like. Moreover, it is not to say that there is (yet) a best or privileged description of any part of reality. Fundamental science is not complete, and as it progresses, better descriptions become available. The important point is that it is not the case that all truths should be reducible to some class of the best available truths. Neither is it the case that we can infer all the truths from such a class of truths.

But there is a sense of "ontologically privileged description" with which I take issue. In this sense, some domain of discourse is ontologically privileged merely if it contains terms that cannot be paraphrased away by any other kind of term. This is then taken as evidence by some philosophers for the existence in reality of entities answering to those terms. My paradigm example of this is the A-theorists in the philosophy of time who argue that because our true ordinary language descriptions of reality are irreducibly tensed, we are thereby committed to the conclusion that reality itself is tensed. But there are other examples. We saw that, for van Inwagen, the fact that many of our true descriptions of reality contain apparently ineliminable property terms, justifies us in concluding that reality contains properties, where these are understood as abstract entities. But the fact that some true sentences contain property terms does not entail that reality contains properties. The truthmakers for those true sentences may involve properties, but equally, they may only involve particulars. The linguistic data, by themselves, do not determine which of these, or of some other possibility, is the case.

We will see in Chapter 7 that proponents of the indispensability argument in the philosophy of mathematics take the ineliminability of mathematical discourse for scientific purposes to establish the ontological claim that mathematical entities exist. Here again, the most that the linguistic data can establish is that mathematical *discourse* is ineliminable for scientific purposes. But this does not entail that mathematical entities exist. They may do so, and they may figure in the truthmakers of true mathematical statements, but equally, they may not exist, and instead some other entities may figure in the truthmakers of true mathematical statements. The linguistic data do not, by themselves, determine what the truthmakers for true, ineliminable, mathematical statements are.

Thus, I reject the component of SLT that says that there is one privileged true description of reality, where that description is taken to be a subset of all the truths that there are, and where the sense in which it is "privileged" is that it contains ineliminable kinds of term. Since I deny that there is a privileged true description of reality in this sense, I also deny that there is a one-to-one correspondence between truths and facts. I think the ratio of truths to facts is many-to-one. This permits there being better and worse descriptions of any fact, in the sense described above. What it does not permit is any inference from the existence of some truth that cannot be paraphrased or translated by another, to the conclusion that there must exist something in reality that can only be described by that truth. Furthermore, as discussed at the beginning of this section, I reject the claim that there need be any structural isomorphism between any truths and the facts they describe. There may be such an isomorphism between some truths and the facts they describe, but we cannot rely on it across the board, so we cannot draw conclusions about the nature and structure of reality from premises about the nature and structure of our true sentences.

Truth conditions and truthmakers

The approach to the relationship between language and reality, or between true descriptions of reality, and the reality that makes them true, that I have been criticizing is patently "top-down." It starts with true representations, and infers ontological conclusions from structural features of those representations. It is fallacious because, as we saw above, many different ontologies are consistent with the way language actually is, so the way language is does not dictate which ontology is the correct one. It may have been encouraged by the ontological significance that truth conditions are thought to have. The idea is that if we know the truth conditions of a sentence, we know what the world must be like to make that sentence true, and so, if a sentence *is* true, we know what the world, as described by that sentence, *is* like.

But it is a mistake to think that a grasp of the truth conditions of sentences can serve as a guide to ontology. For one thing, as we saw in Chapter 2, giving an account of the truth conditions of sentences and then deriving an ontology from that account is just another way of reading off the nature of reality from the nature of a linguistic representation of reality; it takes the metalanguage in which the truth conditions are stated as the language which guides us to our ontology. For another thing, biconditionals such as "'Trees exist' is true if and only if trees exist" can be read both ways. Read left to right they seem to issue in ontological pronouncements. Read right to left, however, they imply that for every way the world is there corresponds a truthbearer (Heil 2003: 55). Since this is false, we should, at the very least, be wary of the ontological pronouncements generated by reading them from left to right.

One unfortunate legacy of Tarski's important work is a tendency to conflate truth conditions with meanings. The conflation was easy to make, as the sentences for which Tarski formulated his T-scheme had no token reflexives or tenses. But once we consider the truth conditions for sentences that do contain token reflexives or tenses, we can see that a sentence's truth condition is not the same thing as its meaning, since two sentences can differ in meaning, yet have the same truth conditions (Dyke 2003b). To treat truth conditions as a guide to ontology is to conflate truth conditions with truthmakers, and there is at least one very good reason why we should not do this. This is that all meaningful sentences have truth conditions, whether they be true or false, but only true sentences have truthmakers.

Another very good reason for not conflating truth conditions with truthmakers is that it is plausible that the truth conditions of sentences are available to competent language users, but there is no reason to think that truthmakers are so available to competent language users. When a language user grasps the truth condition of a sentence, she is able to use that sentence appropriately. To return to an example I have used before, suppose an object, *o*, is lilac, and that the truth condition for the sentence "*o* is lilac" is that *o* appears lilac to a suitable observer in suitable conditions. It is reasonable to think that a competent language user will have a grasp of that truth condition, which enables her to use the sentence appropriately. However, if the sentence "*o* is lilac" is true in virtue of the fact that *o* has molecular structure *P*, it is *not* equally reasonable to think either that competent language users *must* have a grasp of this truthmaker in order to use the sentence appropriately, or that language users competent in the use of the sentence "*o* is lilac" in general *do* have access to this truthmaker. So, language users generally have a grasp of the truth conditions of the sentences they use competently, but there is no reason to think they have a grasp of the nature of the truthmakers of those sentences. To discover what those truthmakers are we have to do some empirical investigation. As Mulligan, Simons and Smith remark "A knowledge of truth-conditions takes us at most one step towards reality: one can, surely, envisage understanding a sentence (knowing its meaning), whilst at the same time having only partial knowledge of the nature of its possible truth-makers" (Mulligan et al. 1984: 299).

As we have seen, a tensed and a tenseless sentence can both be true, and be non-synonymous with each other, while having the same truthmaker. Just because the tensed sentence conveys different information from the tenseless sentence, it does not follow that there is some feature of extralinguistic reality (the property of being past for example) that corresponds to that different information. The same goes for sentences of other domains of discourse. The sentences "*o* is lilac" and "*o* is colored" can both be true and be irreducible to each other, while both being true in virtue of the fact that *o* has molecular structure *P*. Just because the sentence "*o* is lilac" conveys different information from the sentence "*o* is colored," it does not follow that there is some feature in the world, the property of being lilac, that corresponds to that different information.

Adherents of the picture theory see the direction of fit between representations and reality as being *from* the representations *to* reality. They think that we can examine our linguistic representations and derive ontological conclusions from them. However, the true direction of fit is *from* reality *to* the representations. There is much talk, in contemporary philosophy, of language "carving reality at its joints." I take this to mean that our language picks out significant, real divisions existing independently in the world. I do not want to deny that this is the case. I certainly do want to deny that our language somehow creates significant divisions in the world, such that without language there would be no divisions there at all. But language is not privileged in the way many philosophers take it to be. There are many divisions in reality, and some of them are salient to us. To enable us to mark them out we develop concepts and predicates which signify them. The reason why they are salient to us is due in part to the fact that they exist in the world, and we encounter them, and in part to features of us: our perceptual and cognitive make-up, and our interests in reality. The language we use to describe the world has evolved partly as a result of the way we are and partly as a result of the way the world is. Had either of these been different, our language, and our concepts would probably have been different too.

All this should make us wary of thinking that just because we have a predicate or a concept for picking out some respect in which a number of objects are similar, that there must therefore be a property corresponding to that predicate or concept. As Heil notes, "The philosophical mistake is to imagine that sameness of word implies sameness of worldly correspondent" (2003: 49). But we should add to this a further philosophical mistake, which is to think that *difference* of word implies *difference* of worldly correspondent. Just because the predicates of some domain of discourse are not reducible to the predicates of basic physics (or some other acceptable reductionist base), but we still want to say that they apply literally and truly to certain objects, it does not follow that there must be some additional feature of reality to which they correspond. The difference in information conveyed by two different predicates may be a result of a difference in our contribution to the applicability of those predicates, rather than a difference in the contribution made by the world to their applicability.

It is possible that a number of different, true sentences all accurately describe the same portion of reality, but since they do so in different ways, they are not synonymous with each other. Of such sentences we can say that they all have the same truthmaker, but that does not entail that they have the same meaning. Thus, a corollary of my view is that meaning is underdetermined by truthmakers. Since it is possible for two or more sentences to have the same truthmaker but not the same meaning, it should be clear that an investigation into the meanings of true sentences will be unable to yield any certain information about the nature of their truthmakers.

Even though tensed language is not reducible to tenseless language, it does not follow that there is some extra feature of the world to which it refers. We can convey different information about the same portion of reality with a tensed sentence than with a tenseless sentence, but it does not follow that there is some additional feature or entity in reality to which that different information corresponds. The different information conveyed may concern some feature of our interest in that portion of reality, rather than some feature of the portion of reality itself.[2] The same is true of desks. Just because talk of desks cannot be reduced to talk of the constituent particles that make up a desk, it does not follow that the desk is something "over and above" its constituent particles. Difference of word does not imply difference of worldly correspondent. It is probably true too of most of our predicates, except those of fundamental science. There we do seem to have correspondence between predicates and the features of reality they describe. But perhaps this is because it is the aim of fundamental science to describe the world as it is independently of observers, so its descriptions are "better" in the sense described above.

Suppose we have a true sentence, S1 which, it is claimed, involves apparent ontological commitment to a kind of entity, K, and another sentence S2 which, according to some philosopher is an adequate paraphrase of S1, but does not involve apparent ontological commitment to K, although it might involve apparent ontological commitment to some other more respectable kind of entity, L. Within the traditional fallacious program, it was assumed that the structures of sentences have implications for the structure of the reality they describe, so we are forced to accept that reality either has the structure implied by S1 or that implied by S2, (or perhaps that implied by some other paraphrase of S1, but I shall ignore this possibility for the sake of simplicity). Furthermore, the one true, privileged description of reality must include either S1 or S2, so reality itself must include either entities of kind K or entities of kind L. The debate then revolved around whether S2 was an adequate paraphrase of S1, that is, whether S2 conveyed all the same information that was conveyed by S1. According to my view, this is all wrongheaded. We cannot discern the nature of reality from the nature of a description of it. What, then, is the real relationship between S1 and S2, and also between S1 and S2 on the one hand, and reality on the other?

According to my view, the relationship between S1 and S2 is very likely that they have the same truthmaker, but not the same meaning. So the relationship between S1, S2, and reality is that both sentences are made true by the same portion of reality; they both accurately describe that portion of reality, but they do so in different ways, and so are not synonymous. Thus, it is not possible to say all that can be said using S1 by using S2 instead, even though they both describe the same extralinguistic entity. In other words, from the fact that there is something that can be said using S1 that cannot be said using S2, it does not follow that there is some extralinguistic entity referred to by S1 that is not referred to by S2.

From the fact that we can convey more information by uttering a token, u, of the tensed sentence "The enemy is now approaching" than we can by uttering a token, v, of the tenseless sentence "The enemy's approach is simultaneous with u," it does not follow that there is some additional extralinguistic entity referred to by u that is not referred to by v. Indeed, it doesn't follow that there is any difference in the extralinguistic fact described by these two tokens. They can have the same truthmaker even though they differ in meaning. The difference between them in meaning is a difference that resides in the sentences rather than in the extralinguistic entities they describe and which make them true. In this case, the difference is that the tensed sentence is temporally self-locating while the tenseless sentence is not. Thus, the relationship between sentences describing reality and the reality they describe is many-to-one, rather than one-to-one. There is just one way that reality is, but there are many ways of accurately describing it.

Truthmaking and truthmakers

According to my view then, the program of either drawing ontological conclusions from facts about ordinary language sentences or of attempting to find paraphrases of those sentences that have the same meaning, but don't entail those ontological conclusions is fallacious. It assumes that we can "read off" our ontological conclusions from the sentences of ordinary language, or from their paraphrases. The alternative position that is overlooked by this fallacious program holds instead that rather than inspecting our true sentences about reality to find out what reality is like, we should investigate reality itself and find out what it is about the world that makes our true sentences true. I do not mean to suggest by this that language is completely independent of reality, in some "free-floating" sense. Our true sentences are made true by ways parts of the world are, so naturally there is some anchoring of language to reality. While this is not the place for a full-blown theory of truthmakers, or of the truthmaking relation, I want, in this section, to say a bit more about these notions.

I'll start with the truthmaking relation. The first thing to say about the relation that obtains between truth and truthmaker is that it is cross-categorial. It relates linguistic entities (the truths, or truthbearers) with ontological entities (the truthmakers). In general, the truthmakers will be nonlinguistic, but there may be truths about utterances or sentences which would have those linguistic entities as constituents of their truthmakers. For example, the truth "The last thing Beatrice said to me was 'Don't forget to feed the cat,'" has Beatrice's utterance "Don't forget to feed the cat" as part of its truthmaker. But that utterance is part of that truthmaker *qua* ontological entity, rather than *qua* truthbearer. In general, the entities on the linguistic side of the relation, the truthbearers, I take to be sentence-tokens: spoken or written tokens of sentences that are concrete particulars and have a determinate spatiotemporal location. These are the entities to which the predicates "true" and "false" apply.

There is an apparent problem with taking concrete sentence-tokens to be the truthbearers, which is that it seems unable to account for "truths" that are never uttered. I have already addressed this problem in Chapter 2, in the section entitled "The Semantics of Tense." In broad outline, my response is that it is only when a truth exists that the question of what its truthmaker is arises. But the absence of any truths on a particular occasion makes no further difference to the way the world is. The entities that would have been truthmakers for any truths that might have been uttered still exist, but would not stand in the truthmaking relation.

What sort of relation is it that obtains between truth and truthmaker? Since it relates linguistic entities that are capable of being true or false with ontological entities that are not so capable, the relation is not one of entailment. Entailment is a relation that obtains between sentences or sets of sentences. S1 entails S2 if, and only if, it is not possible for S1 to be true and S2 to be false. In order for entailment so defined to hold between two entities, both relata must be capable of being true or false. In order for the truthmaking relation to hold between two entities, by contrast, only the truthbearer, but not the truthmaker, must be capable of being true or false (or rather, must actually *be* true). Hence, truthmaking is not entailment (Heil 2000; 2003: 62–5; Musgrave 2001).

Some philosophers have been tempted by the thought that truthmaking is entailment. For example, John Fox states that, "by a truthmaker for A, I mean something whose very existence entails A" (1987: 189). John Bigelow, too, holds that "Whenever something is true, there must be something whose existence entails that it is true. The 'making' in 'making true' is essentially logical entailment" (1988: 125). Bigelow, however, seems aware of the tension arising from this position when he says, "Truthmaker should not be construed as saying that an *object* entails a truth; rather, it requires that the proposition *that that object exists* entails the truth in question" (1988: 126). But if the truthmaking relation obtains between the truth in question and another proposition (the proposition *that that object exists*) we can still ask whether the latter proposition is true, and if so, what makes it true? Identifying truthmaking with entailment makes the mistake of confining truthmaking to the linguistic or representational realm and leaves unanswered the important question of how the world itself can make our truths true.

Another notion that has been used in an attempt to clarify or explain the nature of the truthmaking relation is that of supervenience. The slogan characterizing this view is that "truth supervenes on being." The idea is that two worlds cannot differ with respect to what is true at them without there being a difference in what exists at them (Bigelow 1988: 132). This is an intuitively attractive idea, but it is less than an explanation, or even a clarification of the truthmaking relation. It has been criticized by Armstrong (2004: 8) and Rodriguez-Pereyra (2002: 32) in the following way. While it is true that truth supervenes on being, it is equally true that being supervenes on truth. Just as there can be no difference in what is true without there also being a difference in what exists, there can equally be no difference in what exists without there being a difference in what is true. The notion of supervenience, despite appearances, does not offer us the asymmetry required of the truthmaking relation. As Rodriguez-Pereyra notes, "The fundamental insight in the idea of truthmaking is that being and truth are importantly and asymmetrically related by a relation of grounding. Truth depends on being in that it is grounded on being – being is the ground of truth" (2002: 33).

We have established that truthmaking is not entailment, and neither is it supervenience. Armstrong opts for the view that truthmaking is necessitation; that is, he thinks that truthmakers necessitate the truths they make true (2004: 5–7). He notes that this would be problematic for one who holds, as I do, that sentence-tokens (including beliefs and judgments) are truthbearers. He asks,

How can truthmakers necessitate truthbearers if the truthbearers are beliefs, statements and so on? How can something in the world, say the state of affairs of the dog's being on the dog-bed, *necessitate* that I have a belief that this is the case, or that somebody states that it is the case?

(Armstrong 2004: 15)

Armstrong is right that the state of affairs of the dog's being on the dog-bed cannot necessitate *that I have the belief that* the dog is on the dog-bed, or *that I state that* the dog is on the dog-bed. To think that would be to think that truthmakers necessitate the *existence* of truths. But why should one think that? If one thinks that truthbearers are concrete particulars like sentence-tokens or beliefs, then what is necessitated by a truthmaker is *that the truthbearer is true*. As I argued above, truthmakers only stand in the truthmaking relation if there is a truth in the vicinity for it to be a truthmaker of. *If* I truly believe that the dog is on the dog-bed, then what makes that belief true is the state of affairs of the dog's being on the dog-bed (assuming, for the moment that Armstrongian states of affairs are legitimate truthmakers). The dog's being on the dog-bed does not necessitate *that I believe that* the dog is on the dog-bed. If the dog was on the dog-bed while nobody was around to believe it, then there would be no truth for that state of affairs to stand in the truthmaking relation with.

Joseph Melia (2005) offers an alternative account of truthmaking. He argues that we are not compelled to see it as a relation holding between entities at all. Instead we can understand the expression "makes true," which occurs in sentences of the form "*A* makes true sentence *S*" as a non-truth-functional connective. The ontological commitments of a sentence of that form are just whatever *A* refers to (and for a nominalist like Melia, this will be just a particular), and the sentence *S*. On this interpretation, as Melia puts it, "*makes true* is as ontologically innocent as *and, or,* and *not*" (2005: 79).

Rodriguez-Pereyra, like Melia, does not see truthmaking as a relation of necessitation. He suggests the following:

(T′) Entity E is a truthmaker of 'S' if and only if E is an entity *in virtue of* which 'S' is true.

(Rodriguez-Pereyra 2002: 34)

He notes that one might object to this formulation because "being true in virtue of" is not a helpful elucidation of "being made true by" (Rodriguez-Pereyra 2002: 35). However, he defends it by claiming that there may be no noncircular definition of truthmaking, but this need not be a problem provided we have a fairly clear understanding of the concept of truthmaking. He thinks, and I agree with him, that we do have an intuitive grasp of the notions of "making true" and "being true in virtue of." That intuitive grasp can be made firmer still with more of an explanation of what the truthmakers for different sentences are.

Before moving on to the question of what truthmakers are, I want to point out how the notion of truthmaking and my notion of the direction of fit between language and reality are mutually illuminating. I suggested above that a useful way of understanding the representational fallacy is that it involves seeing the direction of fit between language and reality as being *from* language *to* reality, but the true direction of fit is from reality to language. Language does not dictate what reality is like. Instead, what reality is like dictates which of our utterances are true. Truths are true in virtue of the way reality is. Notice that grasping this notion of the direction of fit leads us inevitably to the truthmaker principle.

An alternative, indeed the orthodox, approach to questions of ontology is via Quine's criterion of ontological commitment (Quine 1948). According to Quine, the way to find out what there is in the world is to state our best theory of the world in the language of predicate calculus notation and then ask what kinds of things are required as values of its variables in its existentially quantified statements if those statements are to be true. The notion of ontological commitment thus takes language as its starting point and derives an ontology from it. Like truthmaking, it is a cross-categorial relation in that it spans the language–reality divide. But, unlike truthmaking, it sees the direction of fit as being from language to reality. Fraser MacBride has commented that following the truthmaking approach to ontology is "to negotiate an alternative route from language to ontology" from that offered by Quine's criterion of ontological commitment (2005: 117). But that is to miss the full significance of the truthmaking project. It is not an alternative route from language to ontology; it is a route to ontology that does not proceed via language at all. As Rodriguez-Pereyra notes, ontological commitment and truthmaking are converse relations "running from language to world for ontological commitment and from world to language for truthmaking" (2002: 29).

I turn now to the question of what truthmakers are. I'll start with some remarks about what I don't think truthmakers are, which will take me some (but not all) of the way towards saying what they are. I don't think truthmakers are (or need be) structurally isomorphic to the truths they make true. Just because a truth has a certain syntactical structure, it doesn't follow that the entity in the world that makes it true must have an ontological structure that mirrors that syntactical structure. For example, the truthmaker for the truth "The chair is brown" need not consist in a particular answering to the term "chair" possessing the property *being brown*. So truthmakers need not be complex entities consisting of particulars possessing properties. The truthmaker for the truth "The chair is brown" may just be a particular, a spatiotemporal entity, that we can describe as a chair, a wooden object, a collection of molecules, and in many other ways. Some of these descriptions will be better than others, in the sense discussed above.

Another thing truthmakers are not is representational entities. That is, they are not, in general, truthbearers. The truthmaker for the truth "Polly exists" is not, for example, the proposition *that Polly exists*. Instead, it is something nonlinguistic; some part of the furniture of the world, an ontological counterpart to the truth that it makes true. If we were to invoke propositions to be the truthmakers for our truths, then we are merely pushing the truthmaker question back a step. Is the proposition that Polly exists true? If so, what makes it true?[3] In my view, the truthmaker for the truth "Polly exists" is most likely Polly herself.

As I indicated above, this is not the place for a full-blown theory of truthmakers. My project in this book consists in an attack on the methodology employed in some metaphysical disputes, which I think places too much emphasis on language, together with a suggestion for an alternative approach to those metaphysical questions. According to the alternative approach the sentences of some domain of discourse can be literally true, irreducible to any other sentences, and yet not imply the existence of entities peculiar to that domain of discourse. Instead, they can be made true by some other kind of entity, even where there is no logical route from the original sentences to descriptions of those truthmakers. It is, thus, a very general project. The strategy can be filled with content in different ways depending on what one takes to be the truthmakers for the sentences of the domains of discourse in question.[4] The generality of my project, thus, does not require me to commit to any particular view about what sorts of entities truthmakers are. However, I will briefly canvass some of the suggestions that have been made in the literature and then make a tentative suggestion of my own.

Armstrong takes truthmakers to be facts or states of affairs (1997: 2; 2004: 48–9). These entities are composites of particulars instantiating universals. So, in his example discussed above, the truthmaker for "The dog is on the dog-bed" is the fact that the dog is on the dog-bed, or the state of affairs of the dog's being on the dog-bed. More generally, if "*a* is F" is true, and *a* is a particular and F a genuine universal, then the state of affairs of *a*'s being F is the truthmaker for that truth.

Many, most notably nominalists of every stripe, are not prepared to countenance facts or states of affairs so understood. Some even profess to find them puzzling (for example, Bigelow 1988: 153). But the truthmaking project can be carried through without admitting them into one's ontology. Josh Parsons (1999) has argued that the truthmaker principle is consistent with what he calls "thoroughgoing nominalism," according to which there are only concrete particulars. Rodriguez-Pereyra sees the problem of universals as the problem of what the truthmakers are for sentences of the form "*a* is F" or "*a* has the property F," and he argues that his version of resemblance nominalism provides a satisfactory answer to that problem. He does acknowledge the existence of facts, conceived as "complex entities, having different constituents combined or structured in a certain way" (Rodriguez-Pereyra 2002: 85), but holds that their only constituents are resembling particulars. Melia adopts a position he calls "sensible nominalism" and argues that the individuals making up his ontology are sufficient to play the truthmaking role (Melia 2005). Even Armstrong recognizes that one can adhere to the truthmaking principle and be a nominalist (2004: 24).

Another suggestion is that truthmakers are tropes. Mulligan et al. (1984) argue for a position such as this, but call them "moments". According to them, the truthmaker for "Socrates died" is Socrates' death; the truthmaker for "Mary is smiling" is her present smile, and the truthmaker for "This cube is white" is the whiteness of this cube. Similarly, Barry Smith assumes that reality is ultimately physical, but as well as lower-level (in the allowable sense, see above) physical entities such as molecules and atoms, it contains "such common-or-garden substances as you and me, your chair and my table" (1999: 274), which are built up out of the lower-level substances. It also contains 'such common-or-garden tropes ...as headaches, smiles, knots, explosions" (Smith 1999: 274) and these common-or-garden substances and tropes play a role in making true our true sentences.

There is, thus, a variety of ontologies that are, arguably, able to supply truthmakers for truths. As I explained above, for the purposes of my project there is no need for me to opt for any particular ontology. Nevertheless, I shall say a bit more about how I see the truthmaking project offering up truthmakers for particular truths. According to the position I have been arguing for, the truthmaker for a sentence need not include an entity answering to every term in that sentence. A sentence such as "*a* is F" need not have, as part of its truthmaker, a universal, *F-ness*, answering to the predicate "F." One can very well provide a nominalistic truthmaker for that sentence. According to Rodriguez-Pereyra, its truthmaker is that *a* has the property F, but its having that property is accounted for in terms of its resembling all the F-particulars. He uses the term "property" in a neutral sense, which is not intended to refer to any entity over and above the particulars that are said to have it, but only to "an identity of nature between some different particulars" (Rodriguez-Pereyra 2002: 16).

Similarly, Melia argues that "*a* is red *makes true* the sentence '*a* is coloured'" (2005: 78) and takes this to be committed only to the existence of *a* and the sentence "*a* is colored" (2005: 79). But there is something odd about Melia's formulation. It is not grammatical. Surely it would be better to say "The fact that *a* is red makes true the sentence '*a* is colored'"? Presumably the reason Melia does not say this is that he thinks it would commit him to facts, something the sensible nominalist ought to eschew. But this is not so, as Melia himself should realize. He has ably argued that "even in cases where a paraphrase is not possible, it is still possible to recognize that the truthmakers for certain sentences, whatever they may be, do not involve the entities which the sentence apparently refers to or quantifies over" (Melia 2005: 77). The sentence "There is a color that *a* and *b* have in common" does not require the existence of color properties in order to be true. Exactly the same reasoning can be used to deny that the sentence "The fact that *a* is red makes true the sentence '*a* is colored'" commits one to the existence of facts. That the term "fact" occurs in that sentence and, let us suppose, cannot be paraphrased away, does not commit us to the existence of facts. Its truthmaker might just be *a*'s being red standing in the truthmaking relation to the sentence "a is colored," and this the sensible nominalist can perfectly well allow. As he says, the sensible nominalist does not deny that there are red things, round things, square things, and so on.

> One does not describe the world just by listing all the things that there are: one must also *describe* these things correctly, one must say which things are green and which are red.... There is no reason to think that in order to describe something truly the predicate must refer or must carry any ontological commitment.
>
> (Melia 2005: 68)

Having clearly pointed the way out of reading his ontology of language, his unwillingness to talk of facts suggests that he thinks that if he *talks* of them he will be committed to their existence. I am not, here, offering a positive account of what truthmakers are. What I am doing is arguing that the words we use to describe those truthmakers need not commit us to any particular ontology. Just because we find that, in order to be grammatical, we need to employ the term "fact" when describing a truthmaker, it does not follow that we must admit facts (conceived as structured entities consisting of particulars and universals) into our ontology.

In Chapter 2 I argued that two or more non-synonymous truths can have the same truthmaker. It is also the case that one truth can have many truthmakers. Armstrong gives the example of the truth "There exists at least one black swan," which has as separate truthmakers each of the black swans that has existed, exists now, or will exist (1997: 129). I have been focusing on the idea that different truths can have the same truthmaker, so I have talked in terms of the ratio of truths to truthmakers being many-to-one. But once we notice that existential quantifications, as well as disjunctions, whose truthmakers will be whatever makes true any of their true disjuncts, can have many truthmakers, we can see that the ratio of truths to truthmakers is in fact many-to-many. What is important, though, is that the ratio is *not* one-to-one. It is not the case that every truth must have its very own truthmaker, unique to it. To think that the ratio is one-to-one is to think that language dictates ontology; it is to commit the representational fallacy. Something like that thought lies behind the arguments of those, like McGowan, discussed above, who think that every way of truly describing an object picks out a property possessed by that object. Michael Pendlebury calls this the "naïve view" of the making true relation, and notes that it is committed to "a thoroughgoing isomorphism between the structure of the world and the structure of our thought and talk about it" (1986: 177). In other words, to adopt the naïve view is to be committed to the isomorphism component of SLT.

Pendlebury further argues that the logical complexity of a truth is independent from the ontological complexity of its truthmaker. A relatively simple truth, for example, "Smith is a bachelor" is likely to have a very complex set of facts as its truthmaker. While a very complex disjunction may have a very simple fact as its truthmaker, the truthmaker for just one of its disjuncts (Pendlebury 1986: 177; Mulligan et al. 1984: 298). Thus, not only is it not the case that that the ratio of truths to truthmakers is one-to-one, it is also not the case that the logical complexity of a truth is an indication of the ontological complexity of its truthmaker, or vice versa.

Before leaving truthmaker theory, I will mention a couple of problems that it faces. The first of these concerns the question of what the truthmakers are for negative existential statements, such as "There is no hippopotamus in this room"[5] and for statements such as "There are exactly five people in this room." Must we admit negative facts to account for truths of the first sort and totality facts to account for truths of the second sort?[6] That is, is the truthmaker for "There is no hippopotamus in this room" the absence, or lack, of a hippopotamus in the room? That would be a peculiar kind of fact. But a complete inventory of everything there *is* in the room would not preclude there also being a hippopotamus in the room so, on the face of it, would not be an adequate truthmaker for the negative existential statement. Similarly, the five people that are in the room would not, on the face of it, be an adequate truthmaker for "There are exactly five people in this room" as their existence would not preclude there being other people in the room. Do we, therefore, need what Armstrong calls a "totality fact," the fact that these are *all* the people in the room, to provide a truthmaker for sentences like this? These are vexed questions that any positive account of truthmaking must answer. Since I am not offering a positive account of truthmaking here, I will not try to answer them.[7]

The second problem that I will not attempt to answer here is whether truthmaker maximalism[8] is true. That is, does *every* truth have a truthmaker? This question is connected with that of what the primary truthbearers are. If they are propositions which can exist and have truth values even when never thought or uttered, then the question is more pressing, as there are far more of them to furnish with truthmakers than if they are concrete sentence-tokens. Happily, I can avoid the question here as I am only interested in truthmakers insofar as truths have them.

The ontological insignificance of paraphrase

The urge to paraphrase, I believe, grows out of an implicit commitment to SLT. Philosophers who succumb to it reason in the following way. There is an ordinary language sentence that common sense would tell us is true. The paraphraser also thinks it is true but thinks that if we accept it at face value we will be forced to admit into our ontology an entity, or kind of entity, that he does not wish to recognize. He therefore sets about finding another way of saying what the original sentence says that does not force us to admit the problematic entity or entities into our ontology. For example, common sense and our paraphraser would both want to admit, let us say, that the sentence "He had a mischievous grin and a twinkle in his eye" is true. The paraphraser, however, feels uncomfortable in admitting that it is true, because he thinks that by doing so he is admitting the existence of entities answering to the terms "grin" and "twinkle". So he offers a paraphrase of the sentence, for example the somewhat less poetic, "He grinned mischievously and his eye twinkled (or appeared to twinkle)." The paraphrase, he claims, is preferable because it contains no terms that refer to inadmissible entities such as grins and twinkles.

What motivates the paraphraser's reasoning? He dislikes the original sentence (although not enough to reject it as false) because it contains terms that appear to refer to entities whose existence he does not want to recognize. He assumes that by accepting it as true he *thereby* commits himself to their existence. That is, he thinks it would be inconsistent to believe that the sentence is true *and* to deny the existence of those entities. But that, as we have seen, is false. Our discussion of truthmakers in the previous section has shown that there is no need to think that a truthmaker is structurally isomorphic to the truth it makes true. In fact, there are good reasons for thinking that this is not the case. If truthmakers are not structurally isomorphic to the truths they make true, then there is no need to fear that one will be committed to an entity answering to every referring term in a sentence one takes to be true. The truthmaking project undermines the paraphrasing project. Once we recognize this we will realize that there is no need to find a paraphrase for sentences with apparently problematic ontological commitments.

Furthermore, suppose the paraphraser does find a paraphrase of some problematic sentence. Paraphrase is, presumably, a symmetric relation. If a sentence, S1, can be paraphrased by another sentence, S2, then S2 can equally be paraphrased by S1. What, then, determines which of these directions of translation we are to treat as ontologically significant? The paraphraser needs to appeal to considerations external to the paraphrase relation in order to support his case that one of these directions of translation is more fundamental, ontologically speaking, than the other. Examples might be considerations of explanatory power, or of parsimony, or empirical considerations. For example, if S2 involves apparent commitment to fewer kinds of entity than S1, then that might be a reason for thinking that S2 is a more accurate representation of reality than S1. But the point is, that eliminability by paraphrase *by itself* is no guide to ontological relevance.

One philosopher who has recently defended the paraphrase project is Peter van Inwagen (1990). He puts forward a metaphysical theory according to which there are no artifacts, like chairs, and no nonliving "natural" objects, like stones. There are only living organisms and simples. He asserts that if his position is to be taken seriously, "it should be possible to paraphrase the sentences of ordinary language that most philosophers would say expressed facts about things like chairs in language that refers to no material things but simples" (van Inwagen 1990: 108). Why does he think this should be possible? Well, much of our ordinary language appears to refer to objects like tables and chairs, objects which van Inwagen does not wish to admit into his ontology. He does not want to reject these ordinary language sentences as false. As he says, "When someone says 'some tables are heavier than some chairs,' there is obviously something right about what he says. Our technique of paraphrasis enables us to capture what it is that is right about what he says" (van Inwagen 1990: 111). But the assumption that sets van Inwagen, like other paraphrasers, off on his search for a paraphrase, is that the original sentence implies the existence of entities that don't exist. And this is an assumption that we need not accept. We can hold instead that there is something about the world that makes the sentence true and put forward a metaphysical theory about what that truthmaker is. According to van Inwagen, its truthmaker would involve some simples (the xs) being arranged chairwise and some simples (the ys) being arranged tablewise, with the xs being heavier than the ys (1990: 109). Other metaphysicians would put forward different accounts of its truthmaker. Either way, the paraphrase project is doing nothing to further the investigation. It has become redundant.

What about the Quinean indicator of ontological commitment: the quantifier? Surely, it might be thought, if our best theory of the world contains statements which quantify over terms referring to entities of a certain sort, and those statements cannot be paraphrased away, we must be forced to recognize the existence of those entities? For example, that theory may contain the sentence (to adapt an example of van Inwagen's discussed in Chapter 1), "There are some anatomical features shared by spiders and insects." This sentence quantifies over anatomical features, so the paraphraser who does not want to admit such things into his ontology will think that he must find a paraphrase of that sentence. As I indicated above, even if he is successful, we will need an argument for preferring the ontological commitments of his paraphrase to those of the original sentence. Paraphrase by itself will not lead us to the correct ontology. But suppose he is not successful. Are we therefore committed to the existence of anatomical features, where these are universals? No. If we follow the truthmaking route, we bypass the need for paraphrase altogether. Suppose the truthmaker for "There are some anatomical features shared by spiders and insects" is that spiders have a jointed exoskeleton and an open circulatory system and insects have a jointed exoskeleton and an open circulatory system. According to nominalists like Rodriguez-Pereyra and Melia, this truthmaker need include no universals but only particulars. Equally, however, this truthmaker may include universals. What this shows is that the paraphrase project is doing nothing to resolve the issue. The ontology must be arrived at independently. Once it is in place, its proponent will be in a position to explain how the constituents of that ontology provide truth-makers for our truths.

Thus, even when we are faced with quantified statements, there is no guarantee that there are entities answering to the terms over which the quantifiers range. As Melia comments, Quine's "question was not 'what is there?' but 'what must we quantify over?'" (Melia 2005: 77–8). And some dissent has been building in the philosophical literature over whether we are always committed to the existence of things answering to the terms we quantify over. Thomas Hofweber, for example, argues that quantifiers are semantically underspecified, and can make at least two different contributions to the truth conditions of sentences in which they occur (2005: 274). On one reading, the "domain conditions" reading, they *can* be used to establish what must exist for the sentence in which they occur to be true. For example, for the sentence "someone knocked at the door" to be true there must *be* someone such that that person knocked at the door. But they can also be used in what Hofweber calls their "inferential role" reading, and on this reading there is no such close connection between their use and ontology. They perform an inference-preserving role, such that "the inference from 'F(t)' to 'F(Something)' is always and trivially valid, no matter what 't' is" (Hofweber 2005: 274). Very often, a single use of a quantifier can fulfill both roles, but in natural language the roles can come apart. If a quantifier is used just in its inferential-role reading, then from the truth of "F(Something)" we cannot infer that there are any Fs. In order to ascertain whether there are any Fs we must go back to the quantifier-free instances; the instances of F(t).

Another dissenter is Jody Azzouni, who also argues that "*some* uses of the ordinary language 'there is'. . .*do not* carry ontological weight" (1998: 4). Azzouni further argues that a more fruitful way to do ontology than employing Quine's (or any) criterion of ontological commitment is to employ a criterion for what exists. Suffice it to say, then, that even when we are dealing with existentially quantified statements, the paradigm Quinean statement for issuing ontological commitments, it is at least arguable that we cannot read our ontology off them. If we can't do so in that case, then it is consistent to hold that such a statement is true, yet deny the existence of the entities apparently quantified over. If that's right then there is just no point in looking for paraphrases of statements like this, or of any other kind.

Conclusion

The conclusions I have argued for in this chapter are largely negative ones. I have argued that we cannot infer the properties of the world from the properties of language; that SLT, on which many metaphysical debates rest, is false; that we cannot do ontology by looking for an ontologically privileged description of reality and drawing conclusions about its nature by examining that description; that a grasp of the truth condition of a sentence will not tell you what its truthmaker is; that many non-synonymous truths can have the same truthmaker, so the meanings of those truths will not direct us to the nature of that truthmaker; and that the paraphrase project is redundant as a means for doing ontology. I think these negative lessons are important as they inform us how not to do ontology. Failing to heed them will lead us down blind alleys in our metaphysical quest. Are there any positive lessons that we can learn in the wake of this demolition job? I think there are. We should turn our attention to the theories of fundamental science and metaphysical theories that are not derived from considerations of language. We should examine them and judge them on their merits, where these will include pragmatic virtues such as plausibility, explanatory power and ontological economy. Any of the extant metaphysical theories may be right, but considerations of language will not give us a reason for thinking so. Once we realize that considerations of language cannot deliver up a metaphysical theory, we will be free to consider the advantages and disadvantages of the theories themselves. We will not be forced to choose a metaphysical theory on linguistic grounds. Neither will we be forced to abandon what might be the true metaphysical theory on the grounds that it is unable to give adequate paraphrases of certain sentences.

4 The relationship between language and reality

Against the idea of a privileged true description

In Chapter 3, I criticized SLT, the thesis that there is one privileged true description of reality, the sentences of which (a) stand in a one-to-one correspondence with facts in the world, and (b) are structurally isomorphic to the facts with which they correspond. My critique of it in that chapter focused on the latter claims, that true sentences in general stand in a one-to-one correspondence with facts to which they are structurally isomorphic. In this chapter I want to focus on the claim that there is a privileged true description of reality.

Why should anyone think that there is a single, privileged true description of reality? I think the most likely motivation for holding this view is the desire to affirm the realist claim that there is just one way that the world really is, and, furthermore, that the existence of the world, and the way the world is, is independent of human beings and their capacity to think about it; or, in other words, that reality is independent of the mental. If one thinks that there is just one way the world really is, it might seem natural to think that there is just one description of it that accurately captures the way it is. Alternatively, if there are two descriptions of reality that differ in meaning, neither of which is in any way privileged, that might seem to entail that there is a difference in the facts expressed, or the bits of reality described, by those two descriptions. So the existence of two nonequivalent descriptions of reality might be thought to entail the existence of two nonidentical bits of reality described by them. Further support for the view that there is such a privileged true description of reality might seem to come from considering the implications of rejecting it. If there is more than one way of accurately describing reality, where those alternative ways are not mere notational variants of each other, that might be thought to lead to the conclusion that there is more than one way reality really is, or even that there is more than one reality, a distinctly antirealist conclusion.

I want to argue that the ontological thesis of realism, that there is just one way the world is, and that its existence and nature are independent of our means of describing and thinking about it, does not entail SLT. Furthermore, rejecting SLT does not lead to the antirealist conclusions that reality is dependent on the mental, or that there is more than one reality. In other words, it is quite compatible with the ontological thesis of realism that there is more than one way of accurately describing reality, where those descriptions are not equivalent. My support for this view comes from the observation, made in Chapter 2, and developed in Chapter 3, that it is possible for two sentences to have the same truthmaker but not the same meaning. The existence of this possibility shows that some part of reality can be the one way that it is, while there are two or more ways of describing it that are nonequivalent.

What goes for parts of reality also goes for reality as a whole. So, the whole of reality can be the one way that it is while there are two or more ways of accurately describing it that are nonequivalent. This undermines the view that if there is just one way the world is, there must be just one way of accurately describing it. It shows, contrary to the view just outlined that the existence of two nonequivalent descriptions of reality need not entail that the reality described by them, or the facts expressed by them, is different. In fact, to think otherwise is to commit the representational fallacy. It is to assume that the nature of a description of reality has implications for the nature of what it describes.

Consider a token, u, of the tensed sentence "The enemy is now approaching," and a token, v, of the tenseless sentence "The enemy's approach is simultaneous with u." According to the new B-theory of time, these two sentence-tokens do not have the same meaning, but they do have the same truthmaker. Consequently, the fact that they differ in meaning does not entail that there is a difference in the bit of extralinguistic reality that they each describe, or that makes each of them true. What goes for individual sentence-tokens therefore also goes for entire collections of sentence-tokens. Any collection of sentence tokens, S1, that, it is claimed, constitutes a true description of reality might have a different meaning from some other collection of sentence-tokens, S2, yet it may be the case that S1 and S2 both describe the very same extralinguistic reality, or that both S1 and S2 are made true by the very same truthmakers. It follows that it is possible for the ontological thesis of realism to be true (that there is just one way the world is and that the way the world is, is independent of the mental), while it is also the case that there are many nonequivalent ways of accurately describing it. Thus, the ontological thesis of realism is consistent with the denial of SLT.

This conclusion has in fact been argued for by some realists (Heil 1981; Kirk 1999: 149–60) and endorsed by others (Devitt 1991: 229). John Heil considers the following two claims:

(i) It is not the case that there is exactly one way to describe correctly the world and its contents.

(ii) What there is in the world, the way the world is, is independent of our way of describing it.

(Heil 1981: 245)

The first claim effectively constitutes a denial of SLT, and the second is a version of the ontological thesis of realism. Heil suggests that many philosophers who wish to endorse one of these claims do so by denying the other. They take it that the truth of one entails the falsity of the other. Heil, however, argues that they are both true. Consequently, he effectively argues for the position I have been urging: that the ontological thesis of realism is consistent with the denial of the claim that there is just one true, privileged description of reality.

He argues for the truth of (i) as follows:

> I may describe anything imaginable in a variety of ways. The large object I am sitting before may be described as a piece of furniture, as a desk, as something made of metal and plastic, as a material object, as an obstacle, as a collection of molecules, and so on *ad indefinitum*. It is pointless to suggest that some one of these descriptions is privileged, that one is best, that one, in any sense, points more directly to what is really here before me. Of course, we may say that the desk *really is* a collection of molecules. But it really is a desk, a metal and plastic object, an obstacle and all the rest as well. To say that the desk really is a collection of molecules (or to say that it *really is* anything at all), is just to say that such a description is applicable to it. It is not, so far as I can see, to say that it really is this *and nothing more*. The latter claim seems just gratuitous.

(Heil 1981: 245)

The point Heil makes here in defense of (i) supports the contention that I argued for in Chapter 3 that the relationship of representations to reality is many-to-one, rather than one-to-one. That is, if each of the descriptions of the object before me is accurate, and they are non-synonymous, then it follows that there can be many, nonequivalent, true descriptions of the same portion of reality. If that is the case, then it is clearly not possible to derive the nature of reality from the nature of any description of it. To think that the relationship between true representations and reality is one-to-one is to think that there is one privileged description of reality that maps perfectly on to the way reality *really* is. This idea then motivates the view that we ought, in metaphysics, to strive to establish what that privileged description is. As I argued in Chapter 3, it is a short step from there to "reading off" the nature of reality itself from the nature of that privileged description of it.

Heil goes on to suggest that the principal motive for denying (i) is the desire to affirm (ii) together with the tacit belief that (ii) entails the falsity of (i). Similarly, Heil suggests, "there is a *prima facie* absurdity in the denial of what (ii) asserts" (1981: 246). The only plausible motivation for denying (ii) is the belief that (i) is true, and that (i) entails the falsity of (ii). But (i) and (ii) are both true, so it is not the case that they are inconsistent. He then makes what I think is a very important observation, which it is worth quoting in full:

> Assertion (i), on examination appears to involve a claim about language. That claim...boils down to the observation that there are many different co-ordinate systems which might be used to describe things as they are. Assertion (ii), in contrast, reminds us of the fact that co-ordinate systems are, after all, fitted on to an independently existing reality. Thus...a pair of claims which seem at first glance to conflict, in fact are claims about different subject matters: in the one case, language, in the other, reality.
> We are apt to lose sight of this difference because of a tendency to confuse questions about descriptions with questions about things.
> (Heil 1981: 246)

The significance of this observation is that it reinforces my claim that those who think there is just one true, privileged description of reality and who further think that the nature and structure of that description can inform us of the nature and structure of reality commit the representational fallacy. Such philosophers are drawing ontological conclusions about the nature of reality, specifically, the ontological thesis of realism, on the basis of alleged facts about language, specifically, the claim that there is just one way of accurately representing reality. Heil's observation here also undermines another of the possible motivations for asserting that there is just one true, privileged description of reality, which I mentioned above. This was the idea that rejecting it might be thought to entail the conclusion that there is more than one way that reality really is, or that there is more than one reality. But to reject that claim is to reject a claim about language, and this has no ontological implications whatsoever.

Putnam on metaphysical realism

In his later work, Hilary Putnam is an opponent of what he calls "metaphysical realism." He attacks it by attacking the linguistic thesis that he thinks it is committed to, namely, the thesis that there is exactly one true description of the world. I have already argued, and endorsed Heil's arguments, that realism is not committed to this thesis, so Putnam's criticisms of it may be thought to be irrelevant. However, it will be instructive to consider them, if only to illustrate further how realism is consistent with the denial of this thesis.

Putnam characterizes metaphysical realism as follows: "On [the] perspective [of metaphysical realism], the world consists of some fixed totality of mind-independent objects. There is exactly one true and complete description of 'the way the world is'." (1981: 49). So described, metaphysical realism has two components. First, there is the ontological thesis that the world consists of some fixed totality of mind-independent objects. This thesis captures the two dimensions of realism as defended by Michael Devitt (1991: 14–22). These are the existence dimension, according to which the world exists, and the independence dimension, according to which the existence of the world is independent of us and our means of describing or thinking about it.

Second, there is the linguistic thesis that there is just one true and complete description of the way the world is. It should be noted that the linguistic thesis which, according to Putnam, is a component of metaphysical realism, is different from the linguistic thesis I have been discussing. The latter thesis has it that there is just one true, privileged description of reality. Putnam's linguistic thesis states that there is just one true *and complete* description of reality. But no realist need be committed to Putnam's linguistic thesis. That thesis is false if there are any objects in reality without names, which there surely are. Of course, the realist is committed to there being one complete way the world is, but it doesn't follow from this that there is a true and complete description of the way the world is. In what follows, therefore, I shall set aside the completeness component of Putnam's linguistic thesis.

As I noted above, Putnam's criticisms of metaphysical realism focus entirely on the linguistic thesis. He begins by noting that our ordinary, everyday beliefs about the world represent it as being one way, and the sciences represent it as being another way. He then notes that, in the face of this disparity, the metaphysical realist asks "Which is the correct way of representing the world?" According to Putnam, and I agree, this is the wrong question to ask. There are many ways of correctly representing the world, each employing a different system of concepts, which serve different aims and purposes that we have. According to Putnam's metaphysical realist, those representations match, to a greater or lesser extent, what is out there independently of any system of concepts. According to Putnam, however, what is out there is determined, at least in part, and not merely reflected by, the systems of concepts we employ. We cannot say what is out there without invoking one or another system of concepts, and our choice of system depends partly on our own particular interests and desires.

According to Putnam, then, there is no sense at all in the notion of a description of the world that is independent of any conceptual scheme, and yet this is what he thinks the metaphysical realist wants. Putnam's metaphysical realist wants an account of the ontology of the world, where that account is independent of any conceptual scheme. Yet, according to Putnam, this is a contradiction in terms. An *account* of the ontology of the world must be an account in terms of some conceptual scheme or other. For Putnam, ontology, or what there is, is relative to a conceptual scheme. What there is depends, at least in part, on the conceptual schemes we use when describing it.

In propounding his own view, and in criticizing the view he ascribes to the metaphysical realist, Putnam confuses descriptions of reality with reality itself. The realist (as opposed to Putnam's metaphysical realist) can happily accept all that Putnam says about descriptions of reality without being committed to his ontological conclusions. She can accept that there are many ways of representing the world, each of which employs a different conceptual scheme, and that each conceptual scheme reflects our own desires and interests. She can deny that there is exactly one "correct" way of representing the world, which contains a subset of all the truths that there are. And, consistently with all this, she can deny that the way the world is depends on which conceptual scheme we employ when we describe it. Far from establishing that *what there is* depends on the conceptual schemes we employ when we describe the world, all that Putnam has established with his criticisms of the linguistic thesis of metaphysical realism is that *what we say there is* depends in part on the conceptual schemes we employ when we describe the world. But these are two quite different conclusions. The conclusion he claims to have established concerns reality, but the conclusion he has actually established concerns descriptions of reality, and is quite consistent with the ontological thesis of realism.

Putnam's ontological pluralism is an instance of the sort of view that those who defend the claim that there is one true, privileged description of reality are trying to avoid. Such philosophers are typically realists who espouse the ontological thesis of realism: that there is just one way the world is, and that the way the world is, is independent of us and our means of describing it. They further think that they are also committed to the linguistic counterpart of the ontological thesis of realism: that there is just one correct way of describing reality. They take this to imply that the one correct description of reality is restricted in that, for any fact in the world, there is at most one truth contained in the true description that accurately describes it. That is, they assume that their commitment to the ontological thesis of realism commits them to SLT.

It seems to these philosophers that if they deny SLT, they are thereby committed to the denial of the ontological thesis of realism. That is, if there is more than one correct way of describing reality, where those descriptions are non-synonymous, that must mean that there is more than one way reality really is, or that there is more than one reality. This is precisely what Putnam endorses with his thesis of ontological pluralism. It is the desire to avoid this kind of conclusion that leads these philosophers to affirm SLT. However, what I hope I have shown is that it is possible to deny SLT while retaining the ontological thesis of realism. It is possible for there to be more than one correct way of describing reality while there is just one reality, one way reality is, and it is independent of our means of describing it.

A problem arising from accepting SLT

Quine is a philosopher who seems to have endorsed the thesis that there is just one true, privileged description of reality. He endorses the doctrine of physicalism, which, according to him, is the view that the physical facts are all the facts. Physics, according to Quine, has "full coverage." That is, nothing happens in the world without some redistribution of physical states. And he further thinks that this means that, in their quest to discover the ultimate nature of reality, philosophers should concentrate on the language of physics, on what physics tells us the world is like, as that will tell us the true nature of reality. How, then, does he think we should understand those forms of discourse which do not employ the vocabulary of physics? What are we to make of the language of sciences other than physics, such as biology and chemistry, and of everyday discourse? We seem, when employing these discourses, to be describing facts about the world, but if only physics *really* describes facts about the world, are these alternative discourses then not really doing so?

Quine does not think we should, or perhaps even could, dispense with nonphysical forms of discourse. Instead, he suggests that many of our "assertions" should not be seen as attempts to describe reality. Thus, Quine suggests we treat nonphysical discourse as nondescriptive, or noncognitive. Hookway suggests two ways in which we could understand Quine's suggestion for interpreting nonphysical discourses (1988: 65–8). We could understand them as serving an expressive purpose. For example, expressivists about morality take moral judgments not to be describing moral facts, but, rather, to be expressing the moral attitudes of those who make them. Similarly, Quine may be suggesting that ordinary language and nonphysical "descriptions" of reality do not really describe reality, but rather, a speaker who employs such language "projects" a subjective attitude onto reality and thus speaks as if it reflects an objective feature of the world. The use of nonphysical language thus expresses the subjective attitude towards reality of the speaker, rather than describing reality itself. Hookway's second suggestion involves seeing nonphysical "descriptions" of reality as merely a useful technique that help us to carry out our practical activities. Their value is thus wholly instrumental, rather than fact-stating. Ordinary, everyday language does not purport to describe reality, but rather "reflects the framework of normative standards that are employed in controlling our actions and investigations" (Hookway 1988: 67).

Thus, by endorsing the view that there is just one true, privileged description of reality, and that it is the one given to us by the language of physics, Quine is forced into the position of having to give some noncognitive account of every other discourse that does not fall within the domain of physics. Whether we take Quine to be offering an expressivist or an instrumentalist account of all nonphysical language, we must ultimately see him as endorsing the view that almost all of what we say using our ordinary language, and the language of sciences other than physics, is not really descriptive, not really fact-stating, not really true or false, or even capable of being true or false, at all. Indeed Quine often explains away features of our ordinary language by showing that they reflect subjective commitments. For example, talk of necessity expresses our determination not to surrender a proposition too readily, and talk of causes expresses our expectations of how the world will behave. He thinks we are prone to a projectivist fallacy. If we claim that necessity or causation (or colors or value) are real, we mistakenly project a subjective feature of our responses to things on to the world. We treat as objective what is really subjective.

An alternative to Quine's noncognitive treatment of nonphysical language might be some kind of reductionism. That is, rather than giving an expressivist or instrumentalist account of nonphysical language, Quine could instead argue that any apparently descriptive sentence that is not a sentence from the language of physics is reducible to a physical sentence. However, Quine rejects reductionism, and to help explain why, Hookway offers an example designed to show the inadequacy of such a strategy (1988: 75–6). He considers a claim from economic theory, a claim that does not fall within the language of physics. The claim is the economic law that, other things being equal, raising the price of something will lead to a fall in demand for it. He then asks us to imagine a physical predicate that collects together all those events that we would describe as instances of raising prices. Such a predicate will be disjunctive, and extremely long.

There are at least two problems with the idea that the economic law is reducible to a physical law involving that physical predicate. First, the economic law conveys the information that all these events are of the same kind. Without this, the law would have no explanatory force. But this information is lost in an immensely disjunctive physical law. The physical statement can offer no explanation of why these events should be grouped together in a single law. We can only justify this by returning to our economic vocabulary and explaining that all the events are instances of raising prices. Second, since our knowledge of possible economic situations is inevitably incomplete, the disjunctive, physical characterization would also have to be incomplete. Our grasp of the economic vocabulary allows us to recognize very different events as instances of raising prices and to identify new events as such instances. But a mere grasp of the physical descriptions of actual price raisings would not tell us which other physical descriptions should also be added to the disjunction. The economic law finds a significant pattern which cannot be captured in purely physical terms. Hookway goes on to suggest that by rejecting reductionism, Quine wishes to acknowledge all this without having to abandon physicalism.

In a later chapter, Hookway argues that examples such as the one just outlined can be used to undermine Quine's commitment to the thesis that the physical facts are all the facts. Hookway questions Quine's inference from the claim that physics has "full coverage," that all change involves physical change, to the conclusion that the physical facts are all the facts. If statements drawn from economics, or other domains of discourse outside of physics, can provide us with an understanding of phenomena which we could not obtain from the statements of physics, then why should we not claim that they reveal an aspect of reality that is not revealed to us by physics? In spite of the fact that physics has "full coverage," Hookway argues, there are nonphysical facts which we allude to in making sense of ourselves and our surroundings. He writes, "That all change *involves* physical change, does not entail that every fact *is* a physical fact" (1988: 214).

But, if by "fact," Hookway means "bit of reality," then his suggestion seems ultimately to require abandoning Quine's physicalism and even the ontological thesis of realism. We would no longer be entitled to the claim that the way the world is is independent of the way we happen to describe it. Since we are capable of classifying events using the vocabulary of economics, it follows, according to Hookway, that there are facts, bits of reality, that correspond to our ways of classifying them. As well as all the physical events that are described by a physical description of actual price raisings, there is also a further fact in the world, a property, referred to by our economic predicate "is a price raising." Had we chosen to classify events differently, there would have been a different further fact in the world that corresponded to that alternative classification. So, on this view, the way the world is, is not independent of the way we happen to describe it.

If, instead, by "fact" Hookway means "truth," then his suggestion has done nothing to resolve Quine's problem. The truths of physics are the ones that describe the way the world really is, but there are lots of nonphysical truths. If only the physical truths are truly descriptive of reality, then we still need an account of how to deal with the nonphysical truths.

The options for dealing with apparent truths from outside of the domain of physics that we have been presented with so far are these: we should see them as not really describing reality, but as expressing our attitudes towards it; we should see them as reducible to truths statable in the language of physics, or we should see them as expressing facts over and above physical facts. Furthermore, none of these options is particularly attractive. I think there is an alternative to these options, and it has, by and large, been overlooked due to a tacit confusion between descriptions of reality and reality itself. The question at issue is how we are to deal with truths that fall outside of the realms of physics. There is a process of reasoning implicitly adopted by those who see these options as exhaustive, which I believe to be faulty. The first step in this process is to ask whether these apparent truths are indeed truths, and there are two available answers: yes and no. Quine says that they are not truths, and offers an alternative account of their linguistic function. The common sense answer is to say that they are truths. If we want to preserve the common sense answer, while retaining the view that the physical facts are all the facts, then, the thought continues, we must offer some account of how these truths are related to physical truths. The reductionist strategy is to say that they are reducible to physical truths. If the reductionist strategy is unsuccessful, as Quine thinks it is, then we must either revert back to the position that these "truths" are not really truths at all, or we must say that they express facts different from the facts expressed by physical truths. It is in this last step that the error in reasoning occurs.

The implicit, and false, assumption is that if a sentence is irreducible to another kind of sentence, then there must be a difference in the extralinguistic facts they each express. However, as we have seen, it is possible for two sentences to differ in meaning, and so be irreducible to each other, even if they both have the same truthmaker. Accepting the implicit assumption involves endorsing the language-to-reality move that is the representational fallacy. Let's remember that the question at issue concerns *truths*, not extralinguistic facts, and it is possible for a truth to have some truthmaker, while not being in any sense reducible to any other truth which is an alternative description of that same truthmaker. The alternative position that has been overlooked is that truths from outside of the realm of physics are made true by physical facts, facts describable in the language of physics, even though they are not reducible to physical truths. Where Hookway talks about nonphysical "facts," which are revealed to us by language other than the language of physics, all we really need to admit are nonphysical truths and to argue that those truths have physical truthmakers, even though they cannot be translated by, or in any sense reduced to, physical truths. To adapt Hookway's objection to Quine's position, from the fact that all change involves physical change, it does not follow that every truth can be expressed as a physical truth, even though it may have a physical truthmaker.

What causes trouble for Quine's position is that he seems implicitly to endorse SLT. According to his view, the language of physics gives us the privileged true description of reality, the sentences of which stand in a one-to-one correspondence with facts in the world.[1] It is only if he endorses this view that the nonphysical truths will cause him a problem. Only then will he have to adopt some noncognitive account of those "truths," or seek a reduction of them to truths in the physical description, or admit that they refer to facts over and above physical facts. If he rejects SLT, he can freely admit that there are many truths, not all of which are reducible to the truths of physics, while allowing that the truthmakers for all those truths are just physical facts. If the ratio of truths to facts is many-to-one rather than one-to-one, the nonphysical truths will not cause a problem for him.

In Chapter 2, I explained that I use the terms "truthmaker" and "fact" interchangeably to mean "bit of reality" or a way some part of reality is. However, the term "fact" is often used ambiguously to refer, on the one hand, to bits of reality, and on the other hand, to true sentences or propositions. This ambiguity is suggested by talk of, for example, the fact that bananas are nutritious, which might be taken to be about the state of affairs, or the "bit of reality" *that bananas are nutritious*, but it might equally be taken to be about the *truth* "bananas are nutritious." When used in the latter sense, then, talk of facts can be taken to be shorthand for talk of truths. Thus, the use of the term "fact" encourages the confusion between descriptions of reality and reality itself that I am trying to highlight, and avoid. Talk of truthmakers, by contrast, is much more clearly about ontology, rather than about true descriptions of reality.

In my discussion of truthmakers I have argued that it is possible for one and the same truthmaker to make true two or more non-synonymous sentences. When discussing this feature of the relationship of truths to truthmakers, I have often suggested that the truthmaker for a range of non-synonymous truths about it is a physical one. In such a case, the true sentence that describes that truthmaker in the vocabulary of physics, the physical truth, captures more accurately the true nature of that common truthmaker than any of the other truths. However, what I deny is that the other truths are reducible to or derivable from the physical truth. This does not mean that those truths are either not really truths at all, or express facts over and above those expressed by the physical truth. They are simply different ways of describing the same bit of reality.

My reason for suggesting that the truthmaker for a range of non-synonymous truths about it is a physical one has to do with my physicalist persuasion, together with my belief that Ockham's razor supports the conclusion that introducing nonphysical properties such as one denoted by the predicate "is a price raising" into our ontology is otiose. Similarly, when discussing a tensed and a tenseless sentence-token that have the same truthmaker, I suggested that their common truthmaker is the fact that the event the sentence-token is about and the production of it stand in a certain tenseless temporal relation to each other. Here again, my reasons concern the metaphysical and scientific considerations in favor of a B-theoretic metaphysics, discussed in Chapter 2, together with considerations of parsimony. If there is no need to introduce tensed properties or tensed facts into our ontology in addition to tenseless temporal relations, then we should not do so.

However, I want to emphasize that my view of ontology is not dictated by my view of the relationship between language and reality. All that is central to my view is that two or more truths can have the same truthmaker while being non-synonymous. It follows from this (among other things) that we cannot ascertain the nature of a particular truthmaker from examining the linguistic features of any truth that it makes true. Nothing about this view dictates any conclusion about the nature of any truthmaker. I think there are reasons external to this view about the relationship between language and reality for thinking realism, physicalism, and the new B-theory of time true, and I introduce these ontological theses to supplement my view about the relationship between language and reality.

Before drawing this section to a close, I want to return briefly to Quine's notion of the projectivist fallacy. Quine thought that when uttering statements drawn from discourses other than that of physics, we are often guilty of projecting a subjective feature of our responses to things onto the world itself. He further thought, by way of SLT, that only sentences of physical theory are genuinely descriptive of the way the world really is. He thus concluded that nonphysical statements are not descriptive. They do not describe the world as it really is, and so are not fact-stating at all. However, it is possible to agree with Quine about the projectivist fallacy without having to agree with him that we must offer a noncognitive account of nonphysical discourse. Accepting that we do project subjective features of our responses to things onto the world itself does not require us to treat nonphysical statements as not descriptive. We can allow that they are descriptive, that they are determinately either true or false, but some element of them which appears to pick out some extralinguistic feature of reality does not really do so.

Consider tensed discourse. According to the new B-theory, we project our own temporal perspective (a subjective feature of our response to reality) onto objective reality itself and falsely conclude that there is a feature of objective reality, presentness, that is independent of us. But recognizing that we do commit this projectivist fallacy does not require us to reject all tensed sentences as not really descriptive of reality. Instead, we can hold that they are descriptive, they are determinately true or false, but they are made true by facts that do not involve real tense. Similarly, economic truths might plausibly be thought to involve some features of our interest in certain kinds of events, for example, our interest in classifying them in certain ways, and we project those features onto the world itself, falsely concluding that there are objective features of reality corresponding to them that are independent of us. Recognizing this does not require us to reject all economic sentences as not really descriptive of reality. They are descriptive, they do have truth values, but they are made true by physical facts.

The feature of Quine's position that led him to a noncognitive account of nonphysical discourse was his commitment to the claim that there is just one true, privileged description of reality, and it is that given to us by the language of physics. I think he took this to mean that for every fact in the world there is at most one sentence in the one true description that truly describes it. If we reject that claim, then we can accept that some of the ways we truly describe reality incorporate features of our own subjective interests in reality, and occasionally we fallaciously project those features onto reality itself, while also retaining both the views that those descriptions really are determinately true or false and that the physical facts are all the facts. All we are rejecting is that the physical *truths* are all the *truths*.

An objection: what justifies generalizing from the case of tensed language?

It might be objected at this point that I am drawing a general conclusion about the relationship between language and reality on the basis of a particular type of language, and furthermore that my generalization is unjustified because that particular type of language has peculiar and idiosyncratic features not shared by other types of language. Tensed language is context dependent. The truth value of an utterance of a tensed sentence depends on the time at which it is produced. Most language, the objection will continue, is context independent, so it is not justifiable to draw conclusions about all language, and its relationship to reality, on the basis of this small and unrepresentative sample. In response, I want to argue that my inference is justified, and the reason is that much more of language than we ordinarily think is context dependent.

Consider first the example drawn from economic theory discussed above. The sentence-type "Event e is a price raising" is one which can be used to describe any number of a wide variety of events. The predicate "is a price raising" collects together those events and classifies them as all falling into the same category, where the classification itself is determined by our interest in those events, and membership of the category is determined by the natures of the events themselves. As noted above, a physical description of all the events that have so far satisfied that description would be an incomplete description of all the events that could satisfy it. Furthermore, our interest in events of that kind allows us to recognize some new event as falling into that category.

Suppose some particular event, e, satisfies the description "is a price raising," and can also be described using the physical predicate "is P." Then a token of the sentence-type "Event e is a price raising" and a token of the sentence-type "Event e is P" would both be made true by the same fact in the world, namely, the occurrence and nature of e. However, those two sentence-tokens do not have the same meaning as each other. From the fact that we employ the economic sentence-token to describe the event, we can infer something about our interest in that event, namely, that it falls within a category that it is useful for us to delineate. From the fact that we employ the physical sentence-token, we cannot draw that inference, but we can draw another inference about that event, namely, that it has a certain physical nature. In this case, then, the two sentence-tokens are both true, and have the same truthmaker, but they do not convey all the same information. This case is, therefore, relevantly similar to the case of tensed and tenseless sentence-tokens. In that case, both sentence-tokens are true, and they have the same truthmaker, but they do not convey all the same information, because from the fact that we employ the tensed sentence-token, we can infer some additional information about the extralinguistic entity it is about, namely, the utterer's temporal perspective on it.

Of course, an economic sentence and a tensed sentence exhibit different kinds of context dependence. Tensed sentence-types are context dependent in that the truth values of their tokens depend in a systematic way on the time of their production. This is not so for economic sentence-types. But that there can be different types of context dependence does not affect my point. Both economic and tensed sentence-tokens are capable of conveying different information from that conveyed by some other sentence-token that has the same truthmaker. And this is all that is required to reject the view that if a sentence conveys different information from any other sentence (i.e., is irreducible to any other sentence) there must be some feature of extralinguistic reality corresponding to that different information conveyed. Difference in information conveyed does not entail difference in extralinguistic facts described. Some information conveyed by the economic sentence is information about our interest in the extralinguistic fact that is its truthmaker. What is important is not the type of context dependence, but the fact that some aspects of the meanings of some sentences, or of the information conveyed by them, are features not of the extralinguistic entities they describe, but of the context in which they are produced, whether that be the time of utterance or the interests of the utterer.

But there is a further lesson to be learned from the economic example. Since tokens of the economic sentence can be made true by a potentially infinite variety of truthmakers, nothing about the sentence-type itself can inform us of the nature of any particular truthmaker of a given token of it. So, in cases like this, just as in cases involving tensed and tenseless sentences, it should be clear that we cannot draw conclusions about the nature of reality from the nature of any particular sentence describing it. This gives us a further reason for rejecting the language-to-reality move that is the representational fallacy.

Consider now another example. It is commonly argued within the field of the philosophy of mind, that the sentence-type "Organism O is in pain" is multiply realizable.[2] That is, a potentially infinite variety of actual physical states could "realize" (or make true) tokens of that type. I think it is plausible to see the point about multiple realizability as equivalent to the point I made above with respect to economic sentence-types. That is, tokens of the sentence-type "Organism O is in pain" can have a potentially infinite variety of truthmakers. Suppose some organism, O, satisfies the description "is in pain" and also satisfies the description "is in physical state S." Then, a token of the sentence-type "Organism O is in pain" and a token of the sentence-type "Organism O is in physical state S" would both be made true by the same fact in the world, namely, the physical state of organism O. However, those two sentence-tokens do not convey all the same information about their common truthmaker. From the fact that we choose to utter the sentence-token that employs "pain" vocabulary, we can infer something about our way of categorizing certain types of physical states, a way that is of interest to us. From the fact that we choose to utter the sentence-token that employs physical vocabulary, we cannot draw this inference, but we can infer other things about that truthmaker, namely, its physical nature. In this case, then, the two sentence-tokens are both true and have the same truthmaker, but they do not convey all the same information because from the fact that we choose to employ each of these sentence-tokens, we can infer different information about our interest in their common truthmaker. This example is thus also relevantly similar to the example drawn from economics and to the example of tensed and tenseless sentences.

The example just discussed also resembles the example drawn from economics in a further way. I noted, when discussing the economic example, that since tokens of the economic sentence can be made true by a potentially infinite variety of truthmakers, nothing about the sentence-type itself can inform us of the nature of any particular truthmaker of a given token of it. We thus have a further explanation of what is wrong with the representational fallacy. This point also applies to sentences involving pain vocabulary. Since sentences like "Organism O is in pain" are "multiply realizable," tokens of them can be made true by a potentially infinite variety of truthmakers. That being the case, we are not in a position to ascertain anything about extralinguistic reality just by examining the nature of the sentence-types we employ to talk about it.

As a final illustration of my point, I want to return to the example discussed by Heil (1981). The object before me can truly be described as a desk, a metal and plastic object, an obstacle, a collection of molecules, and so on. Which of these descriptions I choose to apply to it depends on me, my interest in it, and the information I wish to convey about it. Thus, when we describe a portion of reality, we do so from a particular perspective, and with certain of our own interests in that portion of reality in place. Our interests in it affect how we choose to describe it. So from each description we choose to apply to an object, we convey different information about it. It is in this way that much of what we say is context dependent. It is dependent on our perspective on, and our interest in extralinguistic reality. That being the case, the fact that I have generalized from lessons learned with respect to tensed language to language in general is justified. Tensed language is explicitly context dependent, while much of the rest of language is less obviously so. But it is, nevertheless, context dependent.

I have argued that the way in which much of what we say is context dependent is that our descriptions of reality are often dependent on our perspective on, and our interest in, extralinguistic reality. Some information conveyed by a descriptive statement concerns the portion of extralinguistic reality it describes, and some other information conveyed by it concerns us and our perspective on, and interest in, that portion of extralinguistic reality. This observation suggests both another line of thought that may have encouraged the representational fallacy, and another reason for seeing it as a fallacy. The line of thought that might have encouraged people to commit the representational fallacy is the idea that if two sentences differ in meaning, that may have been thought to entail that they also differ in the facts they each express, or the bits of reality they each describe. But I have shown that this is not the case. Two sentences can differ in meaning while both being made true by the same bit of extralinguistic reality. Why should we think that the difference in information conveyed by two sentence-tokens necessarily involves a difference in the extralinguistic facts they each pick out, and not merely a difference in our perspective on and interest in the one fact that they each pick out? If the difference in information conveyed by two such sentence-tokens merely concerns us and our interest in reality, then we are not able to conclude from the fact that they convey different information that they must each describe a different fact in reality. This further undermines any reason we might have had for thinking that the way language is reveals to us the way reality is.

Truth, meaning and reality

I have argued that the information conveyed by a sentence can concern two different things. On the one hand, it can concern the extralinguistic entity an expression refers to, or the extralinguistic fact a sentence is about. On the other hand, it can concern language users and their interest in, or perspective on reality. The fact that the information conveyed by what we say is dual faceted in this way is an indication of the fact that much of what we say is context dependent.

Since it is possible for two sentence-tokens to differ in meaning but have the same truthmaker, it follows that truthmakers underdetermine the information conveyed by a sentence-token. This is most clearly seen in the case of overtly context-dependent sentence-types. A token, u, of the sentence-type "The enemy is now approaching" and a token, v, of the sentence-type "The enemy's approach is simultaneous with u" convey different information, despite the fact that they have the same truthmaker. The tensed token conveys some additional information, specifically, the utterer's temporal perspective on the extralinguistic event, the enemy's approach, that the sentence is about. The fact that it conveys this additional information is the reason why tensed language is required for successful communication about extralinguistic reality (Mellor 2001). But the additional information conveyed concerns the language user and her perspective on extralinguistic reality, rather than the intrinsic nature of extralinguistic reality itself. Furthermore, it is conveyed by the fact that the sentence-type of which u is a token is temporally context dependent. Thus, the fact that u conveys more information than v does not entail that there is some additional feature of extralinguistic reality that u, but not v, picks out.

However, the same conclusion can be arrived at with examples of less obviously context-dependent sentences. The tokens "Event e is a price raising" and "Event e is P," where "is P" is a physical predicate that applies to the same event, can have the same truthmaker, while not conveying the same information about e. In this case too, then, truthmakers underdetermine the information conveyed by a sentence-token. We choose to classify events according to whether or not they are price raisings because this serves our purposes and reflects our interest in those events. This information is conveyed by uttering tokens of the economic sentence-type, but not by uttering tokens of the physical sentence-type. The latter sentence fails to reflect our scheme of classification of events in this respect, and so does not convey that information. Thus, just because two such sentence-tokens differ in the information they each convey, it does not follow that there is a difference in the extralinguistic entities they each pick out.

5 The methodological map

Up to now I have been almost entirely concerned with realist strategies in metaphysics.[1] That is, I have concentrated on theories that take a given domain of discourse to be fact-stating, or descriptive of a region of mind-independent reality. I want, in this chapter to expand the boundaries of my investigation to include antirealist treatments of a given domain of discourse as well. I will outline what I call "the methodological map," which details the range of positions generally thought to be available with respect to a given domain of discourse, including both realist and antirealist options. I will further suggest that this range has been thought to be exhaustive, but, as before, I will argue that there is a strategy that has been overlooked, and it is that suggested by the new B-theory of time.

I noted in the introduction that the term "the representational fallacy" does not refer to a particular argument or form of argument. It denotes a general tendency to read metaphysics off language and a variety of philosophical mistakes that follow from yielding to that tendency. In this chapter, I will be concerned with two of these philosophical mistakes. One is the mistake I discussed in Chapter 4 of conflating descriptions of reality with reality itself. The other is the tendency to overlook an occupiable position on the methodological map, which is, I argue, the result of tacitly accepting SLT.

The commonly accepted methodological map

For any particular domain of discourse, there is a range of alternative positions available as to the ontological status of what that discourse is putatively about. The starting point for many metaphysical enquiries is, as we have seen, a domain of discourse of a certain kind, in particular, the true sentences of that domain of discourse. These domains of discourse may include, for example, the language of physics, of ordinary common sense, of morality, modality, mathematics, aesthetics, and so on. Rather than discussing particular domains of discourse at this stage, I will talk of domains of discourse in general, and discuss truths of kind K, or K-truths.

The first possibility is to take the truths of kind K at face value and declare that there are facts of kind K which correspond to the truths of kind

K. K-truths refer to K-facts, and the K-facts make the K-truths true. We might call this view "K-realism." According to K-realism, the domain of K-discourse reflects a realm of reality that includes K-facts.

The next possibility is to treat the truths of kind K as reducible to truths of some other kind, truths of kind L, perhaps. If one takes this route, one denies that there are any K-facts, but this does not make one's K-discourse false. Instead, the K-truths can be analyzed into L-truths, and the L-truths refer to L-facts. This route is appealing to those who find K-facts unattractive, but are quite happy that their ontology should include L-facts. We can call this approach "K-reductionism."

The third and fourth strategies are versions of antirealism about K-discourse, and are typically adopted by those who have antecedently decided that there are no facts of kind K, and who see little chance of success for the strategy of K-reductionism. The first of these is to declare that all the K-"truths" are in fact false, and this is *because* there are no K-facts. K-sentences imply the existence of K-facts, and since there are no K-facts, all the atomic sentences of K-discourse are false. This is an error theory of K-discourse.

The fourth strategy is to treat K-discourse as, despite appearances, not fact-stating at all. On this view, K-"truths" are not truths at all, but not because they are false. Instead it is because they are not candidates for truth and falsity at all. K-discourse seems, on the face of it, to involve assertions about the way the world is, but this is merely an appearance. K-discourse really plays some other, non-assertoric, role in our language. This kind of view is noncognitivism about K-discourse.

The final strategy is also a version of antirealism. According to this view, ontological questions can only legitimately be asked from within a domain of discourse, linguistic framework, or conceptual scheme. The reason for this is that, to think otherwise is to assume that there is a standpoint available to metaphysics that is external to any conceptual scheme, and this view denies that assumption. So, from within the domain of K-discourse we can ask whether there are any K-facts, and the answer to this question will be: yes, there are K-facts "within K-discourse." If we want to know whether there are *really* any K-facts, objectively speaking, and not merely "within K-discourse," our question makes no sense. This view I shall call "conceptual relativism."

In summary, the available positions with respect to K-discourse are these:[2]

1. Truths of kind K refer to facts of kind K (K-realism).
2. Truths of kind K are reducible to truths of kind L, and these refer to facts of kind L (K-reductionism).
3. "Truths" of kind K are actually all false *because* there are no facts of kind K (Error theory of K-discourse).
4. "Truths" of kind K are, despite appearances, not really fact-stating, so they are not candidates for truth or falsity (Noncognitivism about K-discourse).

5. Truths of kind K refer to facts of kind K, so K-facts exist but only relative to the domain of K-discourse (Conceptual relativism).

There is, of course, fundamental disagreement among philosophers who adopt these different approaches to the treatment of K-discourse. But there is, I believe, widespread agreement, at a methodological level, that these options do indeed constitute the range of acceptable answers. In support of this claim, I will show how three philosophers have endorsed a range of options comparable to that described by the methodological map.

In an article entitled "Naturalism and the Fate of the M-worlds," Huw Price (1997) notes that there are areas of human discourse under threat from the rise of modern science. They include morality, modality, meaning and the mental (hence M-worlds). These areas of discourse are, presumably, under threat because they appear to involve reference to features of the world that are not recognized by science. Price begins by noting two possible reactions to this state of affairs. The first is to declare that "at least some of these topics are not worth saving, and that the tide of science does us a favour by sweeping them away" (Price 1997: 247). Price refers to this view as eliminativism. It falls into the third category of the methodological map. According to this view, the areas of discourse in question appear to refer to features of reality, but these alleged features of reality are not recognized by science, so they do not really exist. Consequently, the sentences of those areas of discourse are systematically false.

The second possible reaction, according to Price, is to hold that these areas of discourse "do not need saving, being already out of reach of the waters of science – no part of the scientific landscape, in effect, but no less respectable for that" (1997: 247). Price refers to this view as nonnaturalism, as it recognizes the existence of entities, those referred to by the domains of discourse in question, which are not recognized by science, and hence are nonnatural. This kind of view falls into the first category of the methodological map. Approaches in this category take the domains of discourse in question at face value. Their sentences appear to refer to entities of a certain kind, and since some of those sentences are true, there must be entities of that kind to which they refer. The fact that science does not recognize the existence of these entities tells us merely that science has limits; it cannot tell us about the totality of reality, since there are some features of it that are beyond its boundaries.

Price dismisses both of these views as inadequate. Eliminativism, he says "seems to underestimate the value of what would be lost" (Price 1997: 247), while nonnaturalism offers "no satisfactory account of how there could be a region of the world both out of reach of science, and yet of relevance in human life" (1997: 247). He turns his attention instead to two alternative views, which, he thinks, are more appealing to most philosophical naturalists. These views are noncognitivism and reductionism, which occupy positions 4 and 2, respectively, on the methodological map. As Price notes, noncognitivism offers the naturalist an alternative to the unattractive options of eliminativism and nonnaturalism. He writes, "If moral talk [for example,] isn't in the business of describing reality – if its linguistic *function* is quite different – then we can leave it in place, without conflict with the ontological lessons of the naturalistic view" (Price 1997: 248).

Reductionism offers the naturalist a different alternative. Unlike the noncognitivist, the reductionist takes the domain of discourse in question to be descriptive, so its sentences are capable of being true or false. Unlike the nonnaturalist, however, she does not take there to be any nonnatural properties referred to by the predicates of that domain of discourse. Instead, she argues that for each predicate, "is P," of the domain of discourse in question, there is a physical or natural property, Q, such that, if an object possesses Q, that ensures that the predicate "is P" applies to it. According to the reductionist, the property referred to by the predicate "is P" just is the property referred to by the predicate "is Q," so in this sense the problematic realm is reduced to the unproblematic physical realm. Price does not explicitly discuss the fifth strategy on the methodological map, conceptual relativism, but I shall argue below that the alternative he proposes to the four positions he does consider is a version of conceptual relativism.

Another philosopher who broadly agrees with my view of the acceptable range of positions with respect to any given domain of discourse is John Heil (2003). While discussing, and rejecting, what he calls the analytical project, Heil notes that it typically proceeds as follows. We begin with a particular domain of entities that we take to exist, for example, the items posited by basic physics. These are the Gs. He continues:

> Relative to entities in this favoured realm, entities in some other domain, the Fs, come to be contested....We can ask whether entities in the contested domain, the Fs, are reducible to entities in the favoured domain, the Gs, where reduction is understood as an analytical procedure....The question we take ourselves to be asking is whether Fs exist "over and above" the favoured entities. If reducibility is not in the cards, we must choose between outright eliminativism – there are no Fs – or realism – Fs exist in addition to, "over and above," Gs.
>
> (Heil 2003: 52)

The positions that Heil suggests are available when approaching ontological questions in this way correspond to the first three positions on the methodological map, namely, realism, reductionism, and the error theory, or eliminativism. He later briefly considers the alternative strategy of conceptual relativism. He makes no mention of noncognitivism, but I think it is clear that, with respect to some domains of discourse, it is an option that has been taken up. As I noted above, Heil thinks that this way of approaching ontological questions is flawed and, consequently, that these are not our only options. The alternative that he recommends is one that aligns closely with the view I endorse, and I shall have more to say about this below.

Finally, in his article "The Status of Content," Paul Boghossian (1990) concurs with my account of two of the available antirealist options in the methodological map. He suggests that, with respect to a given domain of discourse, one may be of the opinion that nothing possesses, or even could possess, the sorts of property apparently denoted by its characteristic predicates. In that case, there are two options available. The first is an error conception of that domain of discourse. He writes,

> An error theorist about a given fragment of discourse takes that fragment's semantical appearances at face value: predicates denote properties and (hence) declarative sentences express genuine predicative judgments, equipped with truth conditions. However, the error theorist continues, because nothing actually exemplifies the properties so denoted, all the fragment's (atomic) declarative sentences are systematically *false*.
>
> (Boghossian 1990: 159)

Boghossian goes on to suggest that an error theorist has two options available to her for how to deal with the domain of discourse in question. She can either opt for eliminativism, declaring that the systematic falsity of the sentences of the domain of discourse constitutes sufficient grounds for its elimination and replacement, or she can opt for instrumentalism about the domain of discourse, according to which, in spite of the falsity of its sentences, its continued use serves an instrumental purpose that will not easily be discharged in some other way (Boghossian 1990: 159). The error conception of a given domain of discourse plainly falls into the third category on the methodological map, whether one chooses an eliminativist or an instrumentalist treatment of it.

The second antirealist option available, according to Boghossian, is what he calls nonfactualism. He writes,

> According to this view, although F's declarative sentences appear to express genuine predicative judgments, that appearance is wholly illusory. In actual fact, a non-factualist alleges, F's predicates do not denote properties; nor, as a result, do its declarative sentences express genuine predicative judgments, equipped with truth conditions: seeing as such sentences would be making no claim about the world, so nothing about the world could render them true or false.
>
> (Boghossian 1990: 159–60)

Once again, Boghossian outlines two ways in which a nonfactualist may choose to deal with the fragment of discourse in question. If a nonfactualist holds that the predicates of F fail to refer to a property even though they aspire to do so, then she will very likely recommend that *F* be eliminated. It seems to me that this version of nonfactualism is in fact a version of the error conception, and not of nonfactualism at all. It is constitutive of nonfactualism that the predicates of *F* do *not* aspire to refer to properties, but rather, perform some other function in language. So, anyone who holds that the predicates of *F* aspire to refer to properties is, *ipso facto*, not a nonfactualist. If someone holds that the predicates of *F* aspire to refer to properties, but fail to do so, then she is an error theorist with respect to *F*.

The second option (or, as I see it, the only option) for a nonfactualist is to offer an alternative account of what the declarative sentences of *F* are designed to accomplish. If they are not intended to express statements of fact, then an alternative account of the semantic function of the sentences of *F* must be given. This view, then, falls into the fourth category on the methodological map.

I have argued that there is widespread agreement among philosophers that the range of acceptable positions with respect to a given domain of discourse is exhausted by those presented on the methodological map. Before moving on to look at these options more closely, I want to illustrate that, even in the presentation of these options, the mistake identified in Chapter 4, of confusing descriptions of reality with reality itself is frequently made. For example, in the article discussed above, Price introduces the methodological alternatives by noting that there are areas of human discourse (not of reality, note) that are under threat from the rise of modern science (1997: 247). In presenting the first two responses to this situation, eliminativism and nonnaturalism, he states that eliminativists hold that these topics are not worth saving, while nonnaturalists hold that they do not need saving, as they are beyond the realms of science, but still perfectly respectable. Now, when Price talks of these "topics," is he talking about the domains of discourse, or about the features of reality they purport to describe?

Take the eliminativist view first. The starting point of the eliminativist is the claim that there are no such properties as those apparently denoted by the predicates of a given, questionable domain of discourse. So one interpretation is that they are seeking to "eliminate" these properties in the sense that they want to deny that they exist. But there is another interpretation of the eliminativist project, consistent with Price's comments, which is that they are seeking to eliminate the domain of discourse in question. On this interpretation, they hold that the sentences of the domain of discourse contain empty predicates, and so are false. Their recommendation is that we ought to eliminate the entire domain of discourse on those grounds. This view, that it is the domain of discourse itself that is being recommended for elimination, is also suggested by Boghossian's discussion of the two options available to an error theorist for how to deal with questionable domains of discourse. There, Boghossian suggests that the error theorist can either recommend elimination of the domain of discourse, or some kind of instrumentalist treatment of it.

However, when Price discusses the nonnaturalist alternative, he seems to be talking, not of the domain of discourse, but of the feature of reality it purports to describe. The nonnaturalist is not claiming that the domain of discourse in question is beyond the reach of science. What is beyond the reach of science is the feature of reality to which the discourse refers. His criticism of the nonnaturalist is that she is unable to offer an account of how there could be a region *of the world* that is both beyond the reach of science and of relevance in human life. So Price's use of the term "topics" is ambiguous, as it sometimes refers to domains of discourse, and other times, to the features of reality to which those domains of discourse purport to refer.

Similarly, Heil's presentation of the options available conflates questions about reality with questions about descriptions of reality. He presents the range of alternative options in terms of an ontological question: Are there Fs? He then asks whether there is an analytical route from Fs to Gs. If we think there is, then we are reductionists. If we think there is not, then we must choose between realism, eliminativism and conceptual relativism. But how are we to understand the notion of an *analytical* route from Fs to Gs, if our concern is with ontology? What is it to analyze an F into a G, where what we are talking about are the entities themselves, and not merely descriptions of them? One suggestion might be that we can analyze molecules into their constituent atoms by some chemical process. For example, we can analyze water into hydrogen atoms and oxygen atoms. But this is plainly not the sense of "analytical route" that Heil has in mind. To be sure, we can make sense of analyzing *talk* of Fs into *talk* of Gs, where the relation between the two domains of discourse is that of paraphrase, translatability, reducibility, or the like. But how can we logically analyze an entity into another entity? Logical analysis and reducibility are relations that hold between descriptions of reality, not between portions of reality itself.[3] This criticism, however, does not undermine Heil's presentation of the available options. It merely indicates that confusion can enter the picture at this early stage, with the potential for contaminating entire realms of discussion on the alternative methodological strategies.

Varieties of K-realism

As we have seen, K-realism with respect to a range of K-truths is the view that we should take those truths at face value. Examples of K-realism include realism about moral discourse, such as that espoused by G. E. Moore (1903). According to Moore, the predicates of moral discourse occur in true sentences, and they are not reducible to any nonmoral predicates, so there really are nonnatural moral properties. The A-theory of time, discussed in Chapter 2, is an example of K-realism with respect to tensed truths.

We saw in Chapter 2 how the A-theory of time, in so far as its proponents argue for it on the basis of premises about tensed language, commits the representational fallacy, and I shall argue in Chapter 6 that the same is true of traditional moral realism, such as that endorsed by Moore. The A-theorist commits the representational fallacy by thinking that, just because tensed sentences are true and irreducible to tenseless sentences, it must follow that there is some feature of extralinguistic reality that only they are capable of describing. It is my contention that A-theorists who argue in this way commit the representational fallacy in virtue of the form of their argument. If that is so, then other arguments for K-realism that move from premises about the irreducibility of sentences of some domain of discourse commit the representational fallacy. According to K-realism, we are to take the K-truths at face value. They are true, they are irreducible to any other kind of truth, and they appear to refer to K-facts. Therefore, argues the K-realist, there are K-facts. This is patently to draw ontological conclusions from purely linguistic premises.

A further example of K-realism is the view known as emergentism, as discussed by Jaegwon Kim (2003). According to emergentism, the world is "a hierarchically organized system stratified into 'levels' or 'orders' of entities and their properties, from the bottom level of the most basic bits of matter to higher levels consisting of increasingly complex structures composed of material particles" (Kim 2003: 565). Furthermore, "the heart of emergentism is the claim that some important upper-level properties are 'novel' properties over and above the properties at the lower levels" (Kim 2003: 567). So, emergentism endorses a "layered" model of reality, and holds that to each level there belongs a characteristic set of properties, namely, those that "emerge" at it.

The emergent properties of a given level are those that are denoted by predicates that can truly be applied to entities that exist at that level, but not to entities that exist at any "lower" levels. For example, emergentists think, according to Kim, that when entities at the bottom level are configured into appropriate stable structures, atoms and molecules emerge. When atoms and molecules are configured into more complex systems, with the right kind of complexity, living organisms and their vital properties emerge. Further up in the hierarchy, sensations and consciousness emerge, and then thoughts and rationality. To take the level at which living organisms and their vital properties emerge, the emergentists think that descriptions of reality at that level involve predicates, such as "is a living organism," that are not truly applicable at any lower level, and furthermore those descriptions are true, so there must be properties denoted by those predicates.

I think that emergentism, so conceived, commits the representational fallacy. At each level, according to the emergentist, there are predicates that apply at that level, but not at any lower level. These predicates appear in true sentences describing reality, and the emergentist denies that those sentences are reducible to any other sentences that do not involve those predicates. So the emergentist concludes that there must be properties, features of reality, denoted by those predicates. But the inference is invalid because it is possible for those sentences to be true and irreducible to any other kind of sentence, even if there are no properties answering only to those predicates. Those sentences may have truthmakers that involve no such properties.

We saw in Chapter 3 that a view of this kind, which endorses the layered model of reality, has been criticized by John Heil, along similar lines. Heil argues that philosophers have mistakenly adopted the picture theory, including Principle Φ, that for every meaningful predicate that applies truly to an object, it does so in virtue of designating a property possessed by that object and by every object to which that predicate truly applies, or would apply. Because we have inculcated the picture theory, Heil suggests, we expect to find a property corresponding to every predicate we take to apply literally and truly to the world. Heil discusses the predicate "is in pain." Since this predicate appears in sentences we take to be literally true, we think there must be a property to which it corresponds. However, the predicate may apply to very different organisms, so there may be no single, physical property that is possessed by every organism of which it is true that it is in pain. Pain is multiply realized. It then seems to us that we face a choice between denying that our ascriptions of pain are true, because they involve an empty predicate, or positing some tailor-made, "higher-level," multiply-realizable property, to answer to that predicate, which is dependent on, but distinct from "lower-level" realizing properties.

To endorse the picture theory is to think that we can legitimately arrive at ontological conclusions regarding what sorts of property exist on the basis of purely linguistic data: the sorts of predicate we take to be literally true of the world. Heil rejects the picture theory, and with it the layered model of reality that it generates. He concedes that we may sometimes find it useful to talk of levels of description (Heil 2003: 50), but urges that we must not confuse levels of description with levels of being. I think he is right. We can agree with all the emergentist has to say about predicates, while rejecting her move from predicates to properties. That is, we can accept that there are distinct levels of description of reality, and to each level of description there belongs a characteristic set of predicates, which are not applicable at lower levels, while denying that to each of these predicates there corresponds a property. What "emerges" at each level is a new set of predicates, not a new set of properties. This view then nicely coheres with the alternative methodological strategy I have been arguing for. A pair of sentences, taken from different levels of description, may be non-synonymous, or irreducible to each other, while both being made true by the same fact. Each sentence is simply a different way of describing the same bit of extralinguistic reality. The fact that they are non-synonymous has no ontological implications whatsoever.

Varieties of K-reductionism

K-reductionism is a strategy that denies there are any peculiar properties, or features of reality, associated with K-truths, but does not wish to deny that the K-truths are true, nor that they are capable of being true. It argues for this conclusion by seeking to find some other way of saying what is said by the K-truths, where that alternative does not involve apparent ontological commitment to the dubious entities apparently referred to by the K-truths. Examples of K-reductionism include any theory that employs the method of paraphrase to support its ontological conclusions, which was discussed and rejected in Chapter 3. These theories include the old B-theory of time, nominalist strategies that appeal to the method of paraphrase to avoid ontological commitment to properties, and reductionist versions of naturalism in metaethics, about which I will have more to say in Chapter 6.

An implicit assumption made by K-reductionists is that, were they unable to find any suitable L-truths to which the K-truths can be reduced, they would be committed to the existence of K-facts. So, just like the K-realists, they think that linguistic facts have ontological implications. Their alternative strategy is to find some other language that, they think, more accurately represents reality, and from which we can draw different ontological conclusions from those of the K-realists.

At the end of the section "The Commonly Accepted Methodological Map," above, I noted that talk of reductionism is often prone to confusions between descriptions of reality and reality itself. I raised there the question of how we are to understand the notion of reduction when we are talking about ontology, rather than about descriptions of reality. This very question is raised by Kim (2003). He suggests three ways in which we can understand the notion of reducing one set of properties to another: bridge-law reduction, identity reduction and functional reduction.

The idea of bridge-law reduction derives from Ernest Nagel's (1961) model of intertheoretic reduction, whereby one theory, T, is reduced to another theory, T*, via bridge laws that correlate each predicate of T with a coextensive predicate of T*. The notion of reduction employed here is evidently one that applies to theories, or linguistic entities. Bridge laws are invoked to reduce one theory, or system of sentences, to another theory, correlating the predicates of the one theory to those of the other. Now, whether there can be any chance of success for such a strategy is one question, and Kim, at least, thinks it unlikely.[4] But I think the more important question is: What are the ontological implications, if any, of this reductionist strategy?

According to Kim, the ontological implications of bridge-law reduction are that, if it is capable of providing for each predicate of theory T a coextensive predicate of theory T*, then it will, thereby, have provided for each *property* of T a nomologically coextensive *property* of T*. That is, he takes the correlation of predicates between two theories to imply a correlation of properties between the two theories. He writes,

> To take an ontological turn and speak of properties rather than the predicates, we can say that bridge laws, in a successful Nagel reduction,

> provide for each property in the theory being reduced with a nomologically coextensive property in the base domain. This means that the classificatory scheme of the reduced theory is absorbed into that of the base theory, and we are supposed to be warranted in concluding that each property M in the reduced theory has been reduced to property N in the base domain with which it is connected by a bridge law.
>
> (Kim 2003: 568–9)

But is this "ontological turn" warranted? Only, I want to suggest, if we are warranted in assuming that for every predicate that truly applies to some object, there is a unique property which it denotes. That is, the "ontological turn" is only warranted if we accept Heil's Principle Φ. But, as Heil has argued, we should not accept Principle Φ. There are, he notes, many predicates which fail to satisfy it. The predicate "is red," for example, applies truly to many objects. But, he says, "it is not easy to think of a property that (*a*) all red things share and (*b*) in virtue of which they satisfy the predicate 'is red'" (Heil 2003: 27).

Principle Φ is, therefore, an instance of the representational fallacy. That being the case, we are not entitled to make the "ontological turn" suggested by Kim, and draw ontological conclusions from facts about the possibility or otherwise of securing successful bridge-law reductions between theories. The notion of bridge-law reductions is one which applies to theories, to systems of sentences and not to the features of reality that those theories are about. To reinforce this point still further, I think that very little sense can be made of the idea of "reducing" one property, or set of properties, to another. Suppose we have two predicates, "is *P*" and "is *Q*." It is at least coherent to think that we can reduce one of these predicates to the other. Such a scenario would presumably involve the predicates being at least coextensive. The ontological implications of such a reduction would, again presumably, be that, although we have two different predicates here, we only have one property, to which both predicates refer.

Our only choices, at the ontological level, are that the two predicates either refer to different properties, or they refer to the same property.[5] If they refer to different properties, then all our "reduction" has revealed is that the two properties are coextensive; if any object has one of them it also has the other. But it would be inappropriate to call such a discovery a "reduction." After all, there are still two different properties picked out by these predicates. To be sure, we have discovered a relation between them, but we have not "reduced" one to the other. If, on the other hand, the two predicates refer to the same property, then our reduction has shown that, while we may have thought we had two properties corresponding to our two different predicates, we really only had one, to which they each refer. In this case, it would be more appropriate to call our result a "reduction" as we would have established that there is only one property, and we were mistaken in thinking that there were two. However, it would be more appropriate still to call this result an identity. What we have discovered is that the property referred to by "is *P*" is the very same property as that referred to by "is *Q*."

The second kind of reduction discussed by Kim is identity reduction (Sklar 1967; Block and Stalnaker 1999). This view recognizes the point made in the previous paragraph, that we either have two properties referred to by two different predicates, or just one, and if there are two, then we can't really claim to have "reduced" one to the other. According to identity reduction the fact that justifies a reduction of one predicate to another is that they both refer to the very same property; it is an identity fact. The example of an identity reduction cited by Kim is that an identity, such as "(I): pain = C-fiber stimulation" is used as a bridging principle in the reductive derivation of pain theory from neurophysiology. Identity reductions, then, are reductions from one theory, or set of sentences, to another theory, and what justifies this relation between the two linguistic systems is an identity at the ontological level. The predicates of each theory refer to the very same features of extralinguistic reality. In my view, identity reductions, unlike bridge-law reductions, achieve the necessary separation of linguistic from ontological issues. Reduction is a relation that obtains between theories or predicates, that is, linguistic entities. There is no talk of "reducing" one property to another. *Talk* of pain is (supposedly) reducible to *talk* of C-fiber stimulation, but pain itself is not reducible to C-fiber stimulation; pain just *is* C-fiber stimulation.

However, the fact that, structurally speaking, identity reductions are able to avoid the problem I am concerned with here, namely, that of confusing reality with descriptions of reality, does not mean that they are successful. The main problem they face, which is noted by Kim, is that there are very few, if any, identities available to provide the required bridging principles. Pain is not identical with C-fiber stimulation, since there are many organisms capable of being in pain, which do not have a physiology that incorporates C-fiber stimulation. The predicate "is in pain," as we saw in Chapter 4, is multiply realizable. That is, it applies to many different kinds of organism, and in each kind of organism it is "realized" by a different physiological property. It is the recognition of just this point that, Heil argues, leads many philosophers to think that they must opt for one of two choices: either deny that the predicate "is in pain" denotes a property at all (eliminativism), or posit a "higher-level" property designed specifically to be the property denoted by that predicate. But these are not our only choices. To think that they are is to commit the representational fallacy. That is, it is to think that, just because we have a predicate that occurs in some true sentences, that predicate must either denote a property or be reducible to another predicate that denotes a property, or, contrary to what we thought, the sentences in question are not true at all. However, it *is* possible for a predicate to occur in some true sentences, which are irreducible to any other sentences, even though there is no particular property uniquely denoted by that predicate.

The third kind of reductionism discussed by Kim is functional reductionism. He describes functional reductionism in terms of an example: the reduction of the gene in molecular biology. The first step is to give a functional interpretation of the property of being a gene, that is, a definition of a gene in terms of its causal role. So, being a gene is being a mechanism that encodes and transmits genetic information from parent to offspring. He continues, "The second stage in the reductive process is the actual scientific work of identifying the mechanism that performs this function, and it has turned out that DNA molecules execute the specified task, at least in terrestrial organisms" (Kim 2003: 571).

Once again, Kim has managed to conflate reality with descriptions of reality in his presentation of functional reductionism. He talks of giving a functional definition of the *property* of being a gene. But this is to assume that there is a property designated by the predicate "is a gene." It seems to me, however, that functional reductionism can be presented in a plausible way while keeping talk of predicates, or concepts, and talk of properties, or features of reality, out of each other's hair. The first step involves giving a functional analysis of the *concept* of being a gene, in terms of causal role. This is an analysis of how we use the word "gene," so the first stage in a functional reduction is concerned with linguistic analysis. To adapt Kim's definition, we use the word "gene" to refer to any mechanism that encodes and transmits genetic information from parent to offspring. The second stage in a functional reduction is concerned with ontology; it involves identifying the actual mechanisms, the constituents of reality, to which the concept or word "gene" applies.

One distinct advantage of functional reductionism over both bridge law and identity reductionism, noted by Kim, is that it is consistent with multiple realization, in fact, it anticipates it. He writes,

> When scientists investigate the neural realizers of, say, pain, they would likely focus on a particular population of organisms, say humans or mammals, and try to identify pain's realizer, or realizers, for this population. In this sense, functional reductions are bound to be open-ended projects whose results come in only in a piecemeal fashion. No scientist is likely to attempt to identify pain's realizers for all actual and nomologically possible organisms or pain-capable systems; that is an impossible task.
>
> (Kim 2003: 572)

I agree that this is a definite advantage of this kind of reduction over the two previously discussed. However, Kim continues to talk in terms of *properties* being functionally reducible to, or multiply realized by, other properties, and I think this must be wrong. It seems to me to be simply a category error. How can a property be realized by another property? If the two properties are different, then in what does this realization relation consist? Kim insists that it is more than mere correlation. That is, pain is not merely instantiated in mammals whenever C-fiber stimulation occurs. Rather, pain occurs on a given occasion *only because* C-fibers are stimulated. He notes that token physicalists accept an even stronger relation between the two. While maintaining that pain and C-fiber stimulation are different kinds, any instance of pain is identical with an instance of C-fiber stimulation. Once again, it seems to me that we have two choices here. Either pain and C-fiber stimulation are two different properties, or they are the same property. If they are two different properties, then it is difficult to see how the relation between them can be anything more than mere correlation. If they are the same property, then functional reductionism appears to have reverted to a form of identity reductionism, but that, as we have seen, is unable to account for the phenomenon of multiple realizability.

However, I think that functional reductionism can be saved if we reject talk of properties being realized by other properties, and talk instead of predicates being realized by properties. The predicate "is in pain" is realized in pain-capable organisms by many different physical properties. There is no higher-level property designated by the predicate "is in pain." Instead, there is simply the predicate, which can be applied truly to many different kinds of organisms. Whether or not it does apply to a given organism is determined by whether or not that organism possesses a particular physical property. But it need not be the case that the very same physical property must be possessed by every entity to which the predicate "is in pain" truly applies. We should give up the idea of levels of reality, and the associated idea of certain properties "emerging" at each level. Instead, there are levels of description, with certain *predicates* "emerging," or only becoming applicable, at each level.

Towards the end of his article, Kim briefly considers a suggestion along these lines. He says, "Another alternative is to abandon multiply realizable properties as properties, recognizing only functional concepts or predicates. This would amount to a form of irrealism, and when applied to mental properties...this would be a form of mental eliminativism" (Kim 2003: 581). Kim's reason for thinking that this suggestion would amount to a form of irrealism is presumably that he thinks realism is committed to something like Principle Φ.[6] That is, he thinks that any realist view must be committed to the existence of a property designated by every meaningful predicate that truly applies to some objects. But as we have seen, Principle Φ is false. Furthermore, it is not entailed by realism. As I argued in Chapter 4, it is possible for some sentences to be true, and to have physical truthmakers, even though those sentences cannot be translated by, or reduced to any other (physical) sentence with the same truthmaker. Realism, as we have seen, is the thesis that there is just one way the world is, and that the way it is, is independent of us and our capacity to describe it. This thesis is quite consistent with there being a predicate that truly applies to an object, even though there is no peculiar property that only that predicate designates. It is quite possible for an ascription of pain to be made true by an organism's being in a certain physical state, and another ascription of pain to be made true by a different organism's being in a different physical state, while there is no further property of being in pain, over and above any physical state.

Reductionism, it seems, possibly more than any other strategy on the methodological map, is prone to making the mistake of confusing descriptions of reality with reality itself. It is too easy for the reductionist to talk of "reducing" one property, or set of properties, to another. But, I have suggested, little sense can be made of this idea. Either the reducing property and the property to be reduced are different properties, or they are the same property. If they are different properties, then we are owed an account of that in which the reduction relation that obtains between them consists. And it is difficult to see that it can be anything more than mere correlation, which is not strong enough for the reductionist's purposes. When discussing supervenience, which is thought to be a weaker relation than reduction, Kim notes that,

> Often it is thought, and claimed, that a thing has a supervenient property *because*, or *in virtue of the fact that*, it has the corresponding base property.…Clearly, property covariation by itself does not warrant the use of "because," "in virtue of," etc., in describing the relationship any more than it warrants the attribution of dependence.
> (Kim 1990: 16)

If property covariation is insufficient to establish the required connection between supervenient and base properties, then it will certainly be insufficient to establish the required connection between properties standing in the stronger reduction relation to each other.

On the other hand, if the reducing property and the property to be reduced are the same property, then the "reduction" is actually an identity at the ontological level. This alternative succeeds in avoiding the conflation between reality and descriptions of reality, but is of little use, as there are in fact very few, if any, identities available to play the required role. The fact that many so-called "higher-level" properties are multiply realizable means that they cannot be accounted for in terms of an identity. Even presentations of functional reductionism, such as Kim's, are susceptible to the conflation of descriptions with reality. However, I have suggested that functional reductionism can be set out so as to avoid this mistake.

Two ideas are implicit in the K-reductionist's strategy, neither of which should be accepted. The first is Principle Φ. The K-reductionist must think that if a predicate truly applies to some object, it does so in virtue of designating a property possessed by that object, and by every object to which that predicate truly applies. For some problematic domain of discourse, she accepts that its predicates designate properties, the existence of which she denies. In order to maintain her denial of the existence of those properties, as well as the truth of some of the sentences of that domain of discourse, she seeks to find a way of saying what those sentences say without employing those predicates. If, instead, she relinquished Principle Φ, she could continue to deny the existence of the properties in question, without having to find acceptable paraphrases of the true sentences employing those predicates. The truthmakers for those sentences need not involve the properties whose existence she denies.

The second idea that is implicit in the K-reductionist's strategy is SLT. The K-reductionist must think that if a sentence from some problematic domain of discourse is true and is a part of the one true, privileged description, then it must correspond to a fact in the world distinct from any other fact, since SLT involves the idea that there is a one-to-one correspondence between sentences in the one true description and facts in the world. She thus seeks to show that, although it is true, it is not part of the one true, privileged description of reality. There is no fact that only it describes. Instead it is reducible to some other sentence contained in the one true description that corresponds to a more palatable fact.

If the K-reductionist relinquished SLT, she would be relieved of the burden of having to find acceptable reductionist paraphrases of problematic true sentences. She could accept that such sentences were true without being committed to the view that they correspond to facts in the world that no other sentence corresponds to. She could hold that the ratio of true sentences to truthmakers is many-to-one, so a problematic sentence may have an unproblematic truthmaker.

The way in which proponents of functional reductionism may succeed in avoiding the representational fallacy is by arguing that certain predicates or concepts can be given a functional analysis in terms of their causal role, and then turning to reality to discover which actual entities or properties play that causal role. This approach does not draw ontological conclusions from facts about language. Instead, it offers a linguistic or conceptual analysis of the problematic term in question, to suggest a direction in which the relevant ontological investigation might proceed.

Supervenience theories

Supervenience theories constitute an approach to problematic domains of discourse that does not seem to fit neatly into any of the positions I have classified on the traditional methodological map, so I shall examine them in isolation. Kim presents the core idea of the notion of supervenience as follows:

> Imagine a sculptor working on a statue....When the physical work is finished, his work is finished; there is no *further* work of "attaching" desired aesthetic properties, say elegance and expressiveness, to the finished piece of stone. The aesthetic character of a sculpture is wholly

> fixed once its physical properties are fixed; that is *aesthetic properties supervene on physical properties.*
>
> (Kim 2003: 558)

The notion of supervenience has been adopted in a large number, and wide variety, of metaphysical debates. So, for example, it is said that the mental supervenes on the physical, causal facts supervene on noncausal facts, the moral supervenes on the nonmoral, and so on. One reason why supervenience theories have been so popular is that they are seen as a weaker version of reductionism and so are less susceptible to the criticisms typically aimed at reductionism. For example, Kim notes that "many philosophers saw in it [supervenience] the promise of a new type of dependency relation that seemed just right, neither too strong nor too weak, allowing us to navigate between reductionism and outright dualism" (1990: 16). Similarly, James Klagge notes that "supervenience has been heralded as a relationship between two realms that is weaker than reductionism but stronger than dualism" (1988: 461).

The idea is that the facts referred to by some problematic domain of discourse are not reducible to some other, more palatable range of facts, but neither are they wholly independent of the more palatable facts. So if a reduction from, say, the mental to the physical, is unavailable, we can instead opt for the weaker relation of supervenience and say that the mental supervenes on the physical. Proponents of supervenience theories see themselves as able to retain a naturalistically acceptable view of the world, such that once all the natural, or physical facts are fixed, everything else is thereby fixed, including facts about the mental, the aesthetic, the moral, and so on.

The reason why supervenience theories do not fit naturally into any of the positions on the methodological map is that they attempt to steer a middle path between realism and reductionism. But I want to argue that no such path is available. To simplify my discussion I shall use Kim's example of aesthetic properties, but what I have to say applies equally to supervenience theories about any other issue. In the above quote, Kim states that, "aesthetic properties supervene on physical properties" (2003: 558). Once the physical properties are fixed, everything else is thereby fixed, including the aesthetic properties. Another way of putting it is to say that if two worlds are identical with respect to their physical properties, then they are identical with respect to their aesthetic properties. Specified in this way, a supervenience theory accepts the existence of aesthetic properties in addition to physical properties. As such, it is a version of K-realism, recognizing that the predicates of aesthetic discourse refer to distinctively aesthetic properties, over and above any physical, or non-aesthetic properties. This belies its claim to being a naturalistically acceptable kind of theory, recognizing only naturalistically acceptable properties.

If the idea behind supervenience is that once you have fixed the physical facts, you have thereby fixed the aesthetic facts, but the aesthetic facts exist over and above the physical facts, then supervenience at best recognizes some kind of strong connection between aesthetic and physical facts, but at the same time holds that those facts are not identical, so it is not a reductionist view. I noted above that supervenience theories attempt to steer a middle path between realist and reductionist views, but no such middle path is available. This is because there is no middle ground between asserting and denying the existence of aesthetic properties.

It may, however, be possible to retain the spirit of supervenience-based accounts, while denying that there are such aesthetic facts and properties. Suppose the idea behind supervenience is, instead, this: fix the physical facts and you fix everything else, including *truths* about aesthetics. If that were the underlying thought, then a proponent of supervenience need not recognize the existence of aesthetic facts over and above physical facts. All she need recognize is the possibility of aesthetic *truths* over and above physical facts, such that the physical facts are responsible for making the aesthetic truths true. A supervenience-based account understood in this way would sit well with the strategy that I endorse, and about which I will have more to say in this chapter. What the overlooked strategy, in general, recognizes is that there are domains of discourse which include truths that are not reducible to truths of any other kind. The existence of those truths, however, does not entail the existence of a peculiar kind of fact that can only be referred to by the sentences of that domain of discourse. Instead it is possible that they are made true by other, perhaps physical, facts. According to this modified notion of supervenience, if two worlds are identical with respect to their physical facts, then they are identical with respect to their aesthetic truths. So the physical facts fix the aesthetic truths.

A similar, but not identical distinction is noted by Klagge. He distinguishes ontological supervenience from ascriptive supervenience. Ontological supervenience is "the view, roughly, that, metaphysically speaking, things cannot differ in respect of the possession of properties in one (supervening) class unless they differ in respect of the possession of properties in the other (base) class" (Klagge 1988: 462). Ascriptive supervenience is "the view, roughly, that, logically speaking, a person's judgments of a certain (supervening) kind about things cannot differ unless judgments of the other kind about the things differ" (Klagge 1988: 462). Ascriptive supervenience, as stated, does not quite capture the notion that I have in mind. It is a principle that only constrains the judgments of a given person. In the case of the supervenience of moral judgments on nonmoral judgments, for example, ascriptive supervenience would permit two individuals to make conflicting moral judgments about the very same nonmoral situation. All that is required is that any individual's judgments of the supervening kind (moral judgments) are constrained by their judgments of the base kind (descriptive judgments).

The view that I have in mind, by contrast, is not person-relative in the way that Klagge's is. On my view, there are truths of the supervening kind (be they moral, aesthetic, mental, or whatever), and there are facts describable in the language of basic physics. Those facts serve as truthmakers for any truths of the supervening kind, even though the supervening truths are not reducible to the physical truths.

In general, I think that supervenience theorists typically make the mistake so often made by reductionist theories, of confusing reality with descriptions of it. Their naturalistic proclivities make them sympathetic to the ideal of reductionism, but since it generally fails, they seek to retain its spirit while not having to effect real reductions. They thus talk in terms of natural, or physical facts fixing all the other facts. But are they talking here of facts (bits of reality) or truths? If they are talking of facts, then what they have offered us is a sophisticated version of realism, according to which the predicates of some domain of discourse really do refer to peculiar properties, but there is some deep connection between those properties and the physical properties on which they supervene.[7] But this is in conflict with their naturalistic proclivities that motivated the view in the first place. What I think they ought to do is to talk instead of the physical facts fixing all the other *truths*. Then the sentences of, for example, aesthetic discourse, can be retained as fact-stating, descriptive and (for some of them) true, but there is no need to recognize the existence of peculiarly aesthetic (and nonnatural) properties or facts. Instead, the aesthetic truths have physical truthmakers, even though no reduction from aesthetic truths to physical truths may be available.

Error theories of K-discourse

An error theory of K-discourse, like K-realism, takes the sentences of K-discourse at face value. Ordinarily we take those sentences to be true, and the K-realist accepts this, thus concluding that there must be K-properties designated by the K-predicates. The error theorist, by contrast, rejects our common sense assessment of those sentences as true. She antecedently denies that there are any K-properties, so any sentence employing a K-predicate that ought to designate a K-property must be false. Two examples of this strategy are Mackie's (1977) error theory of moral discourse and Churchland's (1981) eliminativism about folk psychological discourse. According to Mackie, there are no moral properties, such as being right or being good, so moral discourse, which employs moral predicates, is systematically in error. The sentences of moral discourse appear to designate moral properties, but since there are none, those (atomic) sentences are all false. According to Churchland, there are no folk psychological properties or states, such as being in pain or beliefs and desires, so folk psychological discourse, which employs folk psychological predicates is systematically in error. The sentences of folk psychological discourse appear to designate folk psychological properties, but since there are none, those (atomic) sentences are all false.

As noted by Boghossian in connection with error theories, there are two options available to a proponent of this kind of view as to how to deal with the domain of discourse in question (1990). She can either opt for eliminativism, arguing that the systematic falsity of the sentences of the domain of discourse constitutes grounds for eliminating that discourse and replacing it with another that conveys the information it is intended to convey, but whose predicates succeed in designating actual properties, and thus, whose sentences are capable of being true. Or, she can recommend the continued use of the domain of discourse because it serves an instrumental purpose, and it is unlikely that any other domain of discourse could serve that purpose as well as it does. However, these options reflect a practical, or pragmatic issue that need only be taken up if it has been shown that an error theory about a particular domain of discourse is the right strategy.

As I noted above, the error theorist of K-discourse agrees with the K-realist that the sentences of K-discourse should be taken at face value. According to both strategies, the sentences of K-discourse employ K-predicates which appear to designate K-properties. Furthermore, they both appear to accept the following conditional: if a sentence employing a K-predicate is true, then that K-predicate designates a K-property. The K-realist accepts that those sentences are true and concludes, by *modus ponens*, that there must therefore be K-properties. The error theorist of K-discourse denies that there are any K-properties, and concludes, by *modus tollens*, that the (atomic) sentences of K-discourse are systematically false. However, the commission of the representational fallacy occurs at the first stage, on which both strategies agree. It is committed by the acceptance of the conditional.[8] The conditional is in fact false because a sentence employing a K-predicate can be true even if there are no K-properties. The sentence's truthmaker need involve no K-properties.

Varieties of noncognitivism about K-discourse

The fourth strategy on the methodological map is noncognitivism about K-discourse. Like the error theory, this kind of approach denies that the sentences of K-discourse are true. However, it does not thereby conclude that they are false. Instead, it denies that they are even capable of truth or falsity. Even though the sentences of K-discourse appear to be ordinary, declarative, fact-stating sentences, such as are normally either true or false, the noncognitivist argues that this is merely an appearance. Thus, according to the noncognitivist, there are no true sentences of K-discourse, so the fact that they employ K-predicates need not be taken to imply that there are any K-properties.

The noncognitivist goes on to offer an alternative account of the function of K-discourse in our language. An example is noncognitivism about moral discourse. According to this view, while the sentences of moral discourse, such as "some acts of euthanasia are morally acceptable," appear to be declarative, fact-stating sentences, they are really expressions of approval or disapproval. This sentence is an expression of approval of some acts of euthanasia, that might otherwise be expressed by the linguistic construction "Hooray for some acts of euthanasia!" Now, expressions of approval and disapproval, such as this latter construction, are not typically thought to be capable of truth or falsity, so they do not require truthmakers, or facts to which they correspond. Thus, the noncognitivist is relieved of the responsibility of explaining what it is about the world that makes them true or false. The fact that the sentence "some acts of euthanasia are morally acceptable" contains a predicate that appears to designate a property, that of being morally acceptable, has no ontological significance, on this account.

Like K-reductionism and the error theory of K-discourse, noncognitivism is seen as a means of avoiding commitment to the properties and facts apparently referred to by the sentences of K-discourse. That they feel the need to find an alternative such as this is an indication that at least some noncognitivists endorse some kind of language-to-reality move. At the end of the previous section I suggested that it's reasonable to see both K-realists and error theorists of K-discourse endorsing the following conditional: if a sentence employing a K-predicate is true, then that K-predicate designates a K-property. Error theorists deny that there are any K-properties, and employ *modus tollens* to infer that the sentences of K-discourse are false. Noncognitivists essentially make the same move. They endorse the conditional and deny that there are any K-properties, so by *modus tollens* they deny that the sentences in question are true. However, rather than concluding that they are false, they deny that they are even capable of truth or falsity in the first place.

However, for my purposes, these details are irrelevant. What is relevant is that noncognitivists can be seen as endorsing the conditional that licenses the language-to-reality move. If they recognized that the conditional is false, they would no longer have to deny that the sentences of K-discourse are ordinary, declarative, fact-stating sentences, so they would not have to find an alternative interpretation of those sentences. Of course, as with the other positions on the methodological map discussed so far, there may well be *other* reasons for opting for noncognitivism. But if the noncognitivist's reason for taking up this position is that she endorses the conditional while wanting to reject K-realism, then she commits the representational fallacy, and in so doing, misses a viable alternative position on the methodological map.

Conceptual relativism

Conceptual relativism is the view that we are entitled to be realists about any given domain of discourse, but only in a limited, or relativized way. The K-truths refer to K-facts, so we are entitled to say that there are K-facts, but not to say that there are K-facts *simpliciter*. K-facts exist only relative to the domain of K-discourse, or the linguistic framework or conceptual scheme that involves K-truths. The way conceptual relativism arrives at this conclusion is by endorsing the view, suggested and endorsed by Carnap, that there is no absolute, theory-independent, ontological viewpoint available to metaphysics (Carnap 1950). Ontological questions about the entities mentioned in a particular theory or linguistic framework can properly be raised from within that framework (as "internal" questions), but not from a stance outside it (as "external" questions), since, ontologically speaking, there is no such stance. Conceptual relativism has been advanced by, among others, Hilary Putnam (1981).

Since there is no framework-independent stance available to metaphysics, according to Carnap's view, there is no sense to the question: What exists *simpliciter*? We can only ask ontological questions from within a given linguistic framework and answer those questions relative to that linguistic framework. So, are there moral properties? From within the moral framework, *of course* there are. From outside the moral framework, the question makes no sense. This kind of antirealism commits the representational fallacy in perhaps the most pernicious way. Its starting point, as in other strategies that commit the representational fallacy, is the different kinds of language that we employ, and the sentences within those linguistic frameworks that we take to be true. We can ask ontological questions from within those frameworks, and the frameworks themselves will deliver up the answers. So, in a sense, we can't claim to be asserting anything about extralinguistic reality when we assert that there are numbers, or moral properties, or whatever. All we are asserting is that *according to a linguistic framework* there are numbers, or moral properties, or whatever. It is beyond our reach to find out; indeed, it makes no sense even to ask, whether there really are numbers, or moral properties, or whatever. We are, in a sense, imprisoned within our various linguistic frameworks, unable to access the world itself.

Conceptual relativism thus commits the representational fallacy in a very similar way to the varieties of K-realism, which take the sentences of K-discourse at face value, and derive ontological conclusions from them. K-sentences refer to K-facts, and since some of them are true, there must be K-facts. Conceptual relativism makes the same move, but limits its ontological conclusions. According to it, K-facts only exist relative to the linguistic framework of K-sentences. The result is that conceptual relativism makes ontology entirely dependent on language. Language has evolved to include various different domains of discourse, and what there is, is entirely dependent on what those domains of discourse say there is. If language had evolved differently, what there is would have been different too.

Furthermore, conceptual relativism is unable to allow the existence of entities not recognized by our conceptual scheme. The common sense position is surely to say that such entities exist, and it is our conceptual scheme that is limited. Conceptual relativism says instead that it is the world that is limited, as only what is recognized by our conceptual scheme exists. As Ernest Sosa puts it: "is there not much that is very small, or far away, or long ago, or yet to come, which surpasses our present acuity and acumen? How can we allow the existence of such sorts at present unrecognized by our conceptual scheme?" (1993: 624–5).

I want briefly to discuss a view suggested by Price in the article discussed above and to argue that it is a version of conceptual relativism. Price calls his view functional pluralism, and suggests that it bears some similarity to noncognitivism (1997: 248). According to functional pluralism, the sentences of "problematic" domains of discourse, such as those of morality, modality and meaning, are descriptive, or fact-stating, as the realist takes them to be. However, Price says, "these descriptive utterances are functionally distinct from scientific descriptions of the natural world: they do a different job in language" (1997: 252). The similarity between this view and noncognitivism resides in the fact that both views recognize the possibility that utterances can perform different functions in language. However, according to the noncognitivist, utterances are either descriptive, or they perform some entirely different function. Description is merely one of the possible functions of utterances. According to Price, on the other hand, there is a plurality of ways in which an utterance can be descriptive.

How are we to understand this idea of functional pluralism with respect to description? One answer to this question is suggested by a remark of Price's immediately following the sentence quoted above. He says, "They [utterances from 'problematic' domains of discourse] are descriptive, but their job is not to describe what science describes" (Price 1997: 252). This suggests that *what is described* by these utterances is different from what is described by scientific utterances. In other words, the extralinguistic reality described is different in each case. But this would render Price's view a version of K-realism, or nonnaturalism, and he is adamant that his view is both different from nonnaturalism and naturalistically acceptable. So I shall give him the benefit of the doubt and set this possibility aside.

However, the way in which he distinguishes functional pluralism from nonnaturalism is telling. He argues that nonnaturalism, with respect to moral discourse, involves the idea of a single world containing both moral and natural entities, but functional pluralism rejects this idea. He quickly qualifies this with the claim that "I don't mean that it replaces this single world with a bare multiplicity of worlds, which would be equally unappealing" (Price 1997: 252). The multiplicity he does recognize is one of linguistic function. Price's view draws heavily on Carnap's view, described above, which he calls the Carnap thesis. By endorsing the Carnap thesis, and employing it to develop his functional pluralism, Price is effectively developing a version of conceptual relativism, whereby ontological questions and answers are only legitimate from within some conceptual framework.

Price's functional pluralism is the idea that there are many domains of discourse, which may, of course, overlap, and that ontological questions may only legitimately arise from within some domain of discourse. As he says,

> [T]he Carnap thesis tells us that [the choice between reductionism and nonnaturalism] relies on an illegitimate conception of belief: roughly, the idea that beliefs are the mind's attempt to stand in correspondence with a pre-existing World – "pre-existing" in the sense that it is thought of from an external stance which supposedly we occupy as semanticists and ontologists, asking to what our beliefs refer, and what makes them true. But there is no such stance, according to the Carnap thesis....As users of moral language, holders of moral beliefs, we can describe their semantics, and may discover that when our beliefs are expressed in canonical form, they refer to moral properties. We thus find ourselves committed to the existence of moral properties, in the only sense of ontological commitment recognised by the Carnap view.
>
> (Price 1997: 257)

Price's functional pluralism, being reliant as it is on the Carnap thesis, is thus a form of conceptual relativism. Furthermore, we can see from this quote that Price endorses the language-to-reality move that I have suggested is characteristic of conceptual relativism. He asks whether our language, expressed in canonical form, commits us to the existence of moral properties, and finds that it does. So, just like the K-realist, he endorses the conditional: if a sentence employing a K-predicate is true, then that K-predicate designates a K-property. However, since the Carnap thesis is already in place before he makes this move, the resulting position is not K-realism, but conceptual relativism.

The overlooked strategy

I have suggested that K-realists, error theorists and non-cognitivists about K-discourse can all be understood as accepting the following conditional: if a sentence employing a K-predicate is true, then that K-predicate designates a K-property. The alternative strategy that I want to suggest rejects the conditional, but sees the reductionist strategy as unnecessary. A true sentence that employs a K-predicate can have a truthmaker that does not include K-properties, even if no reduction from K-sentences to any other kind of sentence is achievable.

To illustrate my strategy it will be useful to return to Heil's discussion and rejection of the notion of levels of reality (2003: 40–50). Many philosophers begin with the way we represent the world linguistically and ask how this is related to what science tells us the world is like. Some things we say, for example, sentences in the language of basic physics, appear to line up directly with what science tells us exists. Other things we say are reducible, or analyzable, into naturalistically respectable language. But many things we say are not. Reductionist strategies have been overwhelmingly unsuccessful. What are we to do, then, when reductionism fails? We can opt for one of the antirealist options, like eliminativism or noncognitivism. But if these seem unattractive or unworkable, Heil suggests, we are tempted by the alternative that our words do indeed line up with features of the world: higher-level features (Heil 2003: 8). Kim agrees that it is a consideration of these options that has made a hierarchical view of reality seem attractive (2003: 567). He notes that much of the debate concerning the status of "higher-level" properties has centered on the reductionist versus emergentist (or antireductionist) controversy. He further notes that the widespread failure of reductionist strategies has granted antireductionism the status of reigning orthodoxy. He describes this view as follows:

> This position is often called non-reductive materialism (or physicalism). It is materialist in that it accepts ontological materialism (the view that all that exists is material) and supervenience (the claim that physical facts determine all the facts), and yet in denying the reducibility of mental and other special-science properties to physical properties, it is anti-reductionist, embracing a dualism of mental and physical properties.
>
> (Kim 2003: 567–8)

I have argued in this chapter that the range of options here discussed is often seen as exhaustive, due to a tacit commitment to the ontological significance of language. Heil also thinks that this range of options is seen as exhaustive due to an underlying acceptance of the picture theory. If we reject the picture theory, and with it the representational fallacy, we can abandon the notion of levels of reality that seems to fall so naturally out of it. In its place we can put the notion of levels of description. There are many ways in which we can truly describe the world, and many of those ways are not reducible to any other ways of describing the world, but just because this relation obtains between our descriptions, it does not follow that there must be a unique feature of the world that corresponds to every true description of it.

The alternative is to see that there can be some portion of reality that can be described in many different ways. We can even, if we are so inclined, "order" these descriptions into some kind of hierarchical model. That portion of reality can be described as, for example, a collection of atoms, a collection of molecules, a living organism, a sentient being, a conscious being, an intelligent being, a rational being, a moral being, and so on. Each of these descriptions, let us suppose, applies truly to some one portion of reality, just in virtue of the way that portion of reality is. But unless we endorse the picture theory, or the representational fallacy, we need not be committed to the view that there is a distinct property corresponding to each predicate that truly applies to that object. All we need be committed to is the view that there are many ways in which we can truly describe that object, or portion of reality.

The strategy I am suggesting grows out of the conclusions I established in Chapters 2 and 3, that it is possible for two or more sentences to have the same truthmaker while not having the same meaning. It may be that one of those sentences involves a K-predicate, while the other does not. This, in itself, establishes the falsity of the picture theory. If it is possible for two sentences to have the same truthmaker, while only one of them involves a K-predicate, it is not necessary for there to be a K-property designated by that K-predicate in order for the sentence involving the K-predicate to be true. If it was, then it would also be the case that the K-property was part of the truthmaker for the sentence that has no K-predicate since, *ex hypothesi*, both sentences have the same truthmaker. It is simply the case that there are two sentences that truly describe the same portion of reality, where those sentences are couched in whatever language they happen to be couched in, and that language itself has no ontological implications for the nature of that portion of reality.

The problem with the options on the methodological map is that none of them is entirely appealing. K-realism commits us to a proliferation of facts and properties, many of which are not countenanced by science. K-reductionism depends on there being a way of "reducing" or translating talk of one kind of entity into talk of another kind of entity, but there almost never is. The error theory claims that sentences we intuitively accept as true are in fact false; noncognitivism claims that they are not even candidates for truth or falsity in the first place. Conceptual relativism makes what there is depend entirely on what we say there is. The alternative strategy has none of these drawbacks. We can accept, with the K-realist, that the sentences of a given domain of discourse are descriptive, or fact-stating, and true, as common sense would have it, but without being committed to K-realism's proliferation of nonnatural facts and properties. We can find naturalistically palatable truthmakers for these true sentences, without having to follow the lead of the K-reductionist and find naturalistically palatable sentences to which we can "reduce" them. Consequently, none of the antirealist options need even be considered. Our view can be a realist one without the attendant ontological drawbacks of K-realism.

It might be objected that I have said very little about the nature of the truthmakers for the sentences of any given domain of discourse and, consequently, that I have given little in the way of a positive account here that contrasts with the alternatives I am rejecting. I want to both acknowledge this objection and say something in defense of my strategy with respect to it. It is true that I have said very little about the nature of the truthmakers for the sentences of any given domain of discourse, but then, I have not been talking about any particular domain of discourse, except by way of illustration. What I have been talking about is a methodological strategy that can be applied to many different domains of discourse, and in each case, supplied with appropriate content.

Indeed, it is likely that there will be more than one way to supply this strategy with content for any given domain of discourse. This will arise where different accounts of the truthmakers for the sentences of a given domain of discourse are offered. Consequently, what I am offering here is a schema, a strategy, that can be followed and supplied with content by philosophers and scientists working in any of the areas to which this strategy can be applied. It is, therefore, to be expected that I have little to say about the actual ways in which this schema can be filled out. I will, however, be making some suggestions for ways in which it might be applied with respect to moral discourse in Chapter 6, and with respect to some other domains of discourse in Chapter 7. Even in respect of these domains of discourse, however, I expect there will be more than one way in which the strategy can be supplied with content.

6 The overlooked strategy in practice
Moral discourse

In the last chapter, I suggested a methodological strategy for dealing with domains of discourse, and their relationship with reality, that stands opposed to what I suggested were the five main options currently seen as constituting the methodological map. The strategy that I suggested differs from the others in that it does not see facts about the sentences of any given domain of discourse as having any implications for the nature of reality. In this chapter, I will consider how this strategy might be adopted and applied to an entirely different domain of discourse, that of moral discourse, and what the results of that application might look like.

Moral discourse

Moral discourse is typically thought of as one of the most "problematic" domains of discourse and, consequently, has spawned metaphysical theories occupying each of the positions on the methodological map discussed in Chapter 5. It is a domain of discourse involving moral predicates, such as "right," "wrong," "good" and "bad." Sentences of moral discourse that involve moral predicates appear to be either true or false. The options for dealing with moral discourse are, broadly speaking, realism, reductionism, an error theory, noncognitivism, and conceptual relativism.

When discussing the methodological map in Chapter 5, I argued that the alternative strategy that I favor is consistent with the ontological thesis of realism. That is, there is only one way the world is, and the way it is is independent of us and our means of accessing or describing it. However, I denied that it implies or requires the existence of peculiarly K-facts or, in this case, moral facts. The general strategy that I favor is, thus, realism, but without the ontological excesses that realism has traditionally been associated with. That being the case, I want to focus on moral realism and show how the overlooked strategy differs from and improves upon it as it has traditionally been conceived. I will also discuss the other positions on the methodological map in what follows, but mainly for the purposes of comparison.

Moral realism: its motivation and two problems

Moral realism is a theory about the status of moral discourse that has both semantic and ontological components. Its ontological component is that there are distinctively moral facts and moral properties. Its semantic component consists in cognitivism about moral judgments. Cognitivism is the doctrine that moral judgments are capable of truth and falsity. According to moral realism, moral judgments are capable of truth and falsity, and some of them are true.

The principal source of motivation for moral realism is the idea that there are correct answers to moral questions and that when we argue with each other about a particular moral question, we are engaged in a genuine disagreement. If there are correct answers to moral questions, it seems reasonable to think that this is because they correspond to the way things are, independently of what anyone happens to think. This, in turn, suggests that there *is* a way things are morally, and not just a multitude of moral opinions, and that we can be genuinely either correct or mistaken in our moral beliefs. Thus, the domain of moral discourse is treated by the moral realist in a way similar to ordinary, fact-stating discourse. If I ask, "What are the atomic components of water?" there is a correct answer to this question. I can discover that the atomic components of water are hydrogen and oxygen. The sentence "The atomic components of water are hydrogen and oxygen" is a true sentence that corresponds to the facts, independently of what anybody happens to think. Similarly, according to moral realists, if I ask, "Is euthanasia ever morally permissible?" there is a correct answer to this question, and I can discover what it is. There is a fact of the matter about the moral permissibility of euthanasia that corresponds to the way things are independently of what anybody happens to think.

There is an obvious attraction in thinking that moral discourse is objective in this way. If moral disagreements express mere differences of opinion, then there can be no hope of resolving them. Neither could there be any grounds for attributing praise or blame. I could not be praised for rescuing a drowning child, just as I cannot be praised for liking strawberry ice cream. However, one of the most serious objections to moral realism is that it severs the link between moral judgments and our motivations to act in accordance with them (Smith 1994). For while discovering facts about the world can cause me to change my beliefs, it cannot cause me to change my desires, but it must do so if discovering moral facts is to play a role in motivating me to act (Smith 1991). If I believe that it is right to rescue drowning children, and I find myself nearby a drowning child, I will be motivated to rescue that child. Having the moral belief just is my motivation to act in accordance with it. But simply having a certain belief is not normally sufficient for having a motivation to act. I can discover any number of facts about the world, but by themselves they will not cause me to act in one way rather than another. It is only in conjunction with a desire that a belief can provide me with a motivation to act one way rather than another. Thus, if moral judgments correspond to moral facts, we are left without an explanation as to how they motivate us to act in accordance with them.

Another problem for moral realism, indeed a central problem in meta-ethics quite generally, is to present an account of the relation between "is" and "ought." Hume (1738) is credited with establishing that there is a logical gap between statements about what is the case and statements about what one ought to do. Essentially, what this amounts to is that no moral conclusion can be derived from nonmoral premises; no "ought" from "is." G. E. Moore relied on this logical gap in his "Open Question Argument" that moral propositions cannot be reduced to natural, or nonmoral, propositions. To think otherwise, he argued, is to commit the "naturalistic fallacy" (Moore 1903).

Moore believed that ethics is autonomous, that truths of morality cannot be reduced to truths of any other, nonmoral kind. He argued that no moral predicate, such as "good" or "right," is identical with, or reducible to, any nonmoral predicate, for instance, "pleasant" or "desirable." Suppose we take the predicate "good" to denote the same property as that denoted by "pleasant." It would follow from this identification, Moore argued, that finding out that something is pleasant would be sufficient to establish that it is good. But it is not. Even if something is pleasant, it remains an open question whether or not it is good. Thus, according to Moore, no moral property is identical with any nonmoral property; moral properties are nonnatural, *sui generis* properties. Moore's open question argument has certainly been challenged (Pigden 1991), but any moral realist must address the charge that her position commits her to a metaphysically unattractive realm of real, nonnatural, moral properties.

An alternative response to the is/ought distinction is to argue as follows. If moral sentences cannot be reduced to nonmoral sentences, and the truth of some moral sentences requires there to be a range of distinctively moral properties, then it simply follows that no moral sentences are true. This response can be developed in two different ways. First, one could take the line of Ayer (1946), Stevenson (1944), and Hare (1952) and argue that moral discourse does not play the same kind of role in our language as ordinary, fact-stating discourse and so should not be assessed in the same kind of way. Moral sentences do not describe reality, but rather, they express the utterer's approval or disapproval of certain actions or states of affairs, or, alternatively, they prescribe certain actions. To say of some state of affairs that it is good, or of some action that it is right, is not to describe it, and thus attribute the property of goodness or rightness to it. Instead, it is to express one's approval of it, or one's desire that it be brought about. Thus, the entire thrust of Moore's Open Question Argument is avoided by claiming that moral discourse should not be taken to be describing reality, so it is not making any claims about what sorts of facts there are. Instead, moral discourse plays a different kind of role in our language. It expresses approval and disapproval; it is prescriptive rather than descriptive.

The second kind of response along these lines argues that moral discourse should be interpreted as purporting to describe reality, but since reality is not as it describes, it is systematically in error. This also involves rejecting the premise that some moral sentences are true. However, rather than reinterpreting moral discourse, it claims that, since there are no distinctively moral properties, any sentence that makes reference to such properties must be false. This is the line taken by Mackie, who goes on to present an account of our moral discourse and practices that makes no reference to moral facts (Mackie 1977).

Yet another response to the is/ought distinction is to challenge Moore's contention that it establishes that if moral properties are real, they must be nonnatural. This involves responding directly to Moore's arguments that any naturalistic account of moral properties commits the naturalistic fallacy. Charles Pigden carefully dissects the assumptions supporting Moore's arguments and argues that they do not establish the falsity of naturalism. He distinguishes three forms of the autonomy of ethics: logical, semantic, and ontological. Logical autonomy is the thesis that no "ought" can be derived in a valid argument from an "is." Semantic autonomy is the thesis that moral terms do not have the same meaning as any nonmoral terms. Ontological autonomy is the thesis that what makes any true moral judgment true is some *sui generis* moral fact (Pigden 1991: 427). Pigden argues that only ontological autonomy entails the falsity of naturalism, but that Moore's arguments, at best, merely establish semantic autonomy. So, it seems that there is still room for a moral realist who denies that there is a realm of moral facts over and above the facts that can be described using nonmoral language. However, any naturalist moral realist faces a challenge. She must give a reductive analysis of the moral to the nonmoral. This will involve presenting an account of the nature of the naturalistic properties to which moral predicates refer.

To sum up then, the is/ought distinction, together with the threat of committing the naturalistic fallacy, seem to leave available only the following positions on the conceptual landscape with regard to moral discourse and reality. First, one can hold that moral sentences are to be taken as describing reality and that reality is as they describe. They refer to distinctively moral properties and facts, which cannot be identified with natural properties and facts, so reality contains a realm of nonnatural moral properties and facts. Second, one can hold that moral sentences, despite appearances, are not to be taken as describing reality but instead merely express our attitudes towards various actions and states of affairs. Third, one can hold that moral sentences are to be taken as describing reality, but since there are no moral properties, moral predicates are empty and sentences containing them are false. Lastly, one can argue that the logical and semantic autonomy of ethics does not establish the falsity of naturalism;

some kind of reduction of moral predicates to nonmoral predicates is possible. Of these options, only the first and last are available to a moral realist. So the problem for moral realism is that it seems forced either to countenance strange, nonnatural moral properties or to provide an adequate analysis of moral sentences and predicates in terms of nonmoral sentences and predicates.

The argument for moral realism

Characterizations of moral realism typically suggest that one arrives at it from an adequate understanding of the implications of its semantic thesis. For example, Geoffrey Sayre-McCord (1988: 17) characterizes moral realism as a commitment to the following two theses:

1. Moral claims, when literally construed, are literally true or false (cognitivism).
2. Some moral claims are literally true.[1]

From (1) and (2) it is taken to follow immediately that, since moral claims purport to state facts, and some of them succeed in doing so (i.e., are true), there exist in reality some moral facts. A very tight connection is taken to hold between the semantic and metaphysical theses of moral realism (Smith 1991: 402; Brink 1995). We can present the argument for moral realism as follows:

The argument from moral language
1. Some moral predicates are irreducible to nonmoral predicates. (Semantic autonomy of ethics)
2. If (1), then some moral sentences are untranslatable into nonmoral sentences without loss of meaning.
3. Therefore, some moral sentences are untranslatable into nonmoral sentences without loss of meaning.
4. Moral sentences are capable of truth and falsity. (Cognitivism)
5. If there are moral sentences which are untranslatable and true, then there are corresponding irreducible moral facts.
6. Some of those moral sentences (which are untranslatable) are also true. (Semantic thesis of moral realism)
7. Therefore, some irreducible, moral facts exist.

The inference from 1 and 2 to 3 in the argument from moral language is a distillation of my discussion above of the impact of the is/ought distinction on moral realism. If moral predicates are not reducible to nonmoral predicates, then moral discourse cannot be eliminated from natural language without some loss of meaning. But then, given that moral sentences are fact-stating and that some of them are true, it follows that there are some features of reality which moral discourse picks out, namely, moral facts.

The semantics and metaphysics of tense and morality

There are a number of differences between the argument from tensed language (see Chapter 2) and the argument from moral language. First, the argument from moral language contains a sub-argument from 1 to 3, to which there is no counterpart in the argument from tensed language. Step 3 in the argument from moral language is analogous to premise 1 in the argument from tensed language. The fact that there is no corresponding sub-argument in the argument from tensed language merely reflects a difference in focus in each of these areas of debate. In metaethics, the focus has been on the is/ought distinction and the import of the naturalistic fallacy. Debate in the philosophy of time has focused directly on whether or not it is possible to eliminate tense from natural language.

Second, there is no counterpart in the argument from tensed language to premise 4 in the argument from moral language. This is because it has not seriously been questioned that when someone says, for instance, "It is now 4 o'clock," what one says has a determinate truth value. What has been up for debate is what makes such sentences true or false. The nature and function of moral discourse in natural language and in our lives, by contrast, has led some to question whether or not cognitivism about moral sentences is appropriate. Thus, this difference between the arguments is a result of the different contents and functions of moral and tensed discourse. Leaving aside these differences then, we can restate the argument from moral language so that it is structurally analogous to the argument from tensed language as follows:

The revised argument from moral language
1. Some moral sentences are untranslatable into nonmoral sentences without loss of meaning.
2. If there are moral sentences which are untranslatable and true, then there are corresponding, irreducible moral facts.
3. There are moral sentences which are untranslatable and true.
4. Therefore, some irreducible moral facts exist.[2]

In the debate about moral realism, just as in the early debate about tense, it seems to have been unquestioningly assumed that acceptance of cognitivism about moral sentences, together with the claims that moral sentences are irreducible to nonmoral sentences, and that some moral sentences are true, automatically commits one to the existence of a realm of moral facts. When this is combined with Moore's arguments about the irreducibility of moral predicates, the moral realist has found herself committed to a profligate ontology of nonnatural moral facts.

The conceptual landscape surrounding the revised argument from moral language has traditionally offered the following habitable positions. One can accept the argument as sound, perhaps arguing that the conclusion is not as unpalatable as it seems. One can reject premise 3 as well as the suppressed premise that moral sentences are capable of truth and falsity, thus taking a noncognitivist approach to moral discourse. Alternatively one can reject premise 3 while retaining cognitivism, thus arguing that all atomic moral sentences are false, and developing an error theory of moral discourse. Both of these views reject premise 3 and assert instead that there are untranslatable moral sentences, but they are not true. Lastly, one can reject premises 1 and 3, asserting instead that there are true moral sentences, but they are not untranslatable. This is the strategy of naturalism. Naturalism adopts a cognitivist approach to moral discourse, holds that some moral sentences are true, but argues that there are no facts or properties over and above those that can be specified using nonmoral language. So, any true moral sentences must be analyzable in terms of nonmoral sentences. Premise 2 has not yet been called into question.

Compare the responses to the revised argument from moral language with those to the argument from tensed language. The A-theory accepts the argument from tensed language as sound, and is thus the conceptual counterpart to the first response to the revised argument from moral language, moral realism. According to the old B-theory, the argument from tensed language is valid, but premises 1 and 3 are false; there are true tensed sentences, but they are not untranslatable. This response is the conceptual counterpart of the last response to the revised argument from moral language, naturalism. There are no counterparts to either the second or third responses to the revised argument from moral language. The reason for this, as I noted above, is that no one has seriously questioned either the claim that tensed sentences are capable of having a truth value, or that some of them are actually true.[3] It is hard to think what alternative there could possibly be to cognitivism about tensed discourse, and an error theory for tensed discourse would just about have to be an error theory for natural language, since almost everything we say is tensed.

There was a third response to the argument from tensed language, which was to deny the second premise. The new B-theory holds that there can be true tensed sentences that cannot be translated by any tenseless sentence even if there are no tensed facts. Could an analogous position be developed with respect to the revised argument from moral language? Such a position would hold that it is possible for there to be irreducible, truth-assessable moral sentences, and for some of them to be true, while there are no moral facts serving as their truthmakers. This position is to naturalism what the new B-theory is to the old B-theory, so might appropriately be dubbed "new naturalism." However, a more helpfully descriptive name for this metaethical position is: truthmaker naturalism. In the next section I will say some more about how truthmaker naturalism might be filled out.

Truthmaker naturalism

Truthmaker naturalism is a framework for a metaethical theory that can be filled out in different ways, depending on the sorts of nonmoral facts one takes to be the truthmakers for moral sentences. It is beyond the scope of this chapter to consider which sorts of nonmoral facts might best do this job. My aim here is merely to establish that the framework is a viable one, and furthermore to show that it has some advantages over its rivals.

The first thing to say about truthmaker naturalism is that it is a realist position with respect to morality. A typical characterization of moral realism is Sayre-McCord's, which states that it involves commitment to two theses: (1) moral claims, when literally construed, are literally true or false (cognitivism); and (2) some moral claims are literally true (1988: 17). Truthmaker naturalism accepts both these claims. Where it differs from traditional versions of moral realism is in its rejection of any peculiarly moral facts. There is an assumption rife in the literature that commitment to (1) and (2) automatically commits one to the existence of moral facts. After all, the assumption seems to be, if moral claims are irreducible to nonmoral claims, truth-assessable, and some of them are true, doesn't that necessitate the existence of moral facts to make the true ones true? It is just this assumption that is rejected by truthmaker naturalism.

Second, despite their obvious similarity, there is an important difference between naturalism and truthmaker naturalism. Naturalism is a reductive doctrine. It denies the existence of moral properties (goodness, rightness, wrongness, etc.), and reduces talk involving moral predicates to talk involving other, nonmoral predicates. Similarly, the old B-theory is a reductive doctrine, arguing that talk of the pastness, presentness or futurity of something is reducible to talk of its standing in some temporal relation to something else. The new B-theory, by contrast, denies that there is any sense in which tensed language is reducible to tenseless language. It holds instead that tense is an irreducible feature, not of the extralinguistic world, but of our representations of the world. If truthmaker naturalism follows the new B-theory in this regard, it will hold that talk involving moral predicates is not reducible to talk involving nonmoral predicates, but that morality is somehow an irreducible feature, not of the extralinguistic world, but of our representations of it.

To make the distinction between naturalism and truthmaker naturalism more apparent, consider the following naturalist position. A semantic naturalist might hold that, while the moral predicate "good" cannot be replaced in all contexts *salva veritate* by the nonmoral predicate "pleasant" (for example), because the two terms are not synonymous, nevertheless both predicates stand for the same property. So the kind of reduction from the moral to the nonmoral endorsed by semantic naturalism is the same as that between the ordinary language term "water" and its scientific counterpart "H_2O." In a scientific reduction such as this, it is recognized that the two terms do not have the same meaning, but they have a common referent. So the ordinary language term is reducible to the scientific term in so far as it refers to nothing over and above what the scientific term refers to. However, no such claims for a reduction are made by the new B-theory of time, nor by truthmaker naturalism as I am developing it.

The new B-theory of time does not claim that "past" and "earlier than" share a common referent. Rather, tenseless temporal relations figure in the truthmakers for true tensed sentences. A component of tenseless reality is the truthmaker for some tensed sentence, but it does not fully account for the sentence's meaning (Dyke 2003b). Similarly, truthmaker naturalism says that nonmoral properties figure in the truthmakers for moral sentences, but they do not fully account for their meanings. Truthmaker naturalism says that moral expressions contribute, at a semantic level, to the meanings of moral sentences. It is a naturalistic doctrine, in that it postulates nothing in the world, nothing extralinguistic, over and above what can be described using nonmoral expressions, but it is not a reductive doctrine, as naturalism usually is.

The peculiar "tensedness" of tensed language and thought emerges out of the fact that we experience the world and talk about it from some temporal perspective on tenseless reality. Since our perceptions of and interactions with reality are always from some temporal perspective, we tend to locate other events and states of affairs by implicit reference to our own temporal location. Thus, the peculiar "tensedness" of tensed language consists in its being implicitly and essentially temporally self-locating. This is one reason why tensed sentences cannot be translated by tenseless sentences, since the latter are not temporally self-locating. It is open to truthmaker naturalism to argue that the peculiar "moralness" of moral language and thought emerges out of the fact that we bring a moral perspective to bear on a nonmoral reality.

The feature of a true tensed sentence that is not captured by a tenseless description of its tenseless truthmaker is, to use Kaplan's (1989) terminology, its character. The character of a tensed sentence is a function from its context of utterance to its content in that context. A proponent of truthmaker naturalism could argue that moral sentences have a character as well as a content.[4] The character of a moral sentence might be a function from a feature of its context of utterance to its content in that context, where the salient feature of context for moral sentences is a normative system. If the character of a moral sentence is a function from normative systems to moral sentence-tokens with determinate truth values, then when a person asserts a moral sentence she commits herself to a number of normative systems, namely, those that the function takes to true tokens. If this suggestion were taken up by the truthmaker naturalist, then she would be in a position to maintain that no moral sentence means the same as any nonmoral sentence, even though they may have the same content. Furthermore, the aspect of the meanings of moral sentences over and above the nonmoral facts that are their truthmakers would be a fact about the sentence and its use rather than about extralinguistic reality.

One advantage of truthmaker naturalism is that it coheres with the usual motivation for realism that I discussed earlier. The intuitive appeal of moral realism, recall, is that we think there are correct answers to moral questions, and that when we engage in an ethical dispute, there is a genuine disagreement at issue, and not a mere difference of opinion. Since truthmaker naturalism endorses both the thesis that moral sentences are truth-assessable, and that some of them are true, it is consistent with the claim that there are correct answers to moral questions. However, it is not committed to the conclusion that there must be peculiarly moral facts. So it retains this advantage of moral realism without the attendant commitment to dubious metaphysical excesses that has plagued traditional moral realism. In the following section I will argue that truthmaker naturalism has two advantages that render it more attractive than any of its rivals.

Two advantages of truthmaker naturalism

Truthmaker naturalism provides a solution to both of the problems typically faced by moral realism outlined above. It has the resources to provide a solution to the apparent clash between the objectivity of morality on the one hand, and the fact that it provides us with motivations to act on the other. It also permits a plausible account of the is/ought distinction. Both of these advantages are suggested by parallel considerations in the new B-theory of time.

John Perry argued that, while tensed beliefs are irreducible to tenseless beliefs, they are nevertheless indispensable for timely, successful action (1979). In other words, tensed beliefs are indispensable to us even though there are no tensed facts to which they correspond. This has been taken up by proponents of the new B-theory (Mellor 1998, 2001). According to Mellor, we need true tensed beliefs in order to act successfully because we need beliefs that are not true at all times. For example, if I want to be on time for my dentist appointment, and I believe both that my appointment is at 12.30 P.M. and that it takes me half an hour to get to the dentist's, why do I leave my office at noon? My action cannot be explained in terms of my holding the tenseless beliefs that my appointment is at 12.30 P.M., and that it takes me half an hour to get there, as I have had both of these beliefs all morning, yet I only leave my office at noon. No, the belief that motivates me to leave my office is the belief that it is *now* noon. This is an irreducibly tensed belief, one that is only true at noon.

Mellor argues that what causes me to act is not the fact that it is now noon (there are no such facts), but the fact that I come to believe that it is now noon. This can be borne out by the observation that if my watch had stopped and it was actually 1 P.M., but I believed it to be noon, I would still leave my office. However in this scenario my action would not be successful because the relevant tensed belief is false. So, true tensed beliefs are not reducible to tenseless beliefs, but they are indispensable for successful timely action, even though they are not made true by tensed facts. What makes my belief that it is now noon true (if it is true) is the fact that I hold the belief at noon, which is a tenseless fact. The salient point here is that discovering tenseless facts is not sufficient to provide me with a motivation to act. It is only when I acquire an appropriate tensed belief, a belief that is nevertheless made true by a tenseless fact, that I am motivated to act. The motivational force is supplied by the fact that the belief is a tensed one, since any tenseless belief lacks the appropriate motivational force. But the fact that the belief is tensed is a fact about the belief, and not a fact about its truthmaker.

The first objection to moral realism that I outlined above was that, while it safeguards the objectivity of morality, it severs the link between moral beliefs and our motivations to act in accordance with them. But truthmaker naturalism has a response to this problem. In the case of tensed beliefs, we saw that their motivational force is supplied by the fact that they are tensed, which is a fact about the beliefs, and not about the reality those beliefs are about. In the case of moral beliefs, truthmaker naturalism could make a parallel case that the motivational force of a moral belief is a feature of the belief, rather than of the nonmoral fact which makes the belief true. In this way, acquiring a moral belief could be sufficient to provide me with a motivation to act even though coming to believe a nonmoral description of the fact that is its truthmaker would not be. The motivational force of a moral belief would be supplied by the fact that it is irreducibly moral, which is a fact about the belief, and not about extralinguistic reality.

The second problem for moral realism was that it must provide an account of the is/ought distinction. Genuine moral realism regards the two domains of discourse, that about what is the case, and that about what one ought to do, as irreducible to one another, and thus takes itself to be committed to a realm of nonnatural moral facts. Naturalism regards moral discourse as reducible to nonmoral discourse. Truthmaker naturalism, as I have argued, makes no claims that moral discourse is reducible to nonmoral discourse, but neither does it countenance an ontology of irreducibly moral facts. So it must provide an account of the relations between moral and nonmoral expressions, and between moral expressions and nonmoral reality.

Truthmaker naturalism holds that moral beliefs and sentences have nonmoral truthmakers, but it denies that moral beliefs and sentences are reducible to nonmoral beliefs and sentences. So, for example, the sentence "Rescuing that drowning child is the right thing to do," will have a nonmoral truthmaker, such as, for example, the fact that rescuing that drowning child will maximize happiness. But it is not the case that the moral sentence is reducible to a nonmoral sentence that shares its truthmaker, such as the sentence "Rescuing that drowning child will maximize happiness." The moral aspect of a moral belief is a feature only of the belief, and not of the fact that makes it true, which is entirely nonmoral. So, the relation between moral and nonmoral expressions is that they are wholly irreducible to each other. The relation between moral language and nonmoral reality is that the latter serves as truthmaker for any true sentence of the former.

7 Some further applications of the overlooked strategy

In the last chapter I took the methodological strategy that I claim has been largely overlooked by the traditional methodological map, and which is suggested by the strategy of the new B-theory of time and applied it to a different domain of discourse, that of moral discourse. In this chapter, I want to explore whether it can be applied in any other domains of discourse which have traditionally generated both metaphysical controversy and theories that occupy positions on the methodological map. In Chapter 6, I illustrated how the new strategy and its rivals, in both the temporal and moral domains, could all be seen as different responses to arguments from language to reality. As a first step, then, I will reconstruct that argument in general terms and then see whether it is applicable to any other domains of discourse with attendant metaphysical controversies.

The argument from K-language

The argument from K-language is a schematic argument that starts with premises about the nature of a particular domain of discourse, and draws a conclusion about the nature of some feature of reality. Generalizing from the arguments from tensed and moral language, the argument from K-language goes like this:

1. Some K-sentences are untranslatable into non-K-sentences without loss of meaning.
2. If there are K-sentences which are untranslatable and true, then there are corresponding, irreducible K-facts.
3. There are K-sentences which are untranslatable and true.
4. Therefore, some irreducible K-facts exist.[1]

A K-sentence is a sentence that employs a predicate, or other expression, peculiar to the domain of K-discourse, and a non-K-sentence is a sentence that is free of such predicates and expressions. A K-fact is a fact that includes a property, or some other entity, specifically, and only, designated by the expressions of K-discourse.

The various positions on the traditionally accepted methodological map, and the overlooked strategy, can all be illustrated as responses to this argument. The K-realist accepts the argument as sound. The K-reductionist rejects premises 1 and 3, arguing that there are true K-sentences, but they are not untranslatable; a successful reduction from K-sentences to non-K-sentences can be achieved. Error theorists and noncognitivists reject premise 3, holding instead that there are untranslatable K-sentences, but they are not true. Conceptual relativism accepts the argument as sound, but relativizes its ontological conclusion to the domain of K-discourse. Finally, the overlooked strategy rejects premise 2.

Presenting the positions on the methodological map in terms of responses to the argument from language to reality illustrates well the role played in seeing these positions as exhaustive by SLT. The K-realist accepts that K-truths are true and part of the one true description. Since there is a one-to-one correspondence between truths in that description and facts in the world, there must be K-facts for the K-truths to correspond to. The K-reductionist accepts that the K-truths are true but wishes to exclude them from the one true description because she denies that there are any K-facts, so she argues that they are true in virtue of being reducible to some other kind of truth which has a more respectable ontological counterpart. The error theorist denies that there are any K-facts, so denies that the K-"truths" are true. This move is motivated if one thinks that there is a one-to-one correspondence between truths in the one true description and facts in the world. Without that assumption there would be no need to deny that the K-truths are true. The same is true for the noncognitivist, who presents an alternative way of denying that the K-truths are true. If we reject SLT, as the overlooked strategy does, we can accept that the K-truths are true and irreducible, without being committed to the conclusion that there are any K-facts.

My question now is whether there are any other areas of metaphysical debate, the available positions of which can be characterized as responses to different instances of the argument from K-language. In the next five sections I will examine whether the metaphysical debates about material constitution, modality, causation, mathematics and vagueness fit this model.

Material constitution

The problem of material constitution is the problem of the relation objects stand in to the matter that constitutes them. What is the relation between a human being and the cells and particles that constitute it? Between a table and the particles that make it up? Between, to use a much-discussed example, a statue and the lump of clay of which it is made (Gibbard 1975)? Is it identity? Is the statue the very same thing as the lump of clay? In one sense, this answer seems obviously right. After all, it is not the case that there is a lump of clay occupying the region of space (or spacetime) occupied by the statue in addition to the statue. There is just one object there occupying that region of space, or spacetime.

The objection to the view that constitution is identity, however, is that there seem to be some things we can truly say of the statue, that we cannot truly say of the lump of clay, and vice versa. For example, the statue would still exist if a tiny piece of it were chipped off, but the lump of clay would not survive such a change. By contrast, the lump of clay would still exist if it were rolled into a ball, but the statue would not survive such a change. But if constitution is not identity, then we seem to face some unpalatable choices. Either it is not the case that there is just one object standing on a particular plinth, a clay statue. Instead, there are two: a statue and a lump of clay. If we don't want to be committed to the view that there is more than one object occupying a single region of spacetime, we could instead deny that there is any such thing as a statue. All that really exists is the constituent matter that makes up objects that we call statues. But this seems equally unsatisfactory as, along with statues, this maneuver would wipe out books, boats, trees, tables, and even human beings. All of the objects of common sense with which we are so familiarly surrounded are made up out of some sort of constituting material, and if they are neither identical with, nor different from that material, then they do not exist.

Does the problem of material constitution so described fit the structure of the methodological map? I think it does, and to illustrate this I will present the argument from K-language in terms of talk about objects and talk about their constituting matter.

The argument from language about ordinary objects
1. Some sentences about statues are untranslatable into sentences about lumps of clay without loss of meaning.
2. If there are sentences about statues which are untranslatable and true, then there are corresponding facts about statues over and above facts about lumps of clay.
3. There are sentences about statues which are untranslatable and true.
4. Therefore, some irreducible facts about statues exist over and above facts about lumps of clay.

In my presentation of the problem of material constitution above, I suggested that there are at least three available answers to the question about the relationship between a statue and the lump of clay that constitutes it. These are: (1) the statue is identical with the lump of clay; (2) the statue exists and is distinct from the lump of clay; and (3) the statue does not exist, only the lump of clay exists. These positions can be seen as different ways of responding to the argument from language about ordinary objects.

According to the first position, premises 1 and 3 are false. If a statue is identical with the lump of clay that constitutes it, then everything that can truly be said of the statue can truly be said of the lump of clay. According to Leibniz's principle of the indiscernibility of identicals, if "two" things are identical, that is, if "they" are really just one thing, then they must be indiscernible. And if they are indiscernible, it will not be possible to say something truly of one of them that cannot also be truly said of the other. It follows that any true sentence about the statue can be replaced by a true sentence about the lump of clay that preserves the meaning of the original. This position is thus a version of K-reductionism. It sees talk of statues as reducible to talk of the matter that constitutes them. Thus, this response rejects the conclusion of the argument from language about ordinary objects, that there are facts about statues over and above the existence of facts about lumps of clay, and it does so by rejecting premises 1 and 3 and holding instead that there are true sentences about statues, but they are not untranslatable. The problem for this position though, as we saw above, is that there are some things that we can truly say of a statue that we cannot truly say of the lump of clay that constitutes it, and vice versa.

According to the second position, the argument from language about ordinary objects is sound. This position accepts that there are facts about statues, and that they exist over and above facts about lumps of clay. It arrives at this conclusion via consideration of the point made in the previous paragraph that defeats the first position. That is, since there are some things that can truly be said of statues, that cannot truly be said of lumps of clay, and vice versa, it must follow that statues are not identical with lumps of clay. Furthermore, since, according to this view, there are facts about statues, those facts must exist over and above facts about lumps of clay. This view, then, is a version of K-realism. It takes true, ordinary language sentences about statues, that are irreducible to sentences about any other subject matter, to imply the existence of facts about statues, which are not identical to any other kind of fact.

The third response suggested above denies that there are any facts about statues over and above facts about lumps of clay; indeed, it denies that there are any statues, or facts about statues, at all. It thus rejects the conclusion of the argument by rejecting premise 3, and holding instead that there are untranslatable sentences about statues, but they are not true. It is thus a version of the error theory, or eliminativism, about statues. As noted above, along with statues, all the ordinary objects of common sense are also eliminated by this strategy. All that exists is the matter that constitutes these so-called objects, and our ordinary language that purports to refer to them is systematically in error.

The overlooked strategy also has a counterpart in this debate. It is generated by rejecting premise 2 of the argument from language about ordinary objects. It accepts that talk of statues cannot be reduced to talk of lumps of clay, but it is not the case that the only alternative to this is that there are facts about statues over and above facts about lumps of clay. To accept premise 2 is to think that for any domain of discourse, either the expressions of that domain of discourse are replaceable by some other expressions, or the domain of discourse refers to portions of extralinguistic reality that only it is capable of referring to. The overlooked strategy denies all this. According to it, a true sentence about a statue and a true sentence about the lump of clay that constitutes it may have the same truthmaker even though the sentences are irreducible to each other. That being the case, it is possible to be a realist about statues, that is, to think that statues exist as part of extralinguistic reality, and that their existence is independent of our ability to describe them, but they do not exist "over and above," or as entities in addition to, the lumps of clay out of which they are constituted.

I noted above that it is plausible to think that statues cannot be identical with lumps of clay because there are some things that can truly be said of a statue that cannot truly be said of its constituting lump of clay, and vice versa. For example, there are certain changes that a statue could survive, such as being chipped, which the lump of clay would not survive. Conversely, there are certain changes that the constituting lump of clay could survive, such as being rolled into a ball, that the statue could not survive. It is usual, in discussions of the problem of material constitution to describe these differences as differences in the modal properties of each entity. The statue possesses the modal property of being able to survive being chipped, but the lump of clay does not possess this property. The lump of clay possesses the modal property of being able to survive being rolled into a ball, but the statue does not possess this property. The inference to the conclusion that the statue and the lump of clay are not identical is then arrived at by an application of the principle of the indiscernibility of identicals. There are some modal properties that the statue possesses but which the lump of clay lacks, and vice versa, so they are not identical.

The two entities may also differ in their historical properties. The lump of clay may have existed before the statue was formed out of it at time t_1, so the lump of clay would then possess the historical property of having existed before t_1, while the statue lacks that property. Similarly, if the statue was chipped at time t_2, it would continue to exist while the lump of clay would cease to exist at that time, so the statue, but not the lump, would then possess the property of existing after t_2.

What does the overlooked strategy have to say about these alleged differences between the statue and the lump of clay? The traditional discussion of the problem of material constitution moves from saying that there are some things we can truly say about one entity, but not the other, to saying that there are some properties possessed by one entity, but not the other. This move assumes Heil's Principle Φ, that if a predicate applies truly to some object, it does so in virtue of designating a property possessed by that object, and by every object to which it truly applies. It is a move that the overlooked strategy would not make. From the fact that it is true that the statue could survive being chipped, it does not follow that there is a property, *being able to survive being chipped*, that the statue possesses, but which the lump of clay lacks. Similarly, from the fact that it is true that the lump

148 *Some further applications*

of clay, but not the statue, existed before t_1, it does not follow that there is a property, *having existed before t_1*, that the lump of clay, but not the statue, possesses.

However, denying that there are such properties as being able to survive being chipped, and having existed before t_1, does not involve denying that we can truly say of the statue that it can survive being chipped, and of the lump of clay that it existed before t_1. If we can still truly say these things, but the entities in question do not possess these modal or historical properties, what is it that makes true the sentences "The statue can survive being chipped" and "The lump of clay existed before t_1"? I think it is clear that even a very close inspection of the statue, or the lump of clay, would not reveal that it possessed, or lacked, either a modal property, or a historical property. So it is unlikely that anything about the ways the entities actually are can serve as truthmaker for sentences such as these. If the truthmaker is not to be found in the portion of reality that these sentences are about, the only other obvious candidate is that it is to be found in how we apply the concepts *statue* and *lump of clay*. A solution along these lines is suggested by John Heil, and it is worth quoting him at length.

> What makes it true that a lump of bronze can change shape or that it cannot lose bronze particles that make it up? So far as I can see, nothing in the lump of bronze itself makes such assertions true. We can know a priori that these truths hold of lumps of bronze because the truths concern, not properties of the bronze, but the concept of a lump of matter.... Talk of modal properties is a philosophically pretentious, and potentially confusing, way of describing constraints built into concepts we deploy. To say that statues and lumps of bronze possess different modal properties is just an oblique way of calling attention to the evident fact that our statue concept differs from our lump concept.... We decide what is to count as a statue, but an object's satisfying the statue concept is a matter of that object's being a particular way quite independently of how we take it to be.... [W]e decide what is to answer to 'tree', 'mountain', 'beetroot', 'electron', 'lump of bronze', but our application of these terms requires cooperation on the part of the world.
>
> (Heil 2003: 186–7)

According to Heil then, there is no such thing as a modal property. Talk of modal properties arises out of the fact that there are modal truths, which involve modal predicates, and then making the fallacious move from the existence of predicates in true sentences to the existence of properties specifically answering to those predicates. Since there are no modal properties, we should focus on the modal truths and ask what their truthmakers are. According to Heil, modal truths are made true by facts about the correct application of our concepts. A concept has certain constraints built in to it, which dictate what an entity must be like if it is to satisfy that concept, and also what sorts of changes it can undergo while continuing to satisfy it. And it is these conditions of application of our concepts which are the truthmakers for modal truths.

However, this is not to say that the existence of statues and lumps of clay depends on us and the application of our concepts. It is up to us what the concept of a statue is like, and what its conditions of application are. Or rather, what the concept is like and what its conditions of application are are the product of the way our language has evolved. But whether or not anything answers to that concept depends on what the world is like, independently of us and how we happen to describe it. Historical truths will have similar truthmakers. Whether or not a lump of clay exists at a certain time depends on whether or not it has undergone any changes before that time that would disqualify it from continuing to satisfy the concept of a lump of clay, or the same lump of clay as existed at an earlier time.

This account of the truthmakers for modal truths being facts about our concepts and their correct application fits neatly with the thesis I developed in Chapter 4 about language and meaning being partly the product of us and our interest in reality and partly a product of the way reality is independently of us. I argued there that some of the information conveyed by some of our sentences concerns us and our perspective on, and interest in, certain features of extralinguistic reality. For example, sentences employing economic vocabulary, such as "Event e is a price raising" reflect the way we choose to classify certain extralinguistic events, and the way we choose to classify them serves our purposes and reflects our interest in those events. Whether or not anything answers to our concept of a price raising, of course, depends on the way the world is completely independently of us and our schemes of classification.

Another point that is worthy of note is that this application of the overlooked strategy has the effect of making modality an irreducible feature of language and thought about nonmodal reality, and not a feature of mind-independent reality at all. This is analogous to my conclusions with respect to moral and tensed discourse. In this case, the conditions of application of our concepts of ordinary objects are determined by us, so if they generate modal truths, then it is to be expected that the modal nature of those truths is a fact about us and our concepts rather than a fact about the extralinguistic reality to which they apply. I shall have more to say about this in the next section.

Modality

One of the central issues in modality is whether or not modal notions can be given a completely reductive analysis, such that the analysis is entirely free of modal notions. Sider (2003) cites three reasons why one might want to achieve such an analysis. The first is epistemological. Many modal truths are known a priori, yet it seems odd that we can know such truths without the benefit of empirical or sensory evidence. If we can define modal notions in terms of notions for which we have an adequate epistemological basis, then the status of our claims to modal knowledge might be explained. A second reason why we might seek a reduction of the modal to the nonmodal is metaphysical. Sider asserts that "Reductionism is required by any ontology that claims to give a comprehensive account of reality in terms of primitive entities and notions that do not include modal notions" (2003: 184). So, according to Sider, if we want our account of reality to be free of modal notions, we need to exclude them by defining them in terms of nonmodal notions. This is, presumably, so that everything that is ordinarily expressed by a modal term or sentence can be expressed instead by a nonmodal term or sentence. A further metaphysical reason for requiring a reduction of the modal to the nonmodal, noted by Sider, is driven by considerations of parsimony. He writes, "The metaphysician prefers desert landscapes when she can get them; when it is possible to reduce, we should. Of course the reduction might fail; parsimony gives us reason to search, but does not guarantee success" (2003: 185).

Sider's discussion of the reduction of the modal to the nonmodal, and the motivations for it, is carried out in terms of the reduction of modal terms to nonmodal terms. So the aim of the reduction is to replace modal language with nonmodal language. However, the underlying aim of any metaphysician concerned to achieve a reduction of the modal to the nonmodal is surely to show that reality itself is nonmodal. That the real issue is metaphysical rather than merely linguistic is seen more clearly when we consider Sider's third motivation for a reduction of modality stated above, which was from considerations of parsimony. This motivation is surely driven by a desire not to be forced to recognize the existence of modal properties or facts. In other words, the metaphysician does not want to recognize modality as a constituent of extralinguistic reality. As Sider notes, she prefers desert landscapes to more abundant ones. She does not merely prefer desert representations of the landscape, however abundant it may actually be. What this suggests, though, is that by seeking to reduce modal terms to nonmodal terms, a reductionist is really seeking not to have to recognize modal entities as part of extralinguistic reality and also believes that she can achieve this just by concentrating on a reduction of modal language to nonmodal language. Why else, it must be asked, would one bother to seek to reduce modal language to nonmodal language? If one could deny the existence of modal entities without having to effect such a reduction, then that, surely, would be preferable.

What are the alternatives to reductionism in this debate regarding the status of modal discourse? Sider notes two: primitivism and eliminativism. Primitivism is the view that modality is unanalyzable, so is opposed to reductionism, according to which modality is analyzable. So described, primitivism is a view about modal discourse; that it is unanalyzable or irreducible to nonmodal discourse. The ontological dimension of primitivism, though, must be the idea that modality is a feature, or constituent, of reality. Parsimony, recall, can push us to seek reductions of one kind of discourse to another in the hope that we can arrive at the desired representation of a desert landscape, but if a reduction is unavailable, then the dream of a desert landscape, it seems, must be equally unavailable. Eliminativism, like reductionism, denies that modality is a feature of reality, but like primitivism, sees no chance of a successful reduction of modal to nonmodal discourse. According to the eliminativist, reality contains no modal features, so any discourse that appears to refer to such features must be in error, or not be truth-apt.

Can the debate about the status of modal discourse, and about whether or not modality constitutes a feature of reality, be construed as conforming to the methodological map? I think it can be, and to illustrate this, I will present the argument from modal language and show how the positions I have just described can all be seen as responses to that argument.

The argument from modal language
1. Some modal sentences are untranslatable into nonmodal sentences without loss of meaning.
2. If there are modal sentences which are untranslatable and true, then there are corresponding, irreducible modal facts.
3. There are modal sentences which are untranslatable and true.
4. Therefore, some irreducible modal facts exist.

Reductionism denies premises 1 and 3 of the argument from modal language, holding that there are some true modal sentences, but they are not untranslatable. Primitivism accepts the argument from modal language as sound. The desert landscape is simply not to be had when it comes to modality. Eliminativism rejects premise 3, holding that there are some untranslatable modal sentences, but they are not true. What of the overlooked strategy, which rejects premise 2? It maintains that we are not forced to conclude that there are modal facts even if no reductive analysis of modal to nonmodal sentences is available. Instead, we can hold that the true sentences of modal discourse may have nonmodal truthmakers even if no reduction of modal to nonmodal sentences is available.

What sort of nonmodal truthmakers might such a strategy suggest for modal truths? Mondadori and Morton (1976) suggest one answer to that question. They argue, in line with the overlooked strategy, that modal statements can be objectively true, even though it is not possible to provide nonmodal paraphrases of them. They further argue that "when such statements are true...they are true by virtue of actual facts about actual individuals; their truth is not determined by human convention or human knowledge, nor by facts about any exotic metaphysical apparatus" (Mondadori and Morton 1976: 4). Although they do not express it in these terms, it is, I believe, instructive to see theirs as a kind of "multiple realizability" view of modality. They suggest that the sentence "Ljubojevic might win the Petropolis Interzonal," uttered at some time, t, is made true by facts about Ljubojevic's state at t, (his strength and inventiveness), facts about the state of his opponents at t, and facts about the history of the tournament up to t. However, the predicate "might win the Petropolis Interzonal" does not pick out exactly the same physical properties every time it is used. When applied to some other individual, it may result in a true sentence by virtue of that individual possessing quite different physical properties from those possessed by Ljubojevic, together with different facts about the tournament and the other contestants. So, according to Mondadori and Morton, modal predicates cannot be paraphrased by nonmodal predicates, but when they occur in true sentences, the truthmakers of those sentences are physical facts about the actual objects (and their surroundings) to which the modal predicates are applied.

Heil's response to the problem of material constitution discussed above suggests another answer to the question of what the nonmodal truthmakers are for modal truths. Sentences about what is possible or necessary do not describe features of extralinguistic reality. Instead they are, if true, made true by the conditions of correct application of our concepts. Consider a couple of examples. The sentences "It is possible that water is a stimulant" and "It is necessary that no circle is a square" are paradigm modal sentences. Our intuitions suggest that both are true and, as Sider noted, we seem to be able to recognize that they are both true on a priori grounds. According to the suggestion under consideration, what makes each of those sentences true are facts about the conditions of correct application of our concepts.

Take the first sentence first. The embedded sentence "Water is a stimulant" is false, but the attachment to it of the possibility operator results in a sentence that asserts that reality might have been such that water is a stimulant. In order for reality to have been that way, some part of reality would have had to satisfy the concept *water* and also the concept *stimulant*. Nothing about the application of the concept *water* precludes it from applying to something that also satisfies the concept *stimulant*, so the claim that something might have existed that satisfied both concepts is coherent. Thus, we can conclude that the sentence "It is possible that water is a stimulant" is true.

Consider now the second sentence. Here the embedded sentence "No circle is a square" is true, but the attachment to it of the necessity operator results in a sentence that asserts, not just that no circle is in fact a square, but that no circle could possibly be a square. Again, our intuitions are that the modal sentence is true. And the proposal under consideration explains that intuition. In order for reality to be such that some circle is a square, some part of reality must satisfy the concept *circle* and the concept *square*. But the conditions of application of the concept *circle* are such that they preclude anything from satisfying that concept if it also satisfies the concept *square*. Hence, it is not possible for anything to be both a circle and a square, so our modal sentence "It is necessary that no circle is a square" is true.

The proposal that the truthmakers for modal truths are facts about our concepts and their conditions of application has a number of virtues. First, it explains the puzzle, noted by Sider, that generates the epistemological motivation for seeking a reduction of modal to nonmodal discourse. That puzzle concerns how it is possible that we can have a priori knowledge of modal truths. If the truthmakers for such truths are facts about the conditions of application of our concepts, then there is no need to turn to mind-independent reality to discover that they are true. All we have to do is investigate our concepts and how we apply them. Second, there is no need to effect a reduction of modal to nonmodal discourse, or to be an eliminativist, in order to deny that modality is a feature of extralinguistic reality. Since such reductions have been notoriously difficult to come by, and eliminativism is an unattractive option given the extent to which modal discourse is embedded in our thought and language, that is a significant advantage of this approach. The desired desert landscape can, after all, be achieved without having to find a way of reducing modal to nonmodal discourse. Third, as I mentioned at the end of the previous section, one implication of this approach is that modality turns out to be a feature, not of the world, but of us and our thought and language. Since there seems to be no sense in thinking that the truthmaker for "Water might have been a stimulant" or "It is necessary that no circle is a square" exists in the world as part of extralinguistic reality, this seems to me to be a distinct virtue of the proposal under consideration.

It should be noted, however, that the proposal that I have outlined is just one way of developing the overlooked strategy with respect to modality. What is constitutive of this approach is that modal truths do not have to be reducible to nonmodal truths in order to deny any commitment to modal facts. Modal truths can have nonmodal truthmakers while remaining irreducible to nonmodal truths. How one goes about determining what the truthmakers for modal truths are is a matter that is left entirely open by the strategy itself. There are many reductionist strategies with respect to modality, but these are, by and large, problematic (Sider 2003). One particular way in which they are often problematic is that the proposed reductions do not, in general, have the same meanings as the original modal claims. However, any of these strategies could plausibly be adopted within the structure of the overlooked strategy, and the fact that the analyses were not synonymous with the originals would not matter. Thus, one could offer any of the possible worlds analyses of modality (from Lewis's [1986b] analysis in terms of concrete possible worlds, to linguistic, fictional or combinatorial analyses), such that the content of the proposed reduction would play the role, not of analysis, but of stating the truthmakers for modal truths. The fact that statements within these proposed reductions do not have the same meanings as the original modal claims is irrelevant to their ability to be statements describing the truthmakers of the modal claims.

The overlooked strategy, with respect to any domain of discourse, is merely a schematic response to the argument from K-language. It states that we do not have to be committed to K-facts if we are unable to effect a successful reduction of K-discourse to non-K-discourse. It is possible for K-discourse to be irreducible to any non-K-discourse, and yet for its true sentences to be made true by non-K-facts. Just what the nature of those non-K-facts is, is a feature of the account that can potentially be developed in any number of different ways. In the case of modal discourse I have examined two ways in which that aspect of the overlooked strategy can be supplied with content, but there are, doubtless, many more such ways.

Causation

One of the fundamental debates surrounding the issue of causation is over whether causation exists in the world as some kind of necessary connection between events, such that the cause necessitates, or renders inevitable, the effect. David Hume initiated a tradition among empiricist philosophers of denying that there is any such necessity in nature, and of providing an account of causation such that there is nothing more to it than the spatio-temporal relations in which events stand to each other, together with the fact that certain pairs of events are instances of more widespread regularities in nature. Other philosophers have argued that causation does exist in the world as a kind of necessity between causally related events such that the occurrence of the cause makes the occurrence of the effect somehow inevitable. These latter philosophers thus think that there are causal facts in the world over and above facts about the spatiotemporal relations between events and facts about regularities between certain kinds of events. Thus construed, there is reason to think that the debate over whether there are causal facts fits the methodological structure of metaphysical debates that is the focus of this chapter.

Hume's theory of causation, and those that are deemed Humean in character, are typically known as regularity views of causation. According to Hume an event, c, can be said to cause an event, e, if and only if (1) c is spatiotemporally contiguous with e; (2) e temporally succeeds c; and (3) all events of type C (a type of which c is a token) are regularly followed by events of type E (a type of which e is a token) (Hume 1740: 649–50). The regularity view thus takes causation to consist in facts about the spatio-temporal relations between two events and the fact that those events instantiate a more general regularity. Regularity views of causation are therefore reductive in nature. They offer an account of the domain of causal discourse in noncausal terms, and conclude that the domain of causal discourse does not imply the existence of any peculiarly causal facts that make causal sentences true. Other versions of the regularity view of causation seek to analyze causal discourse in terms of necessary and sufficient conditions (Mill 1843: Book III, Chapter 5; Mackie 1974), or in terms of counterfactual conditionals (Lewis 1986a). But these alternative versions of the regularity view of causation share with Hume's the characteristic that they seek to reduce or analyze causal discourse in noncausal terms. This reduction or analysis is typically sought by offering an account of the truth conditions of causal sentences in noncausal terms. The ontological conclusion drawn from this endeavor is that there is no realm of peculiarly causal facts.

There is a range of non-Humean accounts of causation, which differ from the Humean ones in a variety of ways. Some deny that the truth conditions of causal claims can be specified in completely noncausal terms (Anscombe 1971; Tooley 1987). So the fact that it is not possible to completely eliminate all causal expressions is taken to imply that there must be causal facts in the world. Views of this kind differ from the Humean view in that they deny that a completely reductive analysis of causation can be achieved, and in that they hold the ontological view that causation does exist in nature as some kind of necessary connection between events.

Other views take it that the causal relation holds between pairs of events themselves, and not in virtue of those events instantiating some regularity. For example, according to Ducasse (1969), an event, c, causes an event, e, if and only if c was the last, or the only, difference in e's environment before e occurred. Thus, Ducasse's view differs from Hume's in that, according to it, the causal relation holds between a single pair of events just in virtue of the intrinsic nature of that sequence of events itself, and independently of anything that happens at other times and places. According to Hume's view, by contrast, while it can be true to say that a single pair of events are causally related, this is so only in virtue of those events instantiating a regularity, so the fact that a given sequence of events is causal is dependent on what happens at other times and places. However, in another sense, Ducasse's view resembles Hume's. This is that both kinds of view seek to provide a reductive analysis of causation. They differ in the kinds of noncausal facts they take to be the reductive basis of causation, but they both claim to offer an analysis of causation in noncausal terms.

Stathis Psillos suggests that there are three ways of characterizing debates about causation (2002: 127–33). First, the theories can be categorized into generalist and singularist accounts. Generalist accounts are those, like Hume's, that take causation to be dependent on general patterns, or regularities, in nature. Singularist accounts are those, like Ducasse's, that take causation to be a feature of a singular sequence of events. According to singularists, the occurrence of similar sequences of events at other times and places in nature is irrelevant to whether a particular sequence of events is causal.

Second, theories of causation can be categorized into those that take causation to be intrinsic to a sequence of events, or extrinsic to it. According to this categorization, Humean accounts would fall into the extrinsic category, while singularist accounts would fall into the intrinsic category.

According to singularists, whether a sequence of events is causal is an intrinsic feature of that sequence. It is a matter of the way that sequence is in itself, and not at all to do with how it stands with respect to anything else. According to Humean accounts, by contrast, whether a sequence is causal is a matter of whether it instantiates a regularity, so it does concern how that sequence stands with respect to other events. It might be thought that the generalist/singularist distinction and the extrinsic/intrinsic distinction map perfectly onto one another, but Psillos argues that this is not the case (2002: 128–9).

The third way of categorizing theories of causation is into reductive and nonreductive accounts, and it is this distinction that is the most salient for my purposes. According to Psillos, the issue between reductive and nonreductive accounts is "whether causation is ontically autonomous, or whether, instead, it is ontically dependent on non-causal features" (2002: 129). Reductive accounts are those, like Hume's and Ducasse's that take causation to be ontically dependent on noncausal features of the world. Those two particular theories, though, as we have seen, offer quite different accounts of the noncausal facts that constitute the reductive basis of causation. Nonreductive accounts see causation as being "ontically autonomous," that is, as being something in the world over and above, and not dependent on, any noncausal facts. Examples of nonreductive accounts are those of Tooley (1987) and Anscombe (1971).

Psillos suggests that there are two ways in which ontic dependence is normally conceived: full reduction and supervenience. Full reductive accounts take it that the truth conditions of causal claims can be fully specified in noncausal terms. Thus, they do not take causal claims to be synonymous with, or translatable by, noncausal claims. In this respect, then, full reductive accounts of causation are comparable to the truth-condition variant of the new B-theory of time discussed in Chapter 2. Psillos notes that, strictly speaking, supervenience accounts of the notion of ontic dependence are not reductive. According to the supervenience view, if two worlds are identical with respect to their noncausal facts, then they are also identical with respect to their causal facts. The noncausal facts fix all the causal facts. The difference between full reduction and supervenience, then, is this. In a fully reductive account, the prima facie causal facts are identical to the noncausal facts. By stating the truth conditions of causal claims in noncausal terms, the fully reductive account states what noncausal facts are actually specified by a causal claim. In a supervenience-based account, however, the causal facts supervene on the noncausal facts, so the two sets of facts are not identical. This is why a supervenience-based account is not, strictly speaking, reductive.

Since supervenience-based accounts do recognize the existence of peculiarly causal facts, I think it is simply wrong to call them reductive accounts of causation. The difference between reductive and nonreductive accounts is that the former seek to reduce causal discourse to noncausal discourse because they take it that there are no distinctively causal facts. Non-reductive accounts, by contrast, do recognize the existence of distinctively causal facts, and so deny that any such reduction from causal to noncausal discourse is possible. As I argued in Chapter 5, supervenience-based accounts attempt to somehow steer a middle path between the two options of realism and reductionism. With respect to the debate about causation, they do this by arguing that the causal facts are somehow dependent on, or fixed by, the noncausal facts. But no middle path is available, as there is no middle ground between asserting and denying that there are causal facts over and above noncausal facts. Since supervenience-based accounts do accept that there are such causal facts, they must be nonreductive.

Thus, as I see it, the only truly reductive accounts of causation are those that Psillos describes as full reductive accounts. Opponents of full reductive accounts argue that it is not possible to specify the truth conditions of causal claims in entirely noncausal terms. They insist that causal concepts inevitably creep into the analysis, so any such analysis is circular. They further take this as evidence for the claim that causation is an irreducible feature of the extralinguistic world, since the one true description of the world must include causal expressions.

With this preliminary examination of the debate about causation, and of some of the positions that can be taken with respect to it, in place, it is now time to see if an argument from causal language, analogous to the argument from K-language can be constructed, and if so, whether the positions in the debate can be seen as responses to it.

The argument from causal language
1. The truth conditions of some causal sentences cannot be stated in entirely noncausal terms.
2. If there are true causal sentences whose truth conditions cannot be stated in noncausal terms, then there are corresponding, irreducible causal facts.
3. There are causal sentences whose truth conditions cannot be stated in noncausal terms, and which are true.
4. Therefore, some irreducible causal facts exist.

The argument from causal language moves from the alleged impossibility of stating the truth conditions of causal claims in noncausal terms to the conclusion that causal facts exist in the world over and above noncausal facts. A philosopher who accepts this argument as sound is thus a nonreductivist about causation. This position is a version of K-realism about causation, and theories that exemplify it include causal realism, such as that of Tooley and Anscombe, and any supervenience-based account of causation, which takes the supervenient causal facts to be ontologically distinct from the base, noncausal facts. Reductive accounts of causation, such as those of Hume and Ducasse, are versions of K-reductionism about causation, and reject the conclusion of the argument by rejecting premises 1 and 3. They think that the truth conditions of causal claims can be fully stated in noncausal terms, and thus that they are entitled to the conclusion that there are no causal facts in the world over and above any noncausal facts.

Are there any positions in the debate about causation that constitute versions of error theories, or eliminativism about causal discourse? Such a position would seek to reject the conclusion of the argument from causal language by denying premise 3, and holding instead that there are causal sentences whose truth conditions cannot be stated in noncausal terms, but they are not true. One philosopher who can be interpreted as propounding such a position is Bertrand Russell (1918a). He thought that the concept of causation was incoherent. He famously pronounced, "The law of causality, I believe, like much that passes muster among philosophers, is a relic of a bygone age, surviving, like the monarchy, only because it is erroneously supposed to do no harm" (Russell 1918a: 171).[2] If, as Russell believed, the concept of causation was incoherent, it would follow that there is nothing in reality that answers to it. Such a position could be interpreted as claiming that any sentences that employ causal concepts, if understood as descriptive and fact-stating, are false, as they refer to causal facts, but there are no causal facts. A view such as this would be a version of the error theory of causal discourse.

To my knowledge, no philosopher has ever suggested a version of noncognitivism about causal discourse, where that is understood as the view that causal sentences are not capable of truth or falsity, but serve some other function in our language. Huw Price (2007) offers a position that may be thought to come close to such a view. He suggests that "the distinction between cause and effect [is] like the distinction between us and them – a perspectival projection onto a non-perspectival reality" (Price 2007: 254). However, he nowhere suggests that causal statements lack a truth value, which is what would be required by the sort of noncognitivism that rejects premise 3 of the argument from causal language. Instead, Price's view is not that causation doesn't exist, but that the concept *cause* is perspectival.

What of the overlooked strategy with respect to the debate about causation? It would reject the conclusion of the argument from causal language by rejecting premise 2. It would argue that even if full reductive strategies fail, it does not follow that there are causal facts over and above noncausal facts. Instead, the truthmakers for causal sentences may be noncausal facts. Alternatively, the overlooked strategy may accept some reductive account of the truth conditions of causal claims, but deny that this entails that there are no causal facts. A reductive account of the truth conditions of causal sentences could be adopted as an analysis of the semantics of causal sentences, and supplemented with an ontological account of the truthmakers of causal sentences. This would be analogous to the strategy of the truthmaker variant of the new B-theory of time.

Recall my discussion of supervenience-based accounts of causation. I argued there that such accounts are realist in that they accept that there are causal facts over and above any noncausal facts in the world. It may, however, be possible to retain the spirit of supervenience-based accounts, while denying that there are such causal facts. When outlining the thrust of supervenience-based accounts, Psillos has this to say: "So the idea is this: fix the spatiotemporal distribution of local qualities (which, of course, includes the regularities) and you fix everything else, including facts about causal relations" (2002: 129–30).

Thus understood, I want to suggest, proponents of supervenience-based accounts have made the mistake discussed in Chapter 4, of confusing descriptions of reality with reality itself, or of confusing facts with truths. If the idea behind supervenience is that once you have fixed the noncausal facts, you have thereby fixed the causal facts, but the causal facts exist over and above the noncausal facts, then supervenience at best recognizes some kind of strong connection between causal and noncausal facts, but at the same time holds that those facts are not identical, so it is not a reductive view. If, however, we modify the notion of supervenience, being careful to distinguish between truths and facts, it may be possible to keep supervenience-based accounts of causation out of the category of K-realist accounts. Suppose the idea behind supervenience is, instead, this: fix the spatiotemporal distribution of local qualities and you fix everything else, including *truths* about causal relations. If that were the underlying thought, then a proponent of supervenience need not recognize the existence of causal facts over and above noncausal facts. All she need recognize is the possibility of causal truths over and above noncausal facts, such that the noncausal facts are responsible for making the causal truths true.

A supervenience-based account understood in this way would sit well with the overlooked strategy outlined above. What the overlooked strategy, in general, recognizes is that there are domains of discourse which include truths that are not reducible to truths of any other kind. The existence of those truths, however, does not entail the existence of a peculiar kind of fact that can only be referred to by the expressions of that domain of discourse. Instead it is possible that they are made true by other, perhaps physical, facts. According to the modified notion of supervenience, if two worlds are identical with respect to their noncausal facts, then they are identical with respect to their causal truths. So the noncausal facts fix the causal truths. As in the other applications of the overlooked strategy discussed so far, it remains an open question which noncausal facts are the truthmakers for causal truths, so the account can be supplied with content in a number of different ways.

Mathematics

There are various positions available in the philosophy of mathematics with respect to the question of the existence, or otherwise, of mathematical objects. First there is mathematical realism, or Platonism, according to which mathematical objects exist objectively and independently of us. Mark Colyvan characterizes this as the view that "mathematical entities such as functions, numbers, and sets have mind- and language-independent existence or, as it is also commonly expressed, we *discover* rather than invent mathematical theories (which are taken to be a body of facts about the relevant mathematical objects)" (2001: 2). Opposed to mathematical realism is mathematical antirealism, or nominalism. This view is characterized by Colyvan as, "the position that mathematical entities do not enjoy mind-independent existence or, alternatively, we *invent* rather than discover mathematical theories" (2001: 2). An alternative antirealist position, noted by Colyvan, is the view that mathematical entities exist, but are mind- or language-dependent. Colyvan dismisses this view as "of little interest" (2001: 4). Broadly speaking, then, the two available positions with respect to mathematical ontology are that mathematical objects exist, and that they do not, although, as we shall see, there are different ways of developing each of these positions.

One of the most significant problems for mathematical realism is that of providing an adequate epistemology for mathematics. According to many proponents of mathematical realism, the mathematical objects they take to exist independently of us are abstract, acausal, and non-spatiotemporal. But if so, how is it that we come to have knowledge of them (Benacerraf 1973; Cheyne 2001)? Some realists respond to this problem by denying that mathematical objects are abstract after all (Maddy 1990).

There are various different ways of developing antirealist positions with respect to mathematics. One important version of antirealism is fictionalism. Colyvan describes fictionalism as follows: "A fictionalist about mathematics believes that mathematical statements are, by and large, false. According to the fictionalist, mathematical statements are 'true in the story of mathematics' but this does not amount to truth simpliciter" (2001: 4–5). This position has been developed, most notably, by Hartry Field (1980). Other antirealist strategies are reductionist in nature. They involve attempts to reduce mathematical discourse, or discourse that apparently refers to mathematical objects, to some other kind of discourse. Perhaps the most common such strategy is the attempt to reduce mathematics to set theory, which was first propounded by Russell and Whitehead (1910–13).

It is widely agreed that the most significant family of arguments in support of mathematical realism is that of indispensability arguments, especially the Quine–Putnam indispensability argument. This argument has variously been referred to as the best, or even the only, argument for Platonism worthy of consideration (Colyvan 2004). Field asserts that "there is one and only one serious argument for the existence of mathematical entities, and that is the Quinean argument that we need to postulate such entities…in order to do science" (Field 1980: 5). It is thus clearly seen by mathematical realists as providing immensely powerful support for their position, and by mathematical antirealists as a serious obstacle to theirs. It has recently been stated and given a sustained defence by Mark Colyvan (2001), so I shall discuss his formulation of it:

1. We ought to have ontological commitment to all and only those entities that are indispensable to our best scientific theories.
2. Mathematical entities are indispensable to our best scientific theories.
Therefore:
3. We ought to have ontological commitment to mathematical entities.

(Colyvan 2001: 11)

As stated, the argument is, of course, valid. If sound, it establishes the existence of mathematical entities, or more precisely, that we ought to believe in their existence. Thus, for those who accept the argument, it allows them to maintain mathematical realism, or Platonism. Mathematical anti-realists, who deny that mathematical entities exist, faced with this argument and its validity, need to find fault with one or both of its premises in order to affirm their position.

According to Colyvan, premise 2 needs little support. It is uncontroversial that mathematics is widely and diversely applicable to every branch of empirical science, and Colyvan takes this uncontested fact to be all the support necessary for premise 2 of the argument. He writes, "I take as a starting point the simple, undeniable fact that mathematics has such applications.... I'm concerned largely with indispensability arguments, and these arguments purport to yield conclusions about ontology based on this simple, undeniable fact" (Colyvan 2001: 6). The support for premise 1 comes from the doctrines of naturalism and confirmational holism.

Naturalism, in its Quinean guise, is the doctrine that there is no first philosophy and that the philosophical enterprise is continuous with the scientific enterprise (Quine 1981). Furthermore, science, taken to include philosophy, gives us the complete story of the world. Accepting this doctrine requires us to look to our best scientific theories to determine what exists. Since our best scientific theories make indispensable use of mathematics, accepting naturalism thus construed, Colyvan claims, dictates that we ought to believe in the existence of mathematical objects. Naturalism thus provides us with a reason for believing in the existence only of those entities that our best scientific theories say exist. Confirmational holism is then wheeled in to give us reason to believe in all the entities that our best scientific theories say exist. Confirmational holism is the doctrine that theories are confirmed or disconfirmed as wholes (Quine 1951). Thus, if empirical evidence confirms a theory, it confirms the whole theory. Since mathematics constitutes part of every scientific theory, any evidence that confirms any of these theories, also confirms the mathematical part of it. Thus, according to Colyvan, "Naturalism and holism taken together then justify premise 1. Roughly, naturalism gives us the 'only' and holism gives us the 'all' in premise 1" (Colyvan 2004: Section 3).

162 Some further applications

Field's response to the indispensability argument consists of two steps. First, he denies that mathematical statements are true. As noted above, his is a fictionalist account of mathematical discourse. All atomic mathematical statements are false. These statements appear to refer to mathematical objects, but since there are no such objects, they fail to refer, and are thus false. Second, since mathematics is so widely and usefully applicable in scientific theories, and yet he thinks it is false, he needs to show that mathematics need not be true to be useful. He recommends "nominalizing" scientific theories such that any mathematics contained within them does not involve reference to, or quantification over, any mathematical entities. He thus, effectively denies that mathematics, as conceived by the mathematical realist, is indispensable to science, ultimately challenging premise 2 of the indispensability argument.

Another strategy for mathematical antirealists is to undermine the doctrines taken to support premise 1 of the argument, namely, naturalism and confirmational holism. The latter doctrine is the usual target for those adopting this strategy. The idea is that there may be reasons not to take ourselves to be ontologically committed to all the entities referred to, or quantified over, in a scientific theory. Such reasons will need to justify treating some parts of a scientific theory differently from others on the question of ontological commitment. Naturally, those who adopt this strategy will offer reasons why the mathematical constituents of a scientific theory do not carry ontological commitment to mathematical entities, while the other parts of the theory do carry ontological commitment to whatever entities they refer to (quarks, gluons, and so on). Those who have taken up this strategy include Musgrave (1986), Maddy (1992) and Sober (1993).

Yet another strategy for those wishing to reject the conclusion of the indispensability argument is to accept that mathematical claims are true, but deny that they commit us to the existence of mathematical objects. The typical way of achieving this is "to provide a non-platonistic construal of mathematical statements" (Cheyne 2001: 160). Thus, proponents of this strategy see their task as providing a different way of saying what mathematical statements say, or a different (non-Platonist) interpretation of mathematical statements. Geoffrey Hellman, Philip Kitcher and David Lewis are three philosophers who have attempted to reinterpret mathematical statements so as to avoid ontological commitment to mathematical entities. According to Hellman (1989), mathematical claims can be interpreted as asserting the mere possibility of objects exemplifying various structural relationships. According to Kitcher (1984), the assertions of mathematics concern the possible operations of an ideal agent. Finally, according to Lewis (1993), mathematical claims can be interpreted as claims about the mereological properties of some actual concrete wholes and their parts.

It is my contention that all of the positions I have outlined are instances of positions on the traditionally accepted methodological map. Furthermore, the argument that provides the focus for debate among proponents of each of these positions, the Quine–Putnam indispensability argument, conceals a commission of the representational fallacy. First, mathematical realism, or Platonism, is an instance of K-realism. It claims that mathematical entities exist because mathematical statements are true, and they irreducibly refer to, or quantify over, such entities. As we have seen, there are different ways of denying that there are any mathematical entities. Field's strategy is to deny that mathematical statements are true, and to offer a fictionalist interpretation of them, such that they are "true in the story of mathematics." This is an instance of the error theory of K-discourse. It accepts the implicit assumption of the mathematical realist that, if such statements were true, then we would be committed to the existence of mathematical entities, and since it denies that there are any such entities, it denies that mathematical statements are true.

The strategy of attempting to provide a non-Platonist construal of mathematical statements is an instance of K-reductionism about mathematical discourse. Here, the aim is to accept that mathematical statements are true, but to offer an alternative account of what they are about. Just like other forms of K-reductionism, proponents of this strategy offer an alternative interpretation of mathematical discourse that is not committed to the existence of mathematical entities. Furthermore, also like proponents of other forms of K-reductionism, they clearly accept the implicit assumption of the mathematical realist that, were they unable to find another way of saying what is said by mathematical discourse, they would be committed to the existence of mathematical entities.

The strategy that Colyvan dismissed as uninteresting, the position that mathematical entities exist, but are mind- or language-dependent, is a version of conceptual relativism with respect to mathematical discourse. The only strategy outlined above that does not clearly occupy one of the positions on the methodological map is that of taking issue with confirmational holism. This strategy accepts mathematical statements as true, but does not attempt to provide a reinterpretation of them. It merely claims that mathematical statements can be true and yet not be committed to the existence of mathematical entities.

What of the Quine–Putnam indispensability argument? I stated above that I believe it conceals a commission of the representational fallacy, and I will now expand on that accusation. There is a clue to the fact that the representational fallacy is committed by this argument in Colyvan's discussion of it. He says, "Indeed, so important is the *language* of mathematics that it is hard to imagine how some theories could even be stated without it" (Colyvan 2001: 6; emphasis added). The indispensability argument takes as its starting point the indispensability of mathematical *language* to the statement of scientific theories, and draws conclusions from this about mathematical *ontology*. Another clue is to be found in a footnote, where Colyvan notes, "I often speak of certain entities being dispensable or indispensable to a given theory. Strictly speaking it's not the entities themselves that are dispensable or indispensable, but rather it's the *postulation of* or *reference to* the entities in question that may be so described" (2001: 10, n. 18). In his formulation of the indispensability argument, Colyvan's premise 2 states that mathematical entities are indispensable to our best scientific theories. However, as he himself realizes, what it should say is that postulation of, or reference to mathematical entities is indispensable to our best scientific theories. But these are two very different claims. The premise that Colyvan actually employs is about ontology, while the one that he should employ is about language.

Christopher Pincock (2004) criticizes Colyvan's formulation of the indispensability argument along similar lines. He argues that it is illegitimate to omit from premise 2 the idea that it is apparent reference to mathematical entities, rather than the mathematical entities themselves, that is indispensable to our best scientific theories. Hence, he reformulates Colyvan's argument as follows:

1′. We ought to have ontological commitment to all those entities that are indispensable to our best scientific theories.
2′. Apparent reference to mathematical entities is indispensable to our best scientific theories. Therefore:
3′. We ought to have ontological commitment to mathematical entities (metaphysical realism).

(Pincock 2004: 68)

Pincock goes on to note that this argument has been shown to be invalid, since philosophers such as Lewis and Hellman can consistently accept both premises and deny the conclusion.

Colyvan's formulation of the indispensability argument thus illegitimately claims that mathematical entities are indispensable to our best scientific theories, when all it is entitled to is the claim that mathematical language, which involves apparent reference to mathematical entities, is so indispensable. When suitably amended, the argument is seen to be invalid. It moves from a fact about mathematical language, that it is indispensable to the formulation of scientific theories, to a claim about ontology, that mathematical entities exist.

What of the overlooked strategy with respect to the debate about mathematical entities? It would accept that mathematical statements are objectively true or false, and also that they are indispensable to our best scientific theories, but would deny that this implies anything about the existence or otherwise of mathematical entities. Furthermore, it would deny that in order to maintain this position it is necessary to provide a reinterpretation of mathematical statements such that they are seen to be "about" some other kind of subject matter. Of course, different accounts may be developed of what the truthmakers of mathematical statements are, but it is not necessary to show that mathematical statements can be "reduced" (in any sense of that term) to statements describing those truthmakers in other terms. In other words, the truthmakers for mathematical statements may involve nonmathematical entities, even though no reinterpretation from mathematical to nonmathematical statements is available. As in the other applications of the overlooked strategy discussed so far, it remains an open question which facts are the truthmakers for mathematical truths, so the account can be supplied with content in a number of different ways.

I noted above, when outlining the available positions with respect to the existence, or otherwise, of mathematical entities, that one of the extant positions does not obviously occupy a position on the traditionally accepted methodological map. This is the position that results from the strategy of taking issue with confirmational holism. It accepts mathematical statements as true, but does not attempt to provide a reinterpretation of them. It merely claims that mathematical statements can be true and yet not be committed to the existence of mathematical entities. Such a position could be developed along the lines of the overlooked strategy. Colyvan has two major objections to a position such as this. First, he accuses it of having a double standard with regard to the question of ontological commitment. That is, when it suits her, a proponent of this position will accept that her language involves ontological commitment to certain entities, but when it comes to mathematics, she rejects this. And furthermore, this double standard is unmotivated, except perhaps by prejudice. Second, Colyvan claims that a proponent of this position does not meet the desideratum of providing a uniform semantics for all discourse, mathematical and nonmathematical alike. If this position is developed along the lines of the overlooked strategy, then I think it has the resources to meet these objections.

The overlooked strategy never endorses a move from features of language to features of reality, so the double standard objection simply does not apply. What it claims is that, for any domain of discourse, if that domain includes true sentences, then there is something about the world that constitutes the truthmakers for those sentences. The truthmakers for theoretical sentences of scientific theories may involve entities such as quarks and gluons, but if so, the conclusion that quarks and gluons exist is not arrived at by examining the theoretical sentences themselves. Similarly, the truthmakers for mathematical sentences may involve mathematical entities, or they may involve other kinds of entity, but once again, the conclusion that these entities (whatever they may be) exist is not arrived at by examining mathematical sentences. So the proponent of this strategy does not operate a double standard when examining the sentences of different domains of discourse. Instead, she singularly refuses to take features of different domains of discourse as her starting point in developing her ontology. Her question is always "What are the truthmakers for these true sentences?" and never "What entities does the use of this true sentence commit me to the existence of?" By operating in this way, she also meets Colyvan's second objection, because this strategy does constitute a uniform way of treating language, and thus it generates a uniform semantics for all types of discourse.

Vagueness

Many predicates of ordinary language are characteristically vague. Examples of vague predicates are "tall", "bald", "heap", "red", and "child". To describe a predicate as vague is to acknowledge that it has at least two features. First, a vague predicate will have borderline cases. That is, while there are some objects to which the predicate determinately applies and others to which it determinately does not apply, there are some objects for which it is simply unclear whether or not the predicate applies. Thus, for example, some people are determinately bald, others determinately not bald, and still others for which, it seems, it would not be true to say that they are bald, nor that they are not bald; they are borderline cases. Second, vague predicates typically give rise to sorites paradoxes. It is a plausible assumption that a single hair cannot make a difference to whether or not someone counts as bald. Yet if we were to line up a large number of people, starting with a person having a full head of hair, and each differing from his predecessor in having just a single hair less on his head, our plausible assumption would yield the unacceptable consequence that the person at the end of the line, with a single hair on his head, would not count as bald.[3]

Much of the philosophical debate surrounding the issue of vagueness concerns the logic of vague predicates. Suppose we have an object that counts as a borderline case of some vague predicate. For example, suppose Bob is 5 feet 9 inches in height. Is the sentence "Bob is tall" true or false? Or is there, perhaps, some alternative answer to this question? One option is to say that there is a determinate answer to the question of whether or not Bob is tall, but we do not, or even could not, know what that answer is. This option, known as the epistemic view, retains classical two-valued logic, and attributes the vagueness of vague predicates to our ignorance of where the boundaries of their applicability lie. An alternative option is to reject classical two-valued logic, and say that the sentence "Bob is tall" is neither true nor false, or is indeterminate, or even that it is both true and false. This option has been developed in a number of different ways, but their details need not concern me here, as the question that I am interested in is that of the relation between vagueness in language and the ontology that grounds it.

While most of the discussion on the issue of vagueness has focused on the logic of vague predicates, some ontological questions have been raised. Does vagueness in language reflect vagueness in the world? Unlike other issues that I have discussed in this and preceding chapters, however, the issue has not, in general, seemed to be that of whether vague predicates refer to distinctively vague properties.[4] Perhaps this is because it is not really clear what it would be like for a property to be vague. Instead, a more appropriate question seems to be that of whether or not the possession of a property by an object can be indeterminate. Another ontological question that has been raised in discussions on vagueness has been that of whether or not there are vague objects. Discussions of this question have focused on two issues, first, whether objects can have indeterminate spatiotemporal boundaries, and second, whether or not there can be vague identity.

However, in spite of the fact that the issue of vagueness does not seem, on the face of it, to fit as neatly onto the methodological map as other issues I have discussed, there are some positions with respect to vagueness that, I believe, do occupy positions on it. Our question, then, is whether vagueness in language has been thought to have any ontological implications for the existence, or otherwise, of vagueness, however conceived, in the world.

One position with respect to the question of whether there is vagueness in the world is that there is indeed ontic vagueness. This position has been developed in a number of different ways. Some, for example, Michael Tye, argue that there are vague objects in the world, in the sense of objects with fuzzy spatiotemporal boundaries (Tye 1990). Examples, cited by Tye, of vague objects include mountains, islands, countries, and deserts. Such objects are vague because, for some mountain, there are some molecules that are inside it, others that are outside it, and still others for which there is no determinate fact of the matter whether they are inside or outside the mountain. Tye then considers whether there are any remaining molecules, aside from those that are inside the mountain, outside it, or on the borderline. To think that there are additional molecules, he thinks, is to make a metaphysically gratuitous postulation. To think that there are no further molecules, on the other hand, is to recognize sharp boundaries between the molecules inside the mountain, those on the borderline, and those outside the mountain, and this, Tye thinks, is intuitively implausible.

So Tye's response to the question of whether there are any further molecules is to say that it is objectively indeterminate whether there are any remaining molecules. Consequently, the mountain is a vague object (Tye 1990: 535). Tye also recognizes the existence of vague abstract objects, such as sets. He classifies a set as vague if and only if (a) it has borderline members; and (b) there is no determinate fact of the matter about whether there are objects that are neither members, borderline members, nor nonmembers. Finally, he also recognizes some properties as vague. For Tye, a property is vague only if (a) it could have borderline instances; and (b) there is no determinate fact of the matter about whether there could be objects that are neither instances, borderline instances, nor noninstances. Elsewhere (Tye 1994), he offers a three-valued account of linguistic vagueness, which, he argues, requires the world to be vague. He further argues that recognition of this ontic vagueness provides the means to understanding linguistic vagueness.

Terence Parsons and Peter Woodruff (1995) suggest a different way in which the world may exhibit vagueness. They argue that it is at least a coherent possibility that states of affairs can be vague. States of affairs are the having of properties by objects, and Parsons and Woodruff argue that it can be indeterminate whether some object has a given property. This, they suggest, constitutes an objectively indeterminate state of affairs. Thus, on this view, vagueness does not reside in objects, nor in properties, but in the having of properties by objects. The objects and properties concerned may themselves be perfectly precise.

All of the positions with respect to ontic vagueness outlined here, that objects, both concrete and abstract, properties and states of affairs can all be vague, could reasonably be thought to be instances of K-realism with respect to vagueness. That is, they recognize the existence of vagueness in the world, and the evidence for its extralinguistic existence is largely taken to be the existence of vagueness in language, and in how we describe the world.

Another position with respect to vagueness in the world that has been taken by, for example, Peter Unger (1979) and Mark Heller (1988), is to assert that all vague predicates simply lack application. If a predicate is linguistically vague, then it follows that there is nothing to which that predicate applies; its extension is empty. Unger argues that sorites paradoxes for vague predicates, such as "tall," "bald," and "red" show that there are no tall people, no bald people, and no red things. He further argues that sorites paradoxes can be generated for ordinary objects, such as tables and trees. If we start with an ordinary table, and successively remove a single molecule from it, intuition suggests that after each removal we still have a table, but the conclusion of the process would involve a single molecule that would count as a table. He takes this to show that there are no such things as tables, and similarly for all other ordinary objects. A view of this kind could plausibly be thought to be an error theory, or eliminativism, with respect to vague discourse. The starting point of the view is the linguistic data of vagueness in language. Vague expressions appear to describe reality, but there is nothing in reality to which they apply, so they systematically lack application, and so all atomic sentences in which they occur are false.

A third view with respect to the relation between vague language and the ontology that grounds it has come to be known as the epistemic view (Cargile 1969; Williamson 1994). According to the epistemic view, apparently vague predicates have well-defined extensions with sharp boundaries, but we simply do not, or perhaps even could not, know where those boundaries lie. The epistemic view is thus able to retain classical two-valued logic and accept that every vague sentence is either true or false, while admitting that we are ignorant of its truth value. This view, thus, denies that there is any vagueness in the world and recognizes vagueness as merely a feature of our linguistic representations of reality.

There is no suggestion among proponents of the epistemic view that vague sentences can be reduced to nonvague sentences, nor that they have nonvague truth conditions. Thus, it would not be appropriate to see the epistemic view as a version of K-reductionism with respect to vague discourse. According to the epistemic view, the phenomenon of vagueness arises as a result of our ignorance of where the boundaries of the application of our predicates lie. Those predicates, however, do have precise boundaries, so the possession by objects of properties is not a vague matter; it is perfectly precise. So the epistemic view is open to the characterization that vague sentences have nonvague truthmakers, even though they are not reducible to, or translatable by nonvague sentences. Such a characterization would render the epistemic view a version of the overlooked strategy with respect to K-discourse.

Another way of characterizing the epistemic view is in terms of supervenience. Provided we are careful, as recommended in Chapters 5 and 7, to specify supervenience in terms of supervenient truths supervening on subvenient facts, such a characterization would go something like this: If two worlds are exactly alike with respect to all their precise facts, then they are also alike with respect to all their vague truths. In other words, once we fix all the precise facts, we thereby fix everything else, including all the vague truths. According to such a position, there are no vague facts over and above nonvague facts, but there are vague truths in addition to nonvague truths. The truthmakers for vague truths are nonvague facts, so if two objects are exactly alike in all nonvague respects, then all the vague truths about one of them will also be true of the other.

I said at the beginning of this section that the issue of vagueness does not eem to conform as readily to the traditionally accepted methodological map as the other issues that I have discussed, and that this is largely due to discussions of vagueness typically focusing on the logic of vagueness, rather than on ontological questions. In spite of this, however, I have been able to discern three positions with respect to vagueness, two of which occupy positions on the traditional map, and one of which (the epistemic view) can be interpreted as a version of the overlooked strategy. The epistemic view, however, has not explicitly been developed along the lines that I have suggested, because its proponents have been more concerned with epistemological issues surrounding vagueness than with ontological issues. For example, they have been concerned with explaining in what our ignorance with respect to vagueness consists, given that no further information could settle for us the truth value of any vague sentence. However, there clearly is an ontological issue to be addressed with respect to vagueness, and there is potential within the epistemic view to develop an account of that ontological issue that takes its lead from the overlooked strategy.

Conclusion

I have examined five very different metaphysical issues, and I have argued that the debates surrounding them can all be seen as offering positions on the methodological map. I argued in Chapter 5 that the traditional methodological map is flawed because of an implicit, and false, assumption motivating the view that the positions on it exhaust the available options. That assumption is that there is some special relationship between language and reality, such that we can discern the nature of the latter from the nature of some privileged version of the former. One component of this flawed view is SLT, according to which there is one, privileged true description of reality, the sentences of which stand in a one-to-one correspondence with facts in the world and are structurally isomorphic to those facts. I further argued there that there is an overlooked position with respect to the relationship between language and reality which rejects SLT. According to that position, for any domain of discourse, we are not forced to either find some way of eliminating that discourse, or accept its prima facie ontological implications that there is a range of facts that can only be referred to by the expressions of that discourse. Instead, we can leave the domain of discourse in question as it is, and argue that its true sentences have truthmakers that are physically and naturalistically acceptable, even though there is no way of reducing them to physical or naturalistic sentences.

My examination of these debates has shown that the positions that have been advanced with respect to them typically exemplify at least one of the positions on the methodological map. It has also shown that there is a counterpart in each of them to the overlooked strategy, that has, by and large, been overlooked. This position, I suggested, can be supplied with content in each of these debates in a number of different ways. Thus, what I hope to have achieved here is to have suggested a strategy for those working in these fields that can be further advanced and developed, generating new positions in these debates that avoid committing the representational fallacy. It is likely that there are other metaphysical debates too, that are susceptible to a treatment along the lines of those I have offered here.

Notes

1 Metaphysics and the origins of the representational fallacy

1 In 1985, at the University of Sydney, David Stove ran a competition to find the worst argument in the world. He assigned marks to the entries on the basis of the badness of the argument and the extent of its endorsement by philosophers. He awarded the prize to himself for identifying the Gem.
2 For further discussion on the Gem and the part it plays in the philosophy of Kant and the Kantians see Musgrave (1999).

2 A new metaphysical strategy: lessons learned from the philosophy of time

1 Strictly speaking, this is not true of presentists, according to whom only the present moment exists, but I shall ignore this for the purposes of this introduction to the two basic types of theory.
2 For extensive discussion of this issue see Bigelow (1996), Crisp (2003), Keller (2004) and Markosian (2004).
3 I criticize this argument in more detail in Dyke (2003a).
4 In Dyke (2003a), I argue that Craig is not entitled to require of the B-theorist that she show that *ontological* tense is superfluous to human thought and language. He is only entitled to the weaker requirement that she show that *linguistic* tense is so superfluous.
5 This is, in fact, the position of the new B-theory, which I discuss below.
6 The idea that there can be a set of all truths has been shown to be paradoxical (Grim 1984). The idea is that if we assume that there is a set of all truths, then to each subset of it, or element of its power set, there will correspond a unique truth. It follows that there will be at least as many truths as there are elements of the power set. But by Cantor's power set theorem the power set of any set will be larger than the original. It follows that there are more truths than there are members of the original set of all truths. So that set cannot be the set of all truths. However, there are at least three strategies for preserving a non-paradoxical notion of "all the truths." These are the restriction strategy, the class strategy and the nonmaximal strategy (Divers 2002: 245–56). My preference is for the last of these strategies. However, for my purposes, I will simply assume that some nonparadoxical notion of "all the truths" can be preserved which adequately captures the idea that there is one true description of reality which is the collection of all the truths that there are.
7 SLT does not imply that for every fact there is a sentence describing it. To think that there is just one true description of reality need not involve thinking that the description is complete. There have been, are, and will be, many facts that remain for ever undescribed by language-users. Instead, the one-to-one correspondence

between truths and facts alluded to here should be understood as implying that for any fact in the world there is at most one truth in the one true description.
8 For a useful account of the development of the debate between the A- and the new B-theory of time see Oaklander and Smith (1994).
9 S2 states *u*'s truth condition according to the token-reflexive version of the new B-theory. There is an alternative version, the date version, according to which *u*'s truth condition, when it is uttered at time *t*, is that *u* is true if and only if the enemy approaches (tenselessly) at *t*. I discuss the difference between these two versions in Dyke (2002a), but it does not matter for my purposes here, so I shall ignore it.
10 The first premise of this argument is logically redundant, as the argument would be valid without it. However, it is not dialectically redundant, as it allows us to distinguish two different ways of challenging premise 3: either by denying that there are any true tensed sentences that are untranslatable, or by denying that there are any tensed, untranslatable sentences that are true.
11 I argue for this in Dyke (2002b).
12 An objection to the new B-theory along these lines has been put forward by Smith (1993) and Craig (1996).
13 Two B-theorists who deny that McTaggart's paradox establishes the unreality of tense are Sider (2001, 35, n. 19) and Savitt (2000).

3 The representational fallacy or how not to do ontology

1 An example similar to this is discussed in Newman (1992: 12–25).
2 I shall have more to say about this distinction in Chapter 4.
3 This point relates to my argument above that truthmaking is not entailment.
4 I suggest different applications of this strategy in Chapters 6 and 7.
5 The example is from Russell (1918b).
6 Russell (1918b) thought that we needed both negative facts and totality facts. Armstrong eschews negative facts (2004: 54–60) but thinks we do need totality facts (2004: 68–82).
7 However, I direct the reader to Cheyne and Pigden (2006) and Parsons (2006) for a provocative and interesting discussion that furthers the debate on this matter.
8 The term was coined by Armstrong (2004: 5).

4 The relationship between language and reality

1 I shall set aside the "structural isomorphism" component of SLT here, as it is not relevant to this discussion of Quine.
2 I talk here in terms of sentence-types being multiply realizable, while acknowledging that it is more common to talk in terms of properties being multiply realizable. In Chapter 5, I argue that this is the result of confusing properties with predicates.

5 The methodological map

1 Aside, that is, from a brief consideration of Quine's noncognitive treatment of nonphysical discourse in Chapter 4.
2 I am not including a discussion of fictionalism here. This is not because I do not think it a viable metaphysical position. On the contrary. However, fictionalism comes in a variety of subtly different variations. For an indication of the range of fictionalist positions see Kalderon (2005a). Some of these positions can be assimilated to position 3 on the methodological map, that is, to what I have called the error theory or eliminativism about K-discourse. For example, Hartry Field's position with respect to mathematics has it that mathematical discourse involves commitment to the existence of abstract mathematical entities, and since

there are none, it is systematically in error (Field 1980, 1989). Other fictionalist positions take K-discourse to be fact-stating, like K-realism, but argue that the utterance of a K-sentence need not involve assertion. Instead it may involve the expression of some other attitude. See Kalderon (2005b) for an example of this position taken here with respect to moral discourse. Kalderon's view is not so easily assimilated into one of the other positions on the methodological map. Nevertheless, it does not present a novel treatment of K-discourse itself, since it takes K-discourse to be fact-stating. Its novel contribution instead consists in what it says about what we are doing when we utter sentences of K-discourse.
3 I shall have more to say about this below.
4 Robert Kirk also discusses this issue with respect to the possibility of reducing sciences such as biology and chemistry to physics, and sees little chance of success for such a project (Kirk 1999: 156–60).
5 A further possibility is that either one or both of the predicates refer to no property at all. However, advocates of reductionism seem to be assuming that there is at least some designating of properties being achieved by some predicates, so I will not consider these options here.
6 A similar inference is made by Terence Horgan when he considers "preservative irrealism, which would treat higher-order discourse as quite legitimate and perhaps indispensable, while also repudiating its apparent ontological commitments" (Horgan 1993: 581). The only reason for branding a view such as this as irrealism, would be thinking that realism is committed to Principle Φ.
7 This certainly seems to be what Kim has in mind when he talks of A-properties strongly covarying with B-properties (Kim 1990: 13).
8 I am not arguing that the error theorist or the K-realist *must* accept the conditional, but that, insofar as some of them do, they argue fallaciously.

6 The overlooked strategy in practice: moral discourse

1 Sayre-McCord presents a characterization of realism in general, which consists of claims (1) and (2) without any reference to morality. I have added the references to morality in order to keep my discussion focused on moral realism.
2 As in the parallel argument from tensed language, the first premise is logically, but not dialectically redundant. It allows us to distinguish two different ways of challenging premise 3: either by denying that there are any true moral sentences that are untranslatable, or by denying that there are any untranslatable moral sentences that are true.
3 This is not entirely true. Oaklander (2003) defends the thesis that all tensed sentences are logically false.
4 This idea derives from a suggestion by James Dreier (1990, 1999).

7 Some further applications of the overlooked strategy

1 As in the parallel arguments from tensed and moral language, the first premise is logically, but not dialectically redundant. It allows us to distinguish two different ways of challenging premise 3: either by denying that there are any true K-sentences that are untranslatable, or by denying that there are any untranslatable K-sentences that are true. This caveat also applies to subsequent formulations of the argument in this chapter.
2 Russell revised his views on causation in Russell (1948).
3 Keefe and Smith (1996) argue that there is a third feature of vague predicates, namely, that they lack well defined extensions. The difference between this and the first feature will not affect my general presentation of the issues surrounding the notion of vagueness, so I have not included it here.
4 An exception is Tye (1990).

References

Anscombe, G. E. M. (1971) "Causality and Determination," in E. Sosa and M. Tooley (eds), *Causation*, Oxford: Oxford University Press (1993), pp. 88–104.
Armstrong, D. M. (1997) *A World of States of Affairs*, Cambridge: Cambridge University Press.
—— (2004) *Truth and Truthmakers*, Cambridge: Cambridge University Press.
Ayer, A. J. (1946) *Language, Truth and Logic*, 2nd edn, London: Gollancz.
Azzouni, J. (1998) "On 'On What There Is'," *Pacific Philosophical Quarterly*, 79 (1): 1–18.
Balashov, Y. and J. Michel (2003) "Presentism and Relativity," *British Journal for the Philosophy of Science*, 54 (2): 327–46.
Beer, M. (1988) "Temporal Indexicals and the Passage of Time," *Philosophical Quarterly*, 38 (151): 158–64.
Benacerraf, P. (1973) "Mathematical Truth," in P. Benacerraf and H. Putnam (eds), (1983) *Philosophy of Mathematics Selected Readings*, 2nd edn, Cambridge: Cambridge University Press, pp. 403–20.
Bergmann, G. (1959) *Meaning and Existence*, Madison, Wisc.: University of Wisconsin Press.
Bigelow, J. (1988) *The Reality of Numbers: A Physicalist's Philosophy of Mathematics*, Oxford: Clarendon Press.
—— (1996) "Presentism and Properties," in J. Tomberlin (ed.), *Philosophical Perspectives 10: Metaphysics*, Atascadero, Calif.: Ridgeview Publishing Company, pp. 35–52.
Block, N. and R. Stalnaker (1999) "Conceptual Analysis, Dualism, and the Explanatory Gap," *Philosophical Review*, 108 (1): 1–46.
Boghossian, P. (1990) "The Status of Content," *Philosophical Review*, 99 (2): 157–84.
Bourne, C. (2002) "When Am I? A Tense Time for Some Tensed Theorists," *Australasian Journal of Philosophy*, 80 (3): 359–71.
Brink, D. O. (1995) "Moral Realism," in R. Audi (ed.), *The Cambridge Dictionary of Philosophy*, Cambridge: Cambridge University Press, pp. 511–12.
Brueckner, A. (2003) "Tensed Sentences, Tenseless Truth Conditions, and Tensed Beliefs," in A. Jokic and Q. Smith (eds), *Time, Tense and Reference*, Cambridge, Mass.: MIT Press, pp. 199–205.
Cargile, J. (1969) "The Sorites Paradox," *British Journal for the Philosophy of Science*, 20 (3): 193–202.
Carnap, R. (1937) *The Logical Syntax of Language*, London: Kegan Paul, Trench, Trubner & Co.
—— (1950) "Empiricism, Semantics and Ontology," *Revue Internationale de Philosophie*, 4: 20–40.

Castañeda, H.-N. (1967) "Indicators and Quasi-Indicators," *American Philosophical Quarterly*, 4 (2): 85–100.
Cheyne, C. (2001) *Knowledge, Cause, and Abstract Objects: Causal Objections to Platonism*, Dordrecht: Kluwer Academic Publishers.
Cheyne, C. and C. Pigden (2006) "Negative Truths from Positive Facts," *Australasian Journal of Philosophy*, 84 (2): 249–65.
Churchland, P. (1981) "Eliminative Materialism and the Propositional Attitudes," *Journal of Philosophy*, 78 (2): 67–90.
Colyvan, M. (2001) *The Indispensability of Mathematics*, Oxford: Oxford University Press.
—— (2004) "Indispensability Arguments in the Philosophy of Mathematics," in E. N. Zalta (ed.), *The Stanford Encyclopedia of Philosophy*, Fall 2004 edition. Available online at http://plato.stanford.edu/archives/fall2004/entries/mathphil-indis (accessed 28 February 2007).
Craig, W. L. (1996) "Tense and the New B-Theory of Language," *Philosophy*, 71 (275): 5–26.
—— (1997) "Is Presentness a Property?," *American Philosophical Quarterly*, 34 (1): 27–40.
—— (2000) *The Tensed Theory of Time: A Critical Examination*, Dordrecht: Kluwer Academic Publishers.
—— (2001) *Time and the Metaphysics of Relativity*, Dordrecht: Kluwer Academic Publishers.
Crisp, T. M. (2003) "Presentism," in M. J. Loux and D. W. Zimmerman (eds), *The Oxford Handbook of Metaphysics*, Oxford: Oxford University Press, pp. 211–45.
Devitt, M. (1991) *Realism and Truth*, 2nd edn, Oxford: Blackwell.
Divers, J. (2002) *Possible Worlds*, London: Routledge.
Dreier, J. (1990) "Internalism and Speaker Relativism," *Ethics*, 101 (1): 6–25.
—— (1999) "Transforming Expressivism," *Noûs*, 33 (4): 558–72.
Ducasse, C. J. (1969) *Causation and Types of Necessity*, New York: Dover.
Dyke, H. (2002a) "McTaggart and the Truth about Time," in C. Callender (ed.), *Time, Reality and Experience*, Cambridge: Cambridge University Press, pp. 137–52.
—— (2002b) "Tokens, Dates and Tenseless Truth Conditions," *Synthèse*, 131 (3): 329–51.
—— (2003a) "Temporal Language and Temporal Reality," *Philosophical Quarterly*, 53 (212): 380–91.
—— (2003b) "Tensed Meaning: A Tenseless Account," *Journal of Philosophical Research*, 28: 65–81.
Field, H. (1980) *Science without Numbers: A Defence of Nominalism*, Oxford: Blackwell.
—— (1989) *Realism, Mathematics and Modality*, Oxford: Blackwell.
Fox, J. (1987) "Truthmaker," *Australasian Journal of Philosophy*, 65 (2): 188–207.
Gale, R. (1962) "Tensed Statements," *Philosophical Quarterly*, 12 (46): 53–9.
—— (1968) *The Language of Time*, London: Routledge & Kegan Paul.
Gibbard, A. (1975) "Contingent Identity," *Journal of Philosophical Logic*, 4 (2): 187–221.
Goodman, N. (1951) *The Structure of Appearance*, Cambridge, Mass.: Harvard University Press.
Grim, P. (1984) "There Is No Set of All Truths," *Analysis*, 44 (4): 206–8.
Hare, R. M. (1952) *The Language of Morals*, Oxford: Clarendon Press.
Heil, J. (1981) "On Saying What There Is," *Philosophy*, 56 (216): 242–47.
—— (2000) "Truthmaking and Entailment," *Logique et Analyse*, 169–70 (43): 231–42.
—— (2003) *From an Ontological Point of View*, Oxford: Oxford University Press.
Heller, M. (1988) "Vagueness and the Standard Ontology," *Noûs*, 22: 109–31.

Hellman, G. (1989) *Mathematics Without Numbers*, Oxford: Clarendon Press.
Hofweber, T. (2005) "A Puzzle About Ontology," *Noûs*, 39 (2): 256–83.
Hookway, C. (1988) *Quine: Language, Experience and Reality*, Cambridge: Polity Press.
Horgan, T. (1993) "From Supervenience to Superdupervenience: Meeting the Demands of a Material World," *Mind*, 102 (408): 555–86.
Horwich, P. (1987) *Asymmetries in Time: Problems in the Philosophy of Science*, Cambridge, Mass.: MIT Press.
Hume, D. (1738) *A Treatise of Human Nature*, L. A. Selby-Bigge and P. H. Nidditch (eds), Oxford: Clarendon Press, 1978.
—— (1740) *An Abstract of A Treatise of Human Nature*, ed. L. A. Selby-Bigge and P. H. Nidditch (eds), Oxford: Clarendon Press, 1978.
Jubien, M. (1997) *Contemporary Metaphysics: An Introduction*, Oxford: Blackwell.
Kalderon, M. E. (ed.) (2005a) *Fictionalism in Metaphysics*, Oxford: Clarendon Press.
—— (2005b) *Moral Fictionalism*, Oxford: Clarendon Press.
Kaplan, D. (1989) "Demonstratives," in J. Almog, J. Perry, and H. Wettstein (eds), *Themes from Kaplan*, New York: Oxford University Press, pp. 481–614.
Keefe, R. and P. Smith (1996) "Introduction: Theories of Vagueness," in R. Keefe and P. Smith (eds), *Vagueness: A Reader*, Cambridge, Mass.: MIT Press, pp. 1–57.
Keller, S. (2004) "Presentism and Truthmaking," in D. W. Zimmerman (ed.), *Oxford Studies in Metaphysics*, Vol. I, Oxford: Clarendon Press, pp. 83–104.
Kim, J. (1990) "Supervenience as a Philosophical Concept," *Metaphilosophy*, 21 (1–2): 1–27.
—— (2003) "Supervenience, Emergence, Realization, Reduction," in M. J. Loux and D. W. Zimmerman (eds), *The Oxford Handbook of Metaphysics*, Oxford: Oxford University Press, pp. 556–84.
Kirk, R. (1999) *Relativism and Reality: A Contemporary Introduction*, London: Routledge.
Kitcher, P. (1984) *The Nature of Mathematical Knowledge*, Oxford: Oxford University Press.
Klagge, J. C. (1988) "Supervenience: Ontological and Ascriptive," *Australasian Journal of Philosophy*, 66 (4): 461–70.
Laurence, S. and C. Macdonald (1998) "Introduction: Metaphysics and Ontology," in S. Laurence and C. Macdonald (eds), *Contemporary Readings in the Foundations of Metaphysics*, Oxford: Blackwell, pp. 1–7.
Le Poidevin, R. (1991) *Change, Cause and Contradiction*, Basingstoke: Macmillan.
Lewis, D. (1986a) "Causation," in *Philosophical Papers*, Vol. II, Oxford: Oxford University Press, pp. 159–213.
—— (1986b) *On the Plurality of Worlds*, Oxford: Basil Blackwell.
—— (1993) "Mathematics is Megethology," *Philosophia Mathematica*, 1 (1): 3–23.
Loux, M. (2002) *Metaphysics: A Contemporary Introduction*, 2nd edn, London: Routledge.
Lowe, E. J. (1998) *The Possibility of Metaphysics: Substance, Identity, and Time*, Oxford: Clarendon Press.
—— (2002) *A Survey of Metaphysics*, Oxford: Oxford University Press.
Ludlow, P. (1999) *Semantics, Tense, and Time: An Essay in the Metaphysics of Natural Language*, Cambridge, Mass.: MIT Press.
MacBride, F. (2005) "Lewis's Animadversions on the Truthmaker Principle," in H. Beebee and J. Dodd (eds), *Truthmakers*, Oxford: Clarendon Press, pp. 117–40.
McGowan, M. K. (2002) "The Neglected Controversy Over Metaphysical Realism," *Philosophy*, 77 (1): 5–21.

McTaggart, J. M. E. (1927) *The Nature of Existence*, Vol. II, Cambridge: Cambridge University Press.

Mackie, J. L. (1974) *The Cement of the Universe: A Study of Causation*, Oxford: Clarendon Press.

—— (1977) *Ethics: Inventing Right and Wrong*, Harmondsworth: Penguin.

Maddy, P. (1990) *Realism in Mathematics*, Oxford: Clarendon Press.

—— (1992) "Indispensability and Practice," *Journal of Philosophy*, 89 (6): 275–89.

Markosian, N. (2004) "A Defense of Presentism," in D. W. Zimmerman (ed.), *Oxford Studies in Metaphysics*, Vol. I, Oxford: Clarendon Press, pp. 47–82.

Melia, J. (2005) "Truthmaking Without Truthmakers," in H. Beebee and J. Dodd (eds), *Truthmakers*, Oxford: Clarendon Press, pp. 67–84.

Mellor, D. H. (1981) *Real Time*, Cambridge: Cambridge University Press.

—— (1998) *Real Time II*, London: Routledge.

—— (2001) "The Time of Our Lives," in A. O'Hear (ed.), *Philosophy at the New Millennium*, Cambridge: Cambridge University Press, pp. 45–59.

Merricks, T. (1994) "Endurance and Indiscernibility," *Journal of Philosophy*, 91 (4): 165–84.

Mill, J. S. (1843) *A System of Logic: Ratiocinative and Inductive*. Toronto: University of Toronto Press, 1973.

Mondadori, F. and A. Morton (1976) "Modal Realism: The Poisoned Pawn," *Philosophical Review*, 85 (1): 3–20.

Moore, G. E. (1903) *Principia Ethica*, Cambridge: Cambridge University Press.

Mulligan, K., P. Simons and B. Smith (1984) "Truth-Makers," *Philosophy and Phenomenological Research*, 44 (3): 287–321.

Musgrave, A. (1986) "Arithmetical Platonism: Is Wright Wrong or Must Field Yield?" in M. Frické (ed.), *Essays in Honour of Bob Durrant*, Dunedin: Otago University Philosophy Department.

—— (1993) *Common Sense, Science and Scepticism: A Historical Introduction to the Theory of Knowledge*, Cambridge: Cambridge University Press.

—— (1999) "Conceptual Idealism and Stove's Gem," in M. L. Dalla Chiara, R. Giuntini and F. Laudisa (eds), *Language, Quantum, Music*, Dordrecht: Kluwer Academic Publishers, pp. 25–35.

—— (2001) "Metaphysical Realism Versus Word Magic," in D. Aleksandrowicz and R. H. Günther (eds), *Realismus – Disziplin – Interdisziplinarität*, Amsterdam: Editions Rodopi, pp. 29–54.

Nagel, E. (1961) *The Structure of Science*, New York: Harcourt, Brace, & World.

Newman, A. (1992) *The Physical Basis of Predication*, Cambridge: Cambridge University Press.

Oaklander, L. N. (1984) *Temporal Relations and Temporal Becoming: A Defense of a Russellian Theory of Time*, Lanham, Md.: University Press of America.

—— (1991) "A Defence of the New Tenseless Theory of Time," *Philosophical Quarterly*, 41 (162): 26–38.

—— (2003) "Two Versions of the New B-Theory of Language," in A. Jokic and Q. Smith (eds), *Time, Tense and Reference*, Cambridge, Mass.: MIT Press, pp. 271–303.

Oaklander, L. N. and Q. Smith (eds) (1994) *The New Theory of Time*, New Haven, Conn.: Yale University Press.

Parsons, J. (1999) "There Is No 'Truthmaker' Argument against Nominalism," *Australasian Journal of Philosophy*, 77 (3): 325–34.

—— (2006) "Negative Truths from Postive Facts?," *Australasian Journal of Philosophy*, 84 (4): 591–602.

Parsons, T. and P. Woodruff (1995) "Worldly Indeterminacy of Identity," *Proceedings of the Aristotelian Society*, 95 (2): 171–91.
Pendlebury, M. (1986) "Facts as Truthmakers," *The Monist*, 69 (2): 177–88.
Perry, J. (1979) "The Problem of the Essential Indexical," *Noûs*, 13 (1): 3–21.
Pigden, C. R. (1991) "Naturalism," in P. Singer (ed.), *A Companion to Ethics*, Oxford: Blackwell, pp. 421–31.
Pincock, C. (2004) "A Revealing Flaw in Colyvan's Indispensability Argument," *Philosophy of Science*, 71 (1): 61–79.
Price, H. (1997) "Naturalism and the Fate of the M-Worlds," *Proceedings of the Aristotelian Society*, supplement, 71: 247–67.
—— (2007) "Causal Perspectivalism," in H. Price and R. Corry (eds), *Causation, Physics and the Constitution of Reality: Russell's Republic Revisited*, Oxford: Oxford University Press, pp. 250–92.
Psillos, S. (2002) *Causation and Explanation*, Chesham: Acumen Publishing Ltd.
Putnam, H. (1975) "Language and Philosophy," in *Mind, Language and Reality*, Cambridge: Cambridge University Press, pp. 1–32.
—— (1981) *Reason, Truth and History*, Cambridge: Cambridge University Press.
Quine, W. V. O. (1948) "On What There Is," repr. in *From a Logical Point of View*, Cambridge, Mass.: Harvard University Press, 1980, pp. 1–19.
—— (1951) "Two Dogmas of Empiricism," repr. in *From a Logical Point of View*, Cambridge, Mass.: Harvard University Press, 1980, pp. 20–46.
—— (1960) *Word and Object*, Cambridge, Mass.: MIT Press.
—— (1966) "The Scope and Language of Science," in *The Ways of Paradox and Other Essays*, New York: Random House, pp. 228–45.
—— (1969) "Epistemology Naturalized," in *Ontological Relativity and Other Essays*, New York: Columbia University Press, pp. 69–90.
—— (1975) "The Nature of Natural Knowledge," in S. Guttenplan (ed.), *Mind and Language*, Oxford: Oxford University Press, pp. 67–81.
—— (1981) *Theories and Things*, Cambridge Mass.: Harvard University Press.
Rodriguez-Pereyra, G. (2002) *Resemblance Nominalism: A Solution to the Problem of Universals*, Oxford: Clarendon Press.
Russell, B. (1903) *The Principles of Mathematics*, London: Allen and Unwin.
—— (1905) "On Denoting," *Mind*, 14 (56): 479–93.
—— (1915) "On the Experience of Time," *The Monist*, 25 (2): 212–33.
—— (1918a) "On the Notion of Cause," in *Mysticism and Logic*, Harmondsworth: Penguin, 1953, pp. 171–96.
—— (1918b) "The Philosophy of Logical Atomism," in R. C. Marsh (ed.), *Logic and Knowledge*, London: Routledge, 1956, pp. 285–320.
—— (1940) *An Inquiry into Meaning and Truth*, London: George Allen & Unwin.
—— (1948) *Human Knowledge: Its Scope and Limits*, London: Routledge.
Russell, B. and A. N. Whitehead (1910–13) *Principia Mathematica*, Cambridge: Cambridge University Press.
Saunders, S. (2002) "How Relativity Contradicts Presentism," in C. Callender (ed.), *Time, Reality and Experience*, Cambridge: Cambridge University Press, pp. 277–92.
Savitt, S. F. (2000) "A Limited Defense of Passage," *American Philosophical Quarterly*, 38 (3): 261–70.
Sayre-McCord, G. (1988) "The Many Moral Realisms," in G. Sayre-McCord (ed.), *Essays on Moral Realism*, Ithaca, NY: Cornell University Press, pp. 1–23.
Schlesinger, G. (1980) *Aspects of Time*, Indianapolis, Ind.: Hackett Publishers.

Sider, T. (2001) *Four-Dimensionalism: An Ontology of Persistence and Time*, Oxford: Oxford University Press.
—— (2003) "Reductive Theories of Modality," in M. J. Loux and D. W. Zimmerman (eds), *The Oxford Handbook of Metaphysics*, Oxford: Oxford University Press, pp. 180–208.
Sklar, L. (1967) "Types of Inter-Theoretic Reduction," *British Journal for the Philosophy of Science*, 18 (2): 109–24.
Smart, J. J. C. (1949) "The River of Time," *Mind*, 58 (232): 483–94.
—— (1963) *Philosophy and Scientific Realism*, London: Routledge & Kegan Paul.
—— (1980) "Time and Becoming," in P. van Inwagen (ed.), *Time and Cause*, Dordrecht: D. Reidel, pp. 3–15.
Smith, B. (1999) "Truthmaker Realism," *Australasian Journal of Philosophy*, 77 (3): 274–91.
Smith, M. (1991) "Realism," in P. Singer (ed.), *A Companion to Ethics*, Oxford: Blackwell, pp. 399–410.
—— (1994) *The Moral Problem*, Oxford: Blackwell.
Smith, Q. (1993) *Language and Time*, Oxford: Oxford University Press.
—— (2002) "Time and Degrees of Existence: A Theory of Degree Presentism," in C. Callender (ed.), *Time, Reality and Experience*, Cambridge: Cambridge University Press, pp. 119–36.
Sober, E. (1993) "Mathematics and Indispensability," *Philosophical Review*, 102 (1): 35–57.
Sosa, E. (1993) "Putnam's Pragmatic Realism," *Journal of Philosophy*, 90 (12): 605–26.
Stevenson, C. L. (1944) *Ethics and Language*, New Haven, Conn.: Yale University Press.
Stove, D. (1991) *The Plato Cult and Other Philosophical Follies*, Oxford: Blackwell.
Tooley, M. (1987) *Causation: A Realist Approach*, Oxford: Clarendon Press.
—— (1997) *Time, Tense and Causation*, Oxford: Clarendon Press.
Tye, M. (1990) "Vague Objects," *Mind*, 99 (396): 535–57.
—— (1994) "Sorites Paradoxes and the Semantics of Vagueness," in J. E. Tomberlin (ed.), *Philosophical Perspectives 8: Logic and Language*. Atascadero, Calif.: Ridgeview, pp. 189–206.
Unger, P. (1979) "There Are No Ordinary Things," *Synthèse*, 41 (2): 117–54.
Van Inwagen, P. (1990) *Material Beings*, Ithaca, NY: Cornell University Press.
—— (1998) "The Nature of Metaphysics," in S. Laurence and C. Macdonald (eds), *Contemporary Readings in the Foundations of Metaphysics*, Oxford: Blackwell, pp. 11–21.
Wettstein, H. K. (1979) "Indexical Reference and Propositional Content," *Philosophical Studies*, 36 (1): 91–100.
Williams, D. C. (1951) "The Myth of Passage," *Journal of Philosophy*, 48 (15): 457–71.
Williamson, T. (1994) *Vagueness*, London: Routledge.
Wittgenstein, L. (1953) *Philosophical Investigations*, trans. G. E. M. Anscombe, Oxford: Basil Blackwell.

Index

A-series 38, 40, 52–53
A-theory 4–5, 37–39, 111; and the argument from language to reality 40–43, 44, 51, 72; and the new B-theory 53–56, 59–60; and the representational fallacy 9–10, 111–12; resemblance to moral realism 12, 138; and SLT 46–47, 58; and tensed facts 4, 9, 10, 38, 39, 44, 45; and tensed language 40, 42, 51, 54, 111, and tensed sentences 39, 40–41, 42–43, 47, 112; and tenseless sentences 40–41, 42, 51
abstract objects 24, 28, 34, 39, 72, 160, 167–68
Ali, S. ix
Anscombe, E. 155, 156, 157
antirealism 6, 11–12, 21, 89–90, 129; and conceptual relativism 126; mathematical 160–61, 162, in the methodological map 105, 106, 109, 130
Armstrong, D. M. 78–79, 81, 82, 83, 84
Ayer, A. J. 18, 134–35
Azzouni, J. 87

B-series 38, 43, 52–53
B-theory 4, 37, 38, 42, 43, 45–46, 47, 50–51, 59, 60–61; and special relativity 61–62; and tensed facts 38, 42–43; and tensed language 41, 49, 51, 53, 59–60; *see also* old B-theory, new B-theory
Balashov, Y. 62
Beer, M. 52–53
being: addition of 70; levels of 70, 113, 118, 128
belief: moral 128, 133, 142; tensed 141–42

Benacerraf, P. 160
Bergmann, G. 20
Bigelow, J. 61, 78, 81
Block, N. 116
Boghossian, P. 109–10, 124
Bourne, C. 60
Brink, D. O. 136
Brueckner, A. 52

Cargile, J. 168
Carnap, R. 18–19, 20, 31–33, 126, 127–28
Castañeda, H.-N. 44
causal role 117, 120
causation 12, 24, 154–58, 173n2; and the projectivist fallacy 96; reductive analysis of 154–55, 156, 157; regularity views of 154–55; skepticism and 14; and supervenience 121, 156–59
Cheyne, C. ix, 160, 162
Churchland, P. 123–24
co-reporting thesis 52–53
cognitivism 133, 137, 138
Colyvan, M. 160, 161, 163–65
concepts 14–16, 23, 27, 29–30, 31, 36, 37–38, 41, 42, 74–75, 79, 93, 117, 118, 135, 148–49, 152–53; *see also* predicates
conceptual analysis 120 *see also* linguistic analysis
conceptual relativism 111, 125–28, 144, 163; functional pluralism and 127–28; and the methodological map 7, 12, 106, 107, 108, 130; and the representational fallacy 126
conceptual scheme 15, 16, 23, 93–94, 106, 126–27
confirmational holism 161–62

context dependence 44; of language 101–2, 103, 104; new B-theory of time and 57, 58; of tensed language 11, 44, 45, 100, 101, 103, 104
context independence 11, 101–2, 103
Craig, W. L. 39, 40, 42–43, 50, 61
Crane, T. ix
Crisp, T. 171n2

Devitt, M. 90, 93
direction of fit 63–66, 74, 80
discourse: aesthetic 121–22; causal 154–55, 157–58; domain of 11, 74, 81, 143; folk psychological 123–24; mathematical 72, 160, 162, 163; modal 150–51, 153, 154; moral 12, 131, 132–42, 173n2; tensed 12, 49, 100, 137, 138, 149
Divers, J. ix, 170
Dreier, J. 173
Ducasse, C. J. 155, 156, 157

eliminativism 11, 107, 129, 172n2; about causation 158; irrealism and 118; and the methodological map 107, 108, 109, 110, 111; about modality 150, 151; about ordinary objects 146; and the representational fallacy 7; and vagueness 168
emergentism 12, 112–13, 129
empiricism 33–34, 154
entailment 40, 77–78
error theory 3, 110, 123–24, 172n2, 173n8; of causation 58; of mathematics 163; and the methodological map 11, 106, 108–10, 123–24, 125, 128, 130, 144; of morality 123, 132, 138; of ordinary objects 146; and the overlooked strategy 144; and the representational fallacy 7; of vagueness 168
ethics 140–41; autonomy of 134–36
events 7, 27; and the A-theory of time 37–38, 52, 59; and the B-theory of time 37–38, 43, 52–53, 59, 71; and causation 154, 155–56; classification of 101, 104, 149; and the projectivist fallacy 100; reductionism 96, 97; special theory of relativity and 61; tense and 7, 40, 55, 58, 140; as truthmakers 57, 99 101, 104

expressivism 95
facts 38–39; aesthetic 122; causal 121, 154–55, 156–58, 159; extralinguistic 11, 76, 98, 100, 102, 112–13; modal 151; moral 132, 133–34, 135, 141, 142; negative 84; noncausal 155, 156, 157–59; nonmoral 12, 138–39, 142; nonphysical 97; nonvague 169; physical 11, 95, 96–98, 100, 121–22, 123, 152; tensed 39, 141; tenseless 9, 10, 43, 46, 50, 53, 54, 55–56, 141–42; totality 84; vague 169
fictionalism 160, 162, 163
Field, H. 160, 161–62
Fox, J. 78
functional analysis 117

Gale, R. M. 40
Gem, the 16, 22
Gibbard, A. 144–45
Gill, E. ix
God 24
Goodman, N. 43
Grim, P. 171n6
Hare, R. M. 134
Heil, J. ix; on context dependence 103; on language and ontology 64–65, 73, 75; and the methodological map 108–9, 116; on modality 148–49, 152; and the picture theory 68–70, 115, 129, 147
Heller, M. 168
Hellman, G. 162, 164
Hofweber, T. 87
Hookway, C. 95, 96–97, 98
Horgan, T. 173n6
Horwich, P. 60
Hume, D. 134, 154–56, 157

indiscernibility of identicals 146, 147
indispensability argument 72, 160–63, 164
instrumentalism 95, 96, 109
irrealism 118, 173n6 *see also* antirealism

Jubien, M. 31

Kalderon, M. 172n5
Kant, I. 14–15, 17, 19, 171n2
Kaplan, D. 140
Keefe, R. 173n3
Keller, S. 171n2

Kim, J. 112, 119, 120–21, 173n7; on reductionism 114–15, 116, 117–18, 119, 129
Kirk, R. 90
Kitcher, P. 162
Klagge, J. 121, 122–23

language: moral 128, 136–38, 140, 142; ontological significance of 8, 36, 44, 129; of physics 6, 95–96, 98, 100, 105, 128–29; properties of 64–66, 87; structure of 41, 65; temporal viii, 9, 40, 41–43, 44, 47, 51, 54, 56; tensed 11, 55–56, 100–101, 104, 173n2; tenseless 9, 53, 56, 59, 75, 139
Laurence, S. 27
Le Poidevin, R. 60
Lewis, D. 52, 153, 155, 162, 164
linguistic analysis 3, 18, 117
linguistic framework 8, 19, 20, 106, 126
linguistic turn 8, 17–18, 19, 21, 29
logical analysis 9, 17, 18, 19, 20, 111
logical form 9, 17, 18, 20, 35
logical positivists 8, 16, 22, 29, 33, 65; and the linguistic turn 17–19, 20–21
Loux, M. J. 23, 27, 31
Lowe, E. J. 22, 23, 24–27, 31
Ludlow, P. 41–42

MacBride, F. 80
Macdonald, C. ix, 27
Mackie, J. L. 123, 135, 155
Maclaurin, J. ix
Maddy, P. 160, 162
Markosian, N. 61
material constitution 12, 144–49, 152; and identity 145–47
mathematical objects 72, 159–60, 161, 162, 163–64, 165
mathematics 12, 72, 19, 105, 144, 159–66
McGowan, M. K. 66–69, 70–71, 83
McTaggart, J. M. E. 38, 60
McTaggart's Paradox 51, 60
meaning 2, 11, 31, 40, 56, 104, 109; in arguments 42–43, 55–56, 136–37, 143, 145, 151; difference in 58–59, 75–77, 89–90, 98, 103–4, 130; and translation 42–44
Meinong, A. 17
Melia, J. 79, 81–83, 87
Mellor, D. H. 56, 60; tensed language 104, 141–42; B-theory of time 47, 48, 52, 54

Merricks, T. 61
metaethics 114, 137, 138–39
metaphysics: A-theoretic 60–61; Aristotelian conception of 22–23, 31, 63; B-theoretic 4, 50–51, 53, 59–62, 99; Kantian conception of 8, 14–17, 20, 21, 22
methodological map 3, 7, 11–12, 105–31, 69–70, 172n2; commonly accepted positions 107–10; domains of discourse and 7–8, 11, 105, 107, 108, 110, 132, 143–44, 145, 151, 162–63; and mathematics 165; non-cognitivism and 125; supervenience and 120; vagueness and 167, 169
Michel, J. 62
Mill, J. S. 155
modality 12, 52, 105, 144, 147–49, 149–54; problem of material constitution and *see* material constitution
Mondadori, F. 151–52
Moore, G. E. 111–12, 134–35, 137
morality: discourse of 105, 107–8, 132, 133, 142, 143; expressivism about 95; moral realism *see* realism, moral; and realism 173n1; tensed and moral language 42, 56, 75 127; and truthmaker naturalism 141, 142
Morton, A. 151–52
Mulligan, K. 74, 82, 84
multiple realizability 102, 103, 113, 116, 118, 119, 172n2; functional reductionism and 117–18
Musgrave, A. ix, 5, 78, 162
naturalism 108, 121, 139, 140, 142, 161–62; and moral discourse 135, 138; Quinean 26

naturalistic fallacy 134, 135, 137
new B-theory viii, 7, 47, 55–56, 171n5, 172n8; date version of 172n9; overlooked strategy and 11, 12, 105, 143; and the representational fallacy 51–53; and tense 7, 50–51, 54–56, 58–59, 138, 139–40; and tensed facts 48, 50, 52, 53, 55–56, 138; and tensed sentences 6, 10, 47–48, 49–50, 51–53, 54, 55–56, 58–59, 62, 140; and tenseless sentences 6, 52–53, 55, 58–59, 62, 90, 138; token-reflexive version of 172n9; and the truth-condition project 47–48, 49, 50, 51, 54–55, 62; truth-condition variant of

10, 47–54, 53–54, 156; and truthmaker naturalism 138, 139–40, 141; truthmaker variant of 10, 54–56, 62
Newman, A. 172n1
Nolan, D. ix
nominalism 27–28, 34, 64, 65, 81–83, 86; class 64; resemblance 64, 81–82; sensible 81–83
noncognitivism 7, 106, 107–8, 144, 158; methodological map and 11, 124–25, 138; Quinean 11, 95–96, 98, 100
nonfactualism 109–10 *see also* noncognitivism
nonnaturalism 107, 108, 110, 111, 127–28; *see also* realism
normative system 140
numbers 5, 19, 24, 126, 160; *see also* mathematical objects

Oaklander, L. N. ix, 47, 56
Ockham's Razor 2, 43, 99 *see also* principle of parsimony
old B-theory 9–10, 51, 53, 54–55, 59, 62, 139; and tensed facts 9, 10, 43, 44, 55; and tensed sentences 43–44, 47, 55, 138; and tenseless sentences 10, 43–44, 46; translation project of *see* paraphrase project; and SLT 46–47, 58, 71
ontological commitment 1, 2, 47, 76, 83, 85, 128; and the indispensability argument 161–62, 164, 165; Quine's criterion of 79, 86, 87
ontological form 9, 20
ontological pluralism 94
ontology 2, 9, 19, 35, 63–88, 114, 170; and the A-theory of time 37, 39, 46, 42, 54, 59, 62; and the B-theory of time 37; of causation 155, 157; and conceptual relativism 126, 127, 128; and language 64, 65, 129; *see also* language, ontological significance of; mathematical 163, 164; methodological map and 106, 108, 111, 144; modality 151; moral realism 133, 135; new B-theory of time 48–51, 52–53, 54, 59; and paraphrase 84–87; and the representational fallacy 14, 16, 53, 83, 92; and SLT 44, 46, 66–67; truthmakers and 82, 83, 99; of vagueness 166–67
Open Question Argument 134–35

ordinary language 1, 30, 35–36, 49, 84, 87; and material constitution 146; and moral realism 139; paraphrase 9, 28–29, 36, 47, 86; Quine and 95–96; and the representational fallacy 70; vagueness 166
overlooked strategy 4, 12–13, 105, 122, 128–31, 144, 170; causation 158, 159; domain of discourse 13, 122, 146–47, 154, 159, 165, 170; material constitution 146–48; mathematics 164; modality 151–53, 154; moral discourse 132–42, 143; vagueness 165

paraphrase 34–35, 47, 72, 77, 84–85; method of 10, 37, 47, 114; modality and 151; nominalism and 28–29, 83; ontological insignificance of 10, 54, 84–87, 88; project 43–44, 47, 85–86; relation 34, 35–36; and SLT 120; strategy 2–3
Parsons, J. ix, 81
Parsons, T. 167
particulars 39, 64, 69, 79; as truthmakers 63, 72, 77, 80, 81–82, 83, 86
Pendlebury, M. 83–84
Perry, J. 44, 141
perspective 11, 103–4, 149, 158; moral 138; temporal 37, 100, 101, 104, 140
phenomenalism 32–33
philosophy of time viii, 9, 72, 137
physicalism 6, 11, 96, 97, 99, 118, 129
physics 6, 24, 95, 96–98, 99–100, 123, 173n4; entities of 3, 6, 24, 82, 108; language of 95, 102, 119
picture theory 20–21, 22, 68–70, 74, 113, 129–30; principle Φ 70, 113, 115, 118, 118–20, 147, 173n6
Pigden, C. ix, 134, 135
Pincock, C. 164
platonism 27–28, 64, 160–61, 163 *see also* realism, mathematical
possible worlds 24, 153
predicates 34, 69, 83, 113, 130; folk psychological 123; higher-level 69, 113, 118; lower-level 69, 112; modal 148, 152, moral 123, 132, 135–36, 139, nonmodal 152; nonmoral 111, 134, 136, 139, 140; physical 69, 75, 96, 101, 104, 108; reductionism and

114–15, 116, 117, 118–19; vague 166, 168
presentism 39, 41, 61
Price, H. 107–8, 110–11, 127–28, 158
primitivism 150–51
principle of parsimony 2, 43, 99, 150, 151 *see also* Ockham's razor
projectivist fallacy 96, 99–100
proper name 64
properties 6–7, 66–68, 72, 143, 172n2; aesthetic 120–21, 122, 123; emergent 112–13; existence of 27–28; folk psychological 123–24; higher-level 69, 112, 116, 118, 119, 129; historical 147–48; lower-level 69, 112, 113; mind-independent 70; modal 147, 148, 150; moral 5, 123, 126, 128, 133, 134, 139; nonnatural 12, 108, 111, 123, 130, 134, 135–36; and predicates 109, 110, 123–25; physical 113, 118, 120–21, 123, 129, 152; and the picture theory 68, 69, 70, 74, 113, 130; in reductionism 113–20, 173n5 *see also* reductionism; supervenient 122, 123 *see also* supervenience; tensed 38, 39, 43, 52, 99; vague 166–68, 169
propositions 18, 24 78, 81, 96; and facts 38–39; ideal language 19, and metaphysical disputes 27; moral 134; and truthmaker maximalism 84
Psillos, S. 155–56, 157, 159
Putnam, H. 11, 29–30, 31–32, 92–94, 126; and the indispensability argument 160–61, 163

Quine, W. V. O. 11, 28, 43, 26, 33–36, 161; ontological commitment 80, 86–87; privileged description of reality 95–96, 97–98, 100

realism 7, 21, 89, 118, 173n1; about causation 157, 158–59; conceptual relativism and 125, 126, 127; domains of discourse and 106, 111–13, 130, 144, 146–47; error theory and 123–24; existence dimension of 93; immanent 64; independence dimension of 93; mathematical 159–63 *see also* platonism; metaphysical 8, 66–67, 71, 92–94; methodological map and 7, 11–12, 108; moral 12, 111, 112, 132–36, 137, 138, 139 141–42; ontological thesis of 10, 71, 89–92, 93, 94, 97, 132; and the representational fallacy 68, 69, 70
reality 1–3, 4–5, 8; extralinguistic 8, 18–19, 20–22, 103, 113, 147; hierarchical view of 69–70, 129; mind-independent 16, 23, 105, 149, 153; portion of 39, 75, 76, 91, 103, 129–30; structure of 1, 21, 22–23, 25–26, 31, 35–36, 58, 64, 92; temporal 9–10, 40, 42, 43, 44, 48, 50–51, 56, 59–61; true description of *see* strong linguistic thesis
reduction 52, 114, 139, 144, 150–51, 156–57 *see also* reductionism; bridge law 114–15, 116; functional 114, 117–18, 119, 120; identity 114, 116, 117, 118
reductionism 11–12, 96, 97–98, 107–8, 129, 173n5; about causation 157–58, domain of discourse and 97, 106, 108 113–20, 130, 144; functional 117–18, 119, 120 *see also* reduction, functional; mathematics and 160, 163; vagueness and 168
relation: between language and reality 9, 18–19, 20–21, 41, 66, 73, 99, 142, 89–104, 170; causal 155, 159; cross-categorial 77, 80; of inherence 64; of participation 64; spatial 69; spatiotemporal 154; temporal 38, 56–57, 58, 59 99, 140; truthmaking 77–78, 79, 83
relativism 20; conceptual *see* conceptual relativism
representational fallacy 1, 4–5, 7–8, 14–37, 60, 112–13; context dependence and 51–52, 53; domain of discourse and 112, 120; mathematics and 163–64; methodological map and 112, 116, 120, 124, 125, 126; picture theory and 21, 68, 70, 115; tensed sentences and 51, 53, 112; tenseless sentences and 5, 51, 102, 112
Rodriguez-Pereyra, G. 78, 79, 80, 81, 82, 86
Russell, B. 31, 33, 43, 160, 172n5, 172n6, 173n2; error theory of causation 158; logical analysis of language 17–18; relation between language and reality 19–20, 63–64, 65–66; paraphrase 34–36

Saunders, S. 62
Savitt, S. 172n13
Sayre-McCord, G. 136, 139, 173n1
science: fundamental 71, 75–76, 88; language of 95–96, 127, 128–29 and metaphysics 9, 15, 22, 23–25, 26–27, 60; and philosophy 17, 20, 26, 30; description of reality 45, 128–29, 165; functional pluralism 127; functional reductionism and 117; and the methodological map 107, 110, 111, 130; indispensability argument 72, 160–64; new B-theory of time and 4, 5, 59, 60, 61–62; and paraphrase 34–35; phenomenalism 32–33; scientific reductionism 139, 173n4
semantics 2, 5; A-theory of time 41–42; B-theory of time 42, 48, 51, 54; conceptual relativism 128; mathematics 165; methodological map 109, 110; moral realism 133, 135–36, 137; naturalism 139, 140; new B-theory of time 54, 56, 158; and ontology 48–49, 50; primacy of sentence meaning 33; relation to metaphysics 5, 41, 42, 56; tensed sentences and 56–57
sentences: argument from tensed language 55–56; causal 154, 155, 157, 158; context dependent 101, 102, 104; context independent 44, 101; irreducibility of tensed sentences 75, 76; mathematical 165; modal 151, 152–53; moral 12, 134–36, 137–39, 140, 141–42, 173n2; naturalistic 170 *see also* sentence, physical; nonmoral 12, 134, 136, 137, 138, 142; ontological significance of tensed sentences 9, 44, 48, 50, 53; physical 96; tensed viii, 40, 55, 138, 140, 172n10, 173n3; tenseless viii, 74; theoretical 165
sentence-token 57–58, 84, 101, 103; context dependence of 101; economic 100–101, 102, 103, 104; moral 140; as truthbearers 77, 78; truth conditions of 50, 58; truthmakers of 99, 101, 102–3, 104
sentence-type 101; context dependent 58, 104; context independent 58; economic 101, 102, 103, 104; physical 104
Sider, T. 149–50, 152, 172n13

Simons, P. 74
simultaneity: B-series and 38; new B-theory and 48, 52–53, 56–57, 58, 59; truthmakers and 76, 90, 104; special theory of relativity and 61
skepticism 14
Sklar, L. 116
SLT *see* strong linguistic thesis
Smart, J. J. C. ix, 43, 47, 49, 60
Smith, B. ix, 74, 82, 84
Smith, M. 133, 136
Smith, P. 173n3
Smith, Q. 40–41, 49, 50, 53, 61, 133
Sober, E. 162
sorites paradox 166, 168
Sosa, E. 127
spacetime 65, 144–45
special theory of relativity 61–62
Stalnaker, R. 116
state of affairs 2, and discourse 107; language and reality 19, 63; morality and 134, 135; new B-theory and 140; old B-theory and 43; truthmakers and 79, 81, 98
Stevenson, C. L. 134
Stove, D. 15–16, 171n1
strong linguistic thesis 7, 66, 170, 171n1; language and reality 66, 70, 83; and the methodological map 103, 120, 144; paraphrase 47, 54, 84; privileged description of reality and 9–11, 46, 66–67, 71, 72; Quine on 98–100; 172n1; realism and 89–91, 94; representational fallacy 7; tensed facts and 46; tensed sentences and 46, 90; new B-theory and 10, 54–56, 58
substance 64, 65, 69, 82
supervenience 3; causation and 157, 158–59; domain of discourse and 120, 121, 122, 123, 159; methodological map and 12; reductionism and 119, 129, 156, 157; supervenience theories 120–23; and truthmaking 78; and vagueness 169
syntax 19–20, 64, 80

tense: B-theory and 43, 44, 47; ineliminability of 42, 43, 54, 56, 62, 75, 139; in language viii, 41, 42, 173n1; linguistic 171n4; metaphysical status of 9; and morality 137;

ontological 40, 42, 171n4; ontological status of 37; semantics of 54–59
theory of descriptions 34
theory of types 17
Thomasson, A. ix
time, *see also* reality, temporal; A-theory of *see* A-theory; dynamic 37; metaphysics of 4, 41–42, 50–51, 59–62; nature of 4, 53, 54, 61, 62; new B-theory of *see* new B-theory; old B-theory of *see* old B-theory; and the representational fallacy 10; tensed viii, 47, 54; tenseless viii, 49, 55
Tooley, M. 61, 155, 156, 157
tropes 64, 65, 82
truth conditions: antirealism and 109; as a guide to ontology 50, 51, 52, 53, 73; of causal sentences 155, 156, 157–58; and meaning 48, 73; ontological significance of 48, 49, 50, 54, 73; and quantifiers 87; semantic significance of 48, 49, 50; tenseless viii, 48, 49, 51–53, 56, 62; token-reflexive 73, 172n9; and truthmakers 10, 56, 58, 73–74, 88; vagueness 168
truths: aesthetic 122, 123; causal 159; economic 45, 100; historical 149; mathematical 165; modal 148–50, 151, 153; moral 45; nonphysical 97, 98; nonvague 169; physical 11, 97–98, 99, 100, 123; of physics 45, 97; political 45; simpliciter 160; tensed 44, 45, 46, 111; tenseless 45, 46; and truthmakers 77–79, 80–81, 82, 83–84, 85, 88, 99 *see also* relation, truthmaking; vague 169
truthbearers 73, 77, 78–79, 80–81, 84
truthmakers 4, 5, 6, 13, 39, 170; antirealism and 12; causal 158; in common 5, 7, 58, 59, 99, 102; mathematical 72, 164–65; methodological map and 90, 98, 118, 120, 125; modal 148, 149, 154; moral 138, 139, 140, 142; multiple 83, 99; nature of 74, 77, 80–82, 86–87, 88, 99, 130–31; new B-theory and 54, 58, 140; nonmodal 151, 152, 153; of nonsynonymous sentences 5–6, 7, 83, 88, 99, 113; physical 6, 98, 99, 102, 123; presentism and 39; properties and 68, 72, 80; reality and 63; representational fallacy and 11, 103, 113; sentence-tokens and 101–2, 104; of tensed discourse 80–81, 130–31; truth conditions and 72; vagueness and 169
truthmaker maximalism 84
truthmaker naturalism 12, 138–41, 142
truthmaking 10, 77, 78–79, 80, 84, 86–87, 172n3; project 80, 81–82, 85; relation 77–78, 79, 83
Tye, M. 167, 173n4

Unger, P. 168
universals 24, 27–28, 33, 34–35, 64 as truthmakers 81, 82, 83, 86
use-mention confusion 5

vague identity 167
vague objects 167
vagueness 12, 144, 166–69, 173n3; epistemic view of 166, 168–69; in language 166, 168; ontic 167, 168; in the world 166–67, 168
Van Inwagen, P. 27–28, 72, 85–86

weak linguistic thesis 9, 45, 55
Weslake, B. ix
Wettstein, H. 44
Whitehead, A. N. 160
Williams, D. C. 60
Williamson, T. 168
Wittgenstein, L. 18, 19, 30–31, 32, 34, 65
WLT *see* weak linguistic thesis
Woodruff, P. 167–68

eBooks – at www.eBookstore.tandf.co.uk

A library at your fingertips!

eBooks are electronic versions of printed books. You can store them on your PC/laptop or browse them online.

They have advantages for anyone needing rapid access to a wide variety of published, copyright information.

eBooks can help your research by enabling you to bookmark chapters, annotate text and use instant searches to find specific words or phrases. Several eBook files would fit on even a small laptop or PDA.

NEW: Save money by eSubscribing: cheap, online access to any eBook for as long as you need it.

Annual subscription packages

We now offer special low-cost bulk subscriptions to packages of eBooks in certain subject areas. These are available to libraries or to individuals.

For more information please contact webmaster.ebooks@tandf.co.uk

We're continually developing the eBook concept, so keep up to date by visiting the website.

www.eBookstore.tandf.co.uk